John Owen

Travels Into Different Parts Of Europe

1791 - 1792. Vol. I

John Owen

Travels Into Different Parts Of Europe
1791 - 1792. Vol. I

ISBN/EAN: 9783744666398

Printed in Europe, USA, Canada, Australia, Japan

Cover: Foto ©Andreas Hilbeck / pixelio.de

More available books at **www.hansebooks.com**

OWEN's
TRAVELS

INTO

DIFFERENT PARTS OF EUROPE,

In the Years 1791 and 1792.

VOL. I.

TRAVELS

INTO

SEVERAL PARTS OF EUROPE,

In the Years 1791 and 1792.

VOL. I.

TRAVELS

INTO

DIFFERENT PARTS OF EUROPE,

IN THE YEARS 1791 AND 1792.

WITH

FAMILIAR REMARKS

ON

PLACES—MEN—AND MANNERS.

By JOHN OWEN, A. M.
LATE FELLOW OF CORPUS CHRISTI COLLEGE.

Mores, et Studia, et Populos—— VIRG. Georg. Lib. 4.

IN TWO VOLUMES.

VOL. I.

LONDON:
PRINTED FOR T. CADELL JUN. AND W. DAVIES,
(SUCCESSORS TO MR. CADELL,) IN THE STRAND.

1796.

PREFACE.

IT is a subject of equal notoriety and regret, that prefaces have sunk into general disuse, or lost to a great degree their just and original character. The abrupt appearance of an author before the bar of the public is an enterprize of most anxious uncertainty. He seems to be bound by a sort of respect, to present some credentials or submit to some formalities, before he presume upon the ready disposition of so august a judicature to hear and determine his merits. In addition to that duty which respect imposes, a more important claim attaches upon him,

him, from the absolute necessity of some preliminary arrangements, for the purposes of a fair and equitable decision. Yet such is the impatience of the bulk of readers, that all which intervenes between the title and the work is considered as an obstacle in the way of their progress, and treated as a slavish compliance with an obsolete ceremony. The influence of this judgment stops not with readers. It relaxes the strictness of authors themselves; and induces a habit of writing with looseness those very preliminaries, which seem to demand the most cautious precision—an indolence natural to the human mind, which is rarely brought to execute with care, what is not likely to be regarded with attention.

It

It may, however, be affirmed, that the majority of cases in which the merits of writers have been mistaken by the public, might be fairly referred to those defects in the outset of their acquaintance, which a due regard to some prefatory steps would have sufficiently supplied. Works of travel stand particularly exposed to the danger of an erroneous judgment. Presenting in many instances a picture of the times, and embracing a variety of circumstances and events, they may be considered as bearing upon modern history; and therefore, like that, encountering the jealousies, suspicions, and prejudices of minds variously interested, and affected by different, and yet existing, impressions. These obstacles can only be with any colour of expectation diminished, by the establishment of some premises, which the reader may adopt, and to which he may refer, as a rule for interpreting the author's mind on points of critical and delicate decision.

The volumes of travel with which the public are now presented profess to stand on more hazardous ground, in respect to a fair and equitable judgment, than any similar work with which they might be compared; and the author is unwilling to commit them to the world, without anticipating, in some premonitory remarks, the leading objections by which they may be attacked.

1. It may be urged, that books of travel have been greatly multiplied, and that the route which the author pursues has in it no chance of novelty. To this the author, with little variation,

PREFACE.

tion, concedes. He is ready to admit, that the cabinet is already supplied with a numerous catalogue of entertaining travellers; he is ready to admit, that the outline of his tour differs in very few respects from the ordinary track of fashionable travel; and that the places alluded to in the succeeding volumes are, with few exceptions, such as have been repeatedly viewed and repeatedly described. The attention of the public to travelling journals has however, he presumes, not yet been satiated by all that has been, nor will probably be satisfied by all that may be said, of foreign countries and foreign manners. The necessity of supplying some species of light and unelaborate reading is felt by all who are acquainted with the public taste: and no productions are, generally speaking, more readily digested, than those which conduct the fire-side traveller through an extensive tract of country without disturbing him from his arm-chair; and introduce him to all the beauties of a country without exposing him to any of its storms. Relying upon this passion for travelling journals, and the endless variety of an active mind, the author engaged in a correspondence for furnishing expressly the materials of the present volumes. Whether he has rightly judged of the public feelings, and his own powers—will be hereafter decided.

A second objection may probably arise, from the interval which has been suffered to pass between the closing of the Letters and the period of publication. In accounting for this it is is neceſſary to remark, that a conſiderable portion of the Letters had been transferred to private hands for the ſecurity of conveyance, at the time of the author's proceeding upon his expedition into Auſtria; and that the non-arrival of theſe at the period expected very conſiderably delayed the compilation. The publication of Mr. Grey's tour at nearly the ſame period was alſo a ground of diſcouragement. If to this be added the obſtruction occaſioned to the proceſs of printing by the author's diſtance from the metropolis and the preſs, the hiſtory of this delay will have been completely given. The reaſons for ſpecifying theſe cauſes with ſo much minuteneſs, will be ſufficiently obvious to thoſe who are acquainted with the buſy inſinuations of calumny and malice. Events of late

late occurrence have split society into so many factions, that jealousies are now excited, against which too much precaution cannot be employed. The author expects to hear it insinuated, as it has been already candidly rumoured, that the publication was delayed for the convenience of adapting it to the humour of the times. If the circumstances already enumerated had not sufficiently done away this imputation, the very difficulty itself of effecting such a task, in the varying circumstances of the present period, would discover the folly of the charge. To these, however—if these should yet be insufficient—the author is ready to annex his most serious declaration; that in no instance, the most trivial particulars alone excepted, has he shaped or accommodated the original spirit and

and train of the journal; and that a confiderable number of the Letters have been printed, with no other alteration, than that of a literal or verbal correction.

A third objection may poffibly arife in the minds of fome, from the internal character of the Letters themfelves, the circumftances of which they treat, and the unreferved freedom with which thefe circumftances are treated. To this it may be replied, that the author has availed himfelf, in travelling and in writing, of that liberty which has in fuch cafes ever been deemed admiffible: and that as he travelled to fee and report, he conceives that he could only do juftice to himfelf, the public, and his fubject, by depicting, as he has done, manners and fentiments in their natural

tural colours; and expressing, on just occasions, the undissembled feelings of his own mind. If the reader maintains a strict attention—in adjudging these Letters—to the particular periods in which they were written; if he considers the circumstances of the times and the state of public opinion; the author is convinced that his enthusiasm will be pronounced to have been of a venial, if not of a commendable character. But events of such variety, and in many particulars of such importance, have taken place during the lapse of the three last years, that the mind will not, without some difficulty, acquire that temper with which it ought to peruse the reports of a preceding period. Labouring under the influence of some recent impressions, the reader will probably be be led to confound thofe dates which ought to be kept religiouſly diſtinct; and thus condemn, by a reference to fubfequent tranfactions, what in the *then* circumſtances he might have been forward to approve. It muſt not be diſſembled, that the largeſt portion of the author's anxiety for the fate of his work is founded in an apprehenſion of this dangerous, yet almoſt inevitable, confuſion in the public mind of dates and feelings. For his own part, he is free to confefs, that though his mind has been affected with the moſt fenfible emotion at the horrors which have deformed the name of *Liberty*, he yet can fee no reafon for reverſing all the maxims of the wifeſt men and the beſt times; he ſtill can contemplate it—in its genuine characters of benignity and order—as the friend of man, and the happiest cement of civil society. Not all the disorders which have deluged Europe since the æra of the French revolution have induced him to depart from the *principles** which supported his original admiration of this extraordinary event. The downfal of limited monarchy, the irruption of Jacobinism, Brissotinism, and all the modifications of republican tyranny, have cruelly inverted the original picture; but the very hostility which *these* declared against the *first* reformers, and which themselves have experienced from the present less outrageous and democratic rulers, is an argument in favour of the first legislative assembly, which cannot be defeated by any species of regular and ingenuous reasoning.

* Vide Preface to Retrospect.

soning. The evils which have been ingrafted upon this convenient stock, the factions of disorder and equalization, are indisputably lessons of instructive caution against hasty enthusiasm and rash experiment. A torrent of political licentiousness has certainly poured in upon the peaceful and prudent institutions of society; and those who occupy responsible situations are loudly called upon to support the tottering pillars of civil subordination. In the discharge, however, of this duty, no compromise ought to be made of truth and justice; nor should zeal transport us to criminate, what prudence may have forbidden us to admire. So much it seemed expedient to say for the publication of sentiments, whose bearings upon present opinion might else be exposed to misconstruction.

construction. The author is aware that expressions may have been cursorily employed, which the fastidious scruples of some might wish amended or expunged. But he cannot discover any sentiment, with which a candid mind *can*, or a British mind *ought*, to be offended. His opinions on the leading political changes are already before the public; and these will afford a sufficient clue for unravelling and reconciling what might else appear mysterious and inconsistent.

After so much said by way of anticipation, it may now be necessary to say something of the execution. The Letters are short, for the commodiousness of detached reading; and as they were in most instances disposed in packets containing a number, they were originally constructed upon this
concise

concife model, in order to fupport the analogy of chapters in a regular journal. Dates are for the moft part fuperfcribed; but where this is omitted, the Letter is to be confidered as forming a part of a packet, and referred to the date of the preceding. As they are intended for the amufement of the *domeſtic* traveller, they are not charged with any fyftematic calculations of diftance or coin, or any critical adjuftment of names and hiftories. Charts and Itineraries are beft fuited to the minutenefs of the firft, and profeffed difquifitions to the gravity of the laft. The ftyle, it is hoped, will be found not wholly unfuiting the familiarity of the occafions; and the errors and redundancies—if fuch fhould appear—will probably be viewed with fome portion of indulgence,

when

when it is confidered, that the Letters were written in the warmth of youthful impetuofity—and that it would have been a breach of tacit faith to introduce any further emendations, than thofe which are juftified by ufage and acknowledged licence. That the volumes have appeared at all, and that they have not appeared in a lefs correct ftate, are owing to the flattering encouragement and the critical fervices of W. Belſham Efq. to whom thefe Letters were originally addreſſed, and whofe judicious revifion they had the good fortune to receive. In revealing this circumſtance, the author is but difcharging a debt of gratitude to a man, of whofe character—while the public may reafonably differ—his friends can entertain but one opinion. The foundnefs of his judgment, and

the

the accuracy of his taste, were a security to the author for the justness of his corrections; and a friendship of long and strict familiarity, undisturbed by the divisions of politics and theology, have afforded him occasions of general improvement, which it is equally his duty and his pride to acknowledge.

In taking leave of the reader the author has only to request, that a candid distinction may be made in perusing his volumes, between the cast of his mind at the period of his travels, and that which he now professes to have received. The demands of a situation the most grave and important have now engaged him in duties and concerns, which necessarily occupy and solemnize his thoughts; and to the faithful discharge of which, he is desirous of rendering the experience he has acquired, in every respect subservient. He cannot therefore consign his volumes to the public, without confessing, that the Letters discover, in particular instances, a levity, which in his present character he should feel himself bound to condemn. Amongst those errors in the progress of his tour which he has most to regret, and with which the public have the most concern, are the little respect for the solemnities of the Sabbath, and the rare acknowledgment of a beneficent Providence. These it is judged expedient the rather to mention, as they are errors of easy growth, and which it is of the first importance to discountenance and destroy.

The

The cuſtom of travelling on the Sabbath is of great and notorious prevalence; but certainly the law, which devotes it to religious offices, is broken by ſuch abuſe. The looſeneſs of *Catholic*, forms no juſt precedent for an equal licence in *Proteſtant*, diſcipline. Vice is the ſame on an iſland or continent, and cannot alter its nature by any change of meridian. The ſame rule will with equal ſtrictneſs apply, to the general views of events and circumſtances. For if it be an obligation of Chriſtian piety to aſcribe the turns of human felicity to the wiſdom and benevolence of the Deity, this acknowledgment ought in juſtice to pervade the details of a long and eccentric tour, beſet with hazards, and interſperſed with adventure.

With these preliminaries, the author is content to meet the public eye. Convinced that the sentence of the world, when fairly collected, is rarely unjust, he has endeavoured to furnish in the remarks premised, the means of establishing an equitable judgment.

> Speak of me as I am—nothing extenuate,
> Or set down ought in malice—

Such is the rule, by which, as he should judge of others, he wishes himself to be judged.

JANUARY 7, 1796.

CONTENTS.

VOLUME THE FIRST.

LETTER I.

Object and plan of correspondence stated—Variety a species of originality. Page 1

LETTER II.

First sensation of a traveller—French coast—Evils of the antient system—Prospect of final good from the present disorders—Eulogium on the new laws. 4

LETTER III.

Ostend—Ghent—Particulars respecting the Gantois—Aspect of the place—Churches—St.

—*St. Gedule—Criticism and nature not always agreed—Digression on Belgic politics.* - - - Page 8

LETTER IV.

Brussels—Gloomy aspect in Holy Week—Strength of devotion—Religious card-party—Prospect of concluding penance—Consecration of days. - - 15

LETTER V.

Description of a religious ceremony—Devout character of common people—Catholic penance transferable property. - 20

LETTER VI.

Penance concluded—Consequent changes—Theatre—Societies—Comtesse de Choiseul—Chivalry not extinct at Brussels—" Ladies Club." - - 24

LETTER VII.

Politeness exemplified. - . 28

LETTER VIII.

Philosophy of the heart—Instanced in French Noblesse—Their conduct described—Character of a Frenchman traced in his language—Conclusion in favour of philosophy. - - - - Page 30

LETTER IX.

National varieties source of travellers pleasure—Law of etiquette—Fourth law of morals—Defined—Example to the rule—Relation of trifling occurrences defended. 35

LETTER X.

Park—Palace of the arch-duchess—Pillage of the revolutionists—Compared with military law. - - - 39

LETTER XI.

Intention of quitting Brussels—Character of Flemings—Anecdote—Conclusion against them. - - - 43

LETTER XII.

Entrance upon Antwerp—Church of Notre Dame—General state of Antwerp—Amusements—Remains of revolutionary spirit—Political conjectures.   Page 47

LETTER XIII.

Vicissitudes in the history of Antwerp—Siege in 1585—Treaty of Munster—No change in the spirit of fanaticism—Portrait of Van Eupen—his machinations, defeat, and flight.   52

LETTER XIV.

From Antwerp to Breda—Country described—Contrast between Dutch and Austrian Brabant—Breda described—Rendezvous of the late revolutionists—Sketch of some particulars previous to the capture of Brussels—Apology for alluding to Belgic affairs—Different views of Prussia and Holland.   57

CONTENTS.

LETTER XV.

Convenience of travelling through Holland—Entrance of a vessel for Rotterdam—Abrupt separation—Agrémens of land travelling—Passage of the Biesbock—Embarrassed route by land. - Page 64

LETTER XVI.

Dutch Cabaret—Hollanders industrious—Route to Rotterdam—Rotterdam described—Statue of Erasmus—Prudent management of literary honours, - 72

LETTER XVII.

Peculiar character of Rotterdam—Trade the predominant concern—Precipitate departure. - - - 77

LETTER XVIII.

Delft—Its rarities—The Hague—Promenade to Scheveling—Village, &c.—Houses—Palace of the Stadtholder—Churches, Preachers,

Preachers, &c.—The fair—Dress of Dutch girls—Singular hats—Apology for severity. - - Page 80

LETTER XIX.

Passage to Amsterdam—Mode of travelling—Manners of Passengers—Leyden- and Haerlem—Banks of Canals—First coup d'œil of Amsterdam—Pause from narration. - - - 86

LETTER XX.

City of Amsterdam—Eulogium on its commercial character—Compared with its quondam rival Antwerp—Activity of the city—Streets == Stadthouse—Churches—Carriages—Bridge—Proposed account of a contrasted scene. - - - 90

LETTER XXI.

Trip to Broek—View of Amsterdam from Buykstoodt—Approach to Broek—Broek described—Elegant neatness of the houses—
                                          Grotesque

CONTENTS.   xxvii

Grotesque forms of the gardens, &c.—Interior of the houses.—Singular customs—Difficulty of accounting for this neatness—Return to Amsterdam. - Page 96

LETTER XXII.

Passage to Utrecht—The city described—Glance at its history—Anecdote from Duclos—Route to Bommel—Bois-le-duc—Country described—Preparation for advancing. - - - - 103

LETTER XXIII.

Neatness of Hollanders considered—Principally resolvable into necessity—No great personal neatness—Hollanders reputed knavish—Accounted for—Different character of towns and villages—Vindication of the last—Religious anecdotes—Conclusion in favour of their moral virtues. 109

LETTER XXIV.

Singular situation of Holland considered—Goldsmith referred to—Sameness in the aspect of its towns—Gardens criticised—Uncouthness in these consistent with their general habits. - Page 115

LETTER XXV.

Reflections on the national policy of Holland—Orange cockade universal—Attempt to account for this submission—Political disaffection of Hollanders—Spirit of Hollanders unforgiving—Anecdote in proof. 122

LETTER XXVI.

Route from Bois-le-duc described—Maestricht, its lively aspect—Liege, the picture reversed—Spa, its situation—Salubrity of its springs not its only attraction—Dearness of living—Water not the only beverage at Spa. - - 129

LETTER XXVII.

Necessity becoming a virtue—Illustrated in the dress of the female Hollander—Rule applied to salubrious springs—Advantage of the union between amusement and regimen—Its greater disadvantage—Conclusion against Spa. - Page 134

LETTER XXVIII.

Singular grant of indulgence—Departure for Aix—Disgusting effect of invalids—Cathedral, devotion of its worshippers—Same observed at Juliers—Arrival at Dusseldorf. - - - 138

LETTER XXIX.

Works of art best viewed in company—Gallery of the Elector—Chamber of Rubens—Of Vander-Werf—Italian—" La lumière " vraiment soufflée."—The wise and foolish virgins—Holy family—Moral reflection.
142

LETTER XXX.

Cologne described—Bonn, palace, &c.—Picturesque route to Remangen—Improvement of country to Andernach—Reflection on its ruins. - Page 147

LETTER XXXI.

Position of Coblentz—Fair sex—dress of men—Deception of scenery—Two evils which exercise a traveller's fortitude—Singular coachman—Arrival at Mayence. 152

LETTER XXXII.

Mayence described—High mass—Table d'Hôte—Abbés—Comparison of manners at French, Dutch, and German tables—Hauteur of Ecclesiastics—Worms—Entrance into Manheim—Rendezvous of emigrants—Reflections on their fate. - 156

LETTER XXXIII.

Discipline of Manheim—Entrance upon Alsace—Good effects of the revolution—Gaiety

of

of the people—Route to Strasbourg—Vestige of corruption—Religious procession—Apology for defective descriptions. Page 162

LETTER XXXIV.

The revolution considered—Its effects on language—Changes in Strasbourg—Contrast between revolutionists and emigrants—Political aspect of the place—Contrast of antient and modern decrees—Moore no prophet. - - 167

LETTER XXXV.

Want of specie at Strasbourg—Dread of paper-payment—Orderly state of inhabitants—National emolument—Religious worship protected—Rencontre at Mulhausen—Dialogue. - - 172

LETTER XXXVI.

Advance of clock at Basle—Three kings—Beauty of the Rhine—Character of Basle—Simple

—*Simple manners of inhabitants—Best species of poetry.* - - Page 178

LETTER XXXVII.

Dress of women—Eulogium on Basle—Route to Berne—Mountainous varieties—Singular position of Biestal—Soleure—Arrival at Berne. - - 183

LETTER XXXVIII.

Goût for amusements instanced in an emigrant—Position of Berne—Political discussion—Inquisitive character—Route to Geneva.
188

LETTER XXXIX.

Position of Geneva—Lake—Its banks—Mountains—Grand Saleve—Petit—Mole—Glaciers—Aiguilles—Mont Blanc—Rhone and Arve. - 194

LETTER XL.

Effect of King's flight on police of Geneva—on the people—Commotion upon his arrest—Effect

Effect upon Lausanne—Promenades—Politicians—" La belle democrate"—Love—Language. - Page 199

LETTER XLI.

Dress, &c.—Gouté—Genevese dinner—Divisions of Sunday evening—Political state of Geneva. - - 204

LETTER XLII.

Federation celebrated at Ferney—Introduction to company—Speech of Commandant—English toasted—Compliment returned—Effects—Good order of the whole—Voltaire's house. - - 209

LETTER XLIII.

Lausanne—Environs—Swell of lake—Character of Lausanne—Gibbon—First view of Glaciers—Project of tour. 217

LETTER XLIV.

Route to Chamouni—Bonneville—Singular inscription—Cascade at Salenche—Char-à-bancs à-bancs—*Cafcade of Chede*—*Gaieties of St. Gervais.* - Page 221

LETTER XLV.

Glacier de Boiffons—*Its beauty*—*Dangers of its vicinity*—*Afcent of Montanvert*—*Mer-de-glace*—*Environs.* - 226

LETTER XLVI.

Blair's Cabin—*Character of guides*—*Mont Blanc*—*Defcent from Montanvert*—*Source of the Arveron*—*Difcontents of Savoyards*—*Divifion of lands.* - 231

LETTER XLVII.

Evening contemplation—*Paffage of Col-de-Balme*—*Valley of Trent*—*Village.* 238

LETTER XLVIII.

Paffage of Forclay—*St. Blanchier*—*Valley of Entremont*—*Infcriptions on houfes*—*Pofition of Liddes*—*Pilgrim.* 242

LETTER XLIX.

St. Pierre—Flesh of animals—Ascent to St. Bernard—Mule good instructor—Barbarous route—Meal at the convent. Page 247

LETTER L.

Environs of convent—Language of the brothers—Lake—Passage of Hannibal—Institution of the convent—Members. 253

LETTER LI.

Employment of the brothers—Their utility questioned—Storm—Descent from St. Bernard's—Mulish resistance. - 258

LETTER LII.

Position of St. Blanchier—St. Martigny—Butterfly-catcher—Eloquent landlord—Goitrous and Cretins—Sauffure's hypothesis. - - - 263

LETTER LIII.

Cascade of Pissevache—Entrance on territories of Berne—Bex—Salines—Passage through the mountain. - 268

LETTER LIV.

Appearance upon issuing from the Salines—Bex described—Church dispute—Route to Vevai—Chateau de Chillon—Arrival at Lausanne—Reflection on the tour. Page 273

LETTER LV.

Beauties of the country—Rocks of Millerai Character of the Swiss—Marquis de Langle—Chevalier Mehegan—Balance of opinion. - - 278

LETTER LVI.

Political disturbances—Their origin—Strong measures of the Bernois—Reality of the plot doubted—Alledged grievances considered. - - 283

LETTER LVII.

Vineyards—Climate—Prohibition of French language—Severity of government. 289

LETTER LVIII.

Decline of society—and natural beauty—Preparation for Italian tour. Page 293

LETTER LIX.

Departure from Lausanne—Rencontre at Rolle—Geneva—Judgment against theatres. - - - 296

LETTER LX.

Entrance upon Savoy—Aix les Bains—Chamberri—Aigue-belle route described. 300

LETTER LXI.

Inhabitants of Valley—Village triumph—Lannesbourg—Dislocation of carriages, &c. - - - 304

LETTER LXII.

Ascent of Mont Cenis—Appearance of summit—Descent in sledge—Comparison of antient and modern travellers—Novaleze—Particulars of Suze, &c. 307

LETTER LXIII.

Approach to Turin—Dress of inhabitants—His Sardinian Majesty's palace—Equestrian statue—Four seasons, &c.—Chef d'œuvre of Gerard Dow. - Page 314

LETTER LXIV.

University—Museo del Re—Venus, Tripod, &c.—Isiac table, &c.—General hypothesis—Industria. - - 318

LETTER LXV.

Italian opera—Serious best in England—Buffo in Italy—Theatre de Carignano—Italians excell in humorous song—Dancing, vicious taste. - - 322

LETTER LXVI.

Churches—Places, promenades, &c.—Po—Its poetical history not strictly intelligible——Trade of Turin—Reflection on commerce of Britain. - - 325

LETTER LXVII.

Departure from Turin—Trial of pride—Description of route—Late arrival at Villa Nuova—Padrone defined—Village consequence—Italian accommodations—Counsel to travellers. - Page 329

LETTER LXVIII.

Aleffandria—Tortona—Italian fupper—Nafidienus—Garlick. - 333

LETTER LXIX.

Italian Signora—Charms of a red coat—No part of Italy uninterefting—Caftel San Giovanni—Cathedral—Contraft of temple and worfhippers—Reflection on fuperftition.
336

LETTER LXX.

Piacenza—Piazza. Publico—Statues, &c. Cathedral—Dial—Madonna—Altar of St. Anthony—Church of San Agoftino—Wealth of Auguftines—Route to Parma.
340

LETTER LXXI.

Parma—Cathedral—Church San Giovanni —Academy—Chef d'œuvre of Correggio— Its character—Defect of the art—Wooden theatre—Amletto—Italian tragedy—Obstacles to travelling. - Page 343

LETTER LXXII.

Æmilian way—Modena—Tassoni—Cathedral—Singular guide—Chapel San Geminiano—Religious creeping—Secchia— Groundless wars. 349

LETTER LXXIII.

Bologna—Madonna di San Luca—Portico —Virtues of the image—History of its transfer—Moral of the fable. 354

LETTER LXXIV.

View from Saint Luke—Decollation of St. Paul—L'Instituto—Palace Sampieri— Abraham and Hagar—Christ and the Pharisee

Pharisee—St. Paul and St. Peter—Its effects described—Best object of pilgrimage.
Page 360

LETTER LXXV.

Churches—Giovanni in Monte, Cecilia of Raphael—Dominican, Massacre of Innocents, Tomb of Dominique, Death of Virgin —Agnes, Martyrdom—Petronius, Meridian, &c.—Musicals—Route from Bologna—Pietra Mala, &c. - 366

LETTER LXXVI.

Florence—Gallery—Liberality of Grand Duke —Tribune—Venus de Medicis—Progress of artist imagined—Arrotino—Different hypotheses—Conclusion. - 369

LETTER LXXVII.

Wrestlers—Dancing faun—Cabinets of minerals, portraits, &c.—Bust of Alexander —Different opinions—Bust of Brutus— Why unfinished—Conjecture. - 373

LETTER LXXVIII.

Streets—Entrance of city—Palace Pitti, Ceilings, Madonna—Ricardi, Evangelists, &c.—General character of place and people. - - Page 378

LETTER LXXIX.

Cathedral—San Lorenzo, tombs of Michael Angelo, Chapel di Medicis—Santa Annuntiata, bas reliefs, Madonna, &c.—Dominicans—San Spirito—Santa Croce, Monument of Michael Angelo, Galileo—Reflection on the last. - - 381

LETTER LXXX.

Reluctant departure—Peruggia—San Francesco—Resurrection—Raphael indebted to Pietro Perugino—Assumption of Virgin—Analogy of painting and music—Palace Della Penna—Salvator Rosa—General character of Peruggia. - 385

CONTENTS.

LETTER LXXXI.

Foligno — Village politics — Madonna of Raphael—Delicious route to Spoletto—Gothic aqueduct—Importance of Spoletto.
Page 390

LETTER LXXXII.

Cascade of Terni—River Velino—History—Piano del Marmore—Track from village—Points of view—Mode of descent—Height—General effect. - 394

LETTER LXXXIII.

Highest point of Appennine—Birth place of Tacitus—Route to Narni—Nera-bridge—Otriculum—Flexions of Tiber—Città Castellana—Decrease of natural beauty—Entrance of Rome. - - 397

VOLUME THE SECOND.

LETTER LXXXIV.

Delectable embarrassment—Roman capitol—Reflection—Museum—Confined space of capitol—Campo Vaccino—Vestiges of antient structures—Contrast of antient and modern Forum.   Page 1

LETTER LXXXV.

Temple of Peace—Imperial Palace—Arch of Titus—Present state—Jewish delicacy—Sonnet of Baldi—Translation.   6

LETTER LXXXVI.

Temple of Antoninus and Faustina—Peter's miracle—Amphitheatre of Vespasian—Extent, strength, and remains—Miraculous anecdote—Arch of Constantine—Magnificent view—Reflection.   10

LETTER LXXXVII.

Prelude to Christmas—Ceremonies of Nativity—Character of his Holiness—General effect—Papal power on the decline. Page 17

LETTER LXXXVIII.

Multitude of antient monuments—Baths, Dioclesian, Titus—Circuses—Pantheon—Theatre of Marcellus—Aqueducts and baths best testimonies of antient grandeur. 20

LETTER LXXXIX.

Roman burials—Sepulchre of Bibulus—Tombs—Vault of the Scipios—Capo di Bove—Pyramid of C. Cestius—Moles Adriani—Mausoleum of Augustus—Real character of that prince. - 24

LETTER XC.

Fountain of Egeria—Temple of Minerva, Medica—Miscellaneous temples, &c.—Column of Trajan and Antoninus—Roots of bridges

bridges — Cleansing of Tiber — Colour — Diminished reputation.   Page 28

LETTER XCI.

Effect of French revolution upon the Pope—Religious precautions—Devotion of city—Procession—Its effect—Religion and traffic of Rome—Rules for calculating the population. - - 33

LETTER XCII.

Conduct of the Pope upon escape of Louis XVI.—Extract from brief—Spirit of the demand. - - - 37

LETTER XCIII.

Barberini Palace—Four Evangelists, sick satyr, sleeping faun—Spada—Statue of Pompey—Ruspigliosi, Aurora—Villa Albani, Medicis, Borghese—Curtius—Slinging David—Fighting Gladiator—Effect upon the mind. - - 42

LETTER XCIV.

St. Peter's—Street conducting to—Area before—Façade—Ornaments of interior—Ascent to Cross—Vatican—Museum—Additions of Pius—Superiority of antient to modern Rome—Apollo—Laocoon, &c. Page 46

LETTER XCV.

St. John Lateran, relics, &c.—Baptistery—Triclinium, instrument of Pope's authority—Scala Santa—Climbing devotion—Miraculous image—Religious grants. 51

LETTER XCVI.

Santa Maria Maggiore, ornaments, Culla Sacra, &c.—San Paolo, its magnificence, speaking crucifix, &c.—Memorable altars on Ostian way—Santa Maria della Croce—Catacombs of Sebastian, &c.—San Pietro in Carcere, Peter's prison—In Montorio, Transfiguration—In Vinculis, miraculous union of chains, &c.—Miscellaneous miracles. - - 55

LETTER XCVII.

*Coffee-houses—General subsistence—Fondness for theatricals—Serious opera—Description of comic—*Roman *more than* Italian.

Page 61

LETTER XCVIII.

Benediction of horses—Strictly regarded—Romance of scourge—Funeral processions—Efficacy of candles—Existence of miracles. - - 64

LETTER XCIX.

Excursion to Tivoli—Solfaterra, &c.—Cardinal d'Este—Lucan Bridge—Sybils Temple—Villas of Mæcenas, Horace, &c.—Latter disputed—Temple of Tossa—Fall of Anio—Elegant points—Gardens of Este—Adrian's Villa—Village comedy. 68

LETTER C.

Roman jurisprudence—Punishment of the chord—Stiletto—Roman temper vindictive—Anecdote

—*Anecdote—Street affaffination—Roman feelings illuftrated.* - Page 74

LETTER CI.

Amufement of evening—Mildnefs of winter —Roman cloak—Sacred days—Pleafures of higher and lower ranks—Celebrated emigrants — Academia — Englifh and Roman dance—Defective education of ladies—Reafon affigned—Morals—Darknefs of ftreets. - 80

LETTER CII.

Carnival—Promenade of mafks—Interchange of dreffes between the fexes—Races—Project of retiring—Ultimate effect of carnival on the mind. - - 86

LETTER CIII.

Change in travelling fince Horace—Velletri —Humours of place—Tre-ponti—Improvement of Pontine Marfh by reigning Pope—Approach to Terracina—Characterific of Terracina—Monte Circello— Route

CONTENTS.

Route from Terracina—Beauties of Fondi—Sinuessa—Gaeta—Modern Capua—Reflection on its change. - Page 89

LETTER CIV.
Morals of Naples—Close of carnival—Masquerade—Singular mask—Language of natives corrupt—Great use of term mo—*Objection to its study.* - 95

LETTER CV.
Bay—Prospect from hotel—Promenades—Beauties of country—Corruption of manners—Accountable in lower orders—Lazzaronis—Their character and use—Assassination—Royal decision. - 99

LETTER CVI.
Profligacy of higher orders not easily accountable—Opera—Academia—Display of apartments—Music no object of meeting. 103

LETTER CVII.
Visit to Vesuvius—Ascent—View from base—Lava—Cicerone—Caccia del Re—Pain de Sucre

CONTENTS.

Sucre—Difficult ascent to Crater—Its appearance—Descent to Hermitage—Inhabitants—Dangers reconciled—Power of habit.   -   -   Page 106

LETTER CVIII.

Pompeia—Perfect street—Plan of houses and shops, &c.—Subterraneous vaults—Slow progress of clearing — Reasons—Anecdote of King of Naples.   112

LETTER CIX.

Changes upon coast—Pozzuolo, Temple of Serapis, &c.—Baiæ, Temple of Venus, Mercury, &c.—Bauli—Piscina Mirabile—Elysian Fields—Live only in description—Grotto del Cane—Phenomenon yet unaccounted for—Baths of Nero—Pisciarella—Soil generally impregnated with heat.
   118

LETTER CX.

Musæum at Portici—Court-yard—Repository of antiques—Different cabinets— Ruins

Ruins of Herculáneum—Entrance of lava into houses, &c.—Insensibility of natives—Provision of nature—Uncertainty of soil—Climate, &c.   -   Page 124

LETTER CXI.
Farnese Bull—Hercules—Tomb of Virgil—Happy tradition—Cicerones—Their character—Case of conscience decided—Honorable credentials. - 129

LETTER CXII.
Eruption of Vesuvius—Ascent of the mountain—Appearance—Flow of Lava—Crater, &c. described—View upon mountain—Nature of the discharge—Departure. 133

LETTER CXIII.
Re-entrance of Rome—Difference of impression—Little attraction in Roman society—Excellence of Roman accent—Oaths—Reverse of Cardinal de Bernis—Royal aunts—Abbé Mauri—Decline of papal power—Political

—*Political precautions—Emigrants distinguished.* - - Page 138

LETTER CXIV.

Route to Sienna—Highest point of Appennine—Sienna, cathedral—Itinerant preacher—Religious policy. - 144

LETTER CXV.

Contrast of Campagna and Tuscany—Attempt to account for evils of the former—Severe impost—Magnitude of farms, &c.—Means of reformation—Obstacle to experiment. - 148

LETTER CXVI.

Leghorn described—Political rumours—No effect on commercial cities—Contrast of objects at Leghorn and Rome—Corruption of Romish church—Probable mischiefs of its overthrow. - - 152

CONTENTS.

LETTER CXVII.

Voyage to Genoa—Felucca described—Passengers—Their character—Subject of Lotto—French revolution—Sailor's judgment—Virtuoso's amendment. - Page 156

LETTER CXVIII.

*Carrara—Its marbles—Port of Lerici—Entertainment, &c.—Spezia—English navy—*Capitano *Cook—English prodigies—Passion for stones, best attachment—Successful virtu—Piedmontese education—Prince of Carignano and English prince.*
160

LETTER CXIX.

Coast from Lerici—Land route—Robbers—Francesconi—Port of Carucci—Genoese orator—French and English character contrasted—Virtuoso discouraged—Entrance into harbour of Genoa. 166

LETTER CXX.

Approach to Genoa defcribed—Structure of houfes, &c.—Streets, &c.—Ponte di Carignano—Induftry and public fpirit.

Page 170

LETTER CXXI.

Palaces—Francefco Balbi—Palazzo Roffo—Head of Holofernes—Ornaments of interior, &c.—Durazzo—Anecdote of poffeffor. - - - 174

LETTER CXXII.

Albergo de Poveri—Its good adminiftration and ufes—Paupers Church, &c.—Proceffion of children—Extent of building—Hofpital—Sala de Feriti—Church of Carignano—Statues, &c.—Sedan—Doge—General effect of city. - 178

LETTER CXXIII.

Departure from Genoa—Sailor's devotion—Lerici—Rencontre—Company—Crifis—Contrary

Contrary wind—Land expedition—Arrangement. - Page 184

LETTER CXXIV.

Exchange of Sarzana and Leghorn—Carriages defcribed—Order of proceffion—Day-light—German gutturals—Arrival.
188

LETTER CXXV.

Pifa—Cathedral, &c.—Torre Pendente—Mechanics no defence againſt fear—Baths, &c.—Route to Florence—Dreſs of females. - - 191

LETTER CXXVI.

Rigours of Quareſima, &c.—Second view—Ponte della Trinità—Police—Fair ſex—Morals. - - 195

LETTER CXXVII.

Appennine—Pietra Mala—Aſpect of ground, &c.—Cicerone—Loiano—Sanctity of Good Friday

CONTENTS. lvii

Friday—Advantages of mechanical devotion. - - Page 198

LETTER CXXVIII.

Functions at Bologna—Sepulture of Christ—Italian oratory—Musical solemnity—San Michaele in Bosco—Pleasures of its vicinity—Revisit to Sampieri—Painting reconsidered, &c. - 203

LETTER CXXIX.

Easter-Eve—Pilgrims, processions, &c.—Easter-Day, Cardinal Legate, Gonfalonier, &c.—Wealth, &c. of city—Defeated by superstition—Papal yoke—Probability of its decline. - - 207

LETTER CXXX.

Route to Ferrara—Altered aspect of town—State of superstition—Humours of Rovigo—Delicious village—Communicative landlord—Mountain of the seven churches—Relics of Saints—Terrace—Religious curiosities.
212

CONTENTS.

LETTER CXXXI.

Change of miracle—Defcent of Brenta—Banks of canals, &c.—Approach to Venice—Tour of city—Place of St. Mark—Columns, caffe's, &c.—Rendezvous—Cafinos, &c.—Church of St. Mark, relics, &c.
                                        Page 218

LETTER CXXXII.

Church of San Zacharia, Angel and violin—San Giovanni e Paolo, Saviour and the Levite—St. Roche—Santa Maria della Salute—Scalzi—Frari—Precious depofit—Titian's tomb—Reflection.   223

LETTER CXXXIII.

Palace Pifani, Family of Darius—San Georgio Maggiore, Marriage of Cana—Luxuries of the convent—Grand Canal—Ponte di Rialto—Prices of gondolas—Population—Paths and gondolas.   228

LETTER CXXXIV.

Origin of Venice—Advancement—State of Defence—Person of Venetians—Dress— Masking—Amusements—Gondola described —Gondoliers—Political restraints.

Page 232

LETTER CXXXV.

Police defective—Use of the knife—Skirmishes of Sclavonians—Licentiousness tolerated—Reason assigned—Departure from Venice—Village gratitude. - 237

LETTER CXXXVI.

Padua — Sarcophagus, Antenor — Church, St. Antony—Santa Justina—Prato della Valle, Livy, &c.—University town—Vicenza—Olympic Theatre, interior described —Madonna del Monte Berrico—Inhabitants—Courtesy. - 241

CONTENTS.

LETTER CXXXVII.

Route to Verona—Amphitheatre, interior described—Churches, &c.—Reflections on leaving Italy—Route to Trent—Bolzano, loquacious landlord—Route to Brixen—Change of country—Passing to Inspruck—Dress and manners of Tyrolians. Page 246

LETTER CXXXVIII.

German tragedy—State of Inspruck, &c.—Change of costume—Review of route through Tyrol—Objects of superstition—Different in Italy and Tyrol—Catholic church-yard—Alliance of Catholic to poetic rite. - - - 253

LETTER CXXXIX.

Augsbourg, state of country, &c.—Gold and silver head-dress—Political events—Route to Lindau—Boden See—Circuit of lake—Rosbach, &c.—Constance—Emigrant rendezvous—Power of adversity. 259

LETTER CXL.

Sympathy—Emigrant sufferings—Surviving Politesse—Polonese princess—State of Constance—Environs, &c.—Route to Schaffhouse—Encounter. - Page 264

LETTER CXLI.

Equilibrium restored—Fall of Rhine—Level, rocks, &c.—Points of view—Imagination indulged—Minute beauties—Sole defect—Bridge of wood—Safety against speculation—Route to Zurich—Eglisau—Diverting landlord. - 269

LETTER CXLII.

Mind's caprice—Zurich described—Fair sex —Government severe—Effects of politics on Geneva—Only objects not changed. 274

LETTER CXLIII.

Villa at Lausanne—Its beauty—Change of possessor—Reasons—Bad effects of defeated opposition

opposition—New law respecting travellers—Its operation—Gibbon—Changes felt in society—Not felt by lower orders.
Page 279

LETTER CXLIV.

Amusements discover nature—Flask and valz—Sunday diversions—Jeu de l'Epingle—Questions et reponses—Ariosto quoted—Intellectual character of the Swiss—Pleasant repartee. - - 283

LETTER CXLV.

Rustic enthusiasm—Heloise—Forcible address to passions—Corrupt tendency—Merits considered—Character of writer—Epitaph on Rousseau—Id. on Voltaire. 288

LETTER CXLVI.

Polish princess—Political character—Vivacity, &c.—Bon-mot of Stanislaus—Forced marriage—Italian law—Anecdote—Ariosto wrote from other models—English manners contrasted. - - 292

LETTER CXLVII.

Swiss mourning for massacre of 10th of August—New plans of travel—Project to Egypt defeated—Courteous adieu of emigrants—Advantage of difficulties.
                                                          Page 297

LETTER CXLVIII.

Second tour to Glaciers—Review on route—Jura, Geneva, &c.—Track to Bonneville, environs, &c.—Picturesque approach to Cluse—Valley of Maglan—Cascade—New hotel at Salenche—Cascade of Chede, lake, &c. — Boissons — Montainvert—Guides, Cachat—His atchievements—Saussure, &c. —Unsuccessful expedition to Mont Blanc—Aiguille de Dru—Source of Arveron changed—Arrival at Geneva—Prospect of change of scene. - 302

LETTER CXLIX.

Excursion to Lyons—Addition of company—Patriotic adieu—French boundary—Colonges

longes—Village tactics—National troops—Cerdon—Expensive privilege—Montluel—Female politician—Entrance of Lyons—Place Bellecourt—Hotel, &c. Page 313

LETTER CL.

Table à Hôte—Discussion—City described—Low population—Indignities of statue of Louis XIV.—Gala procession. 318

LETTER CLI.

Burning of royal portraits, and books, &c.—Order of proceeding—Setting fire to pile—Ashes of Louis XIV.—Temper of populace—Dialogue—Farther introduction—Bourgeois guard—Finale of fête. 323

LETTER CLII.

Picture inverted—Prediction—Theatre—Paysan Magistrat—Marseillois march—Symptoms of disorder—Confirmation—Insurrection—Massacre—First victim—Consequences—Procession of mob—New victims—Disco-

very — Calm — Morning deliberation — Paſſports—Retreat projected. Page 328

LETTER CLIII.
Plan of mob—Unfortunate officer—Origin of mob—Conduct of Municipality—Affiches—Counter advertiſements—Orderly defence—Carriage engaged—Manners brutalized—Eſcape anticipated. 336

LETTER CLIV.
Return to Geneva—Second addreſs of Mayor—Iſſue from Lyons—Montleuil—Fugitive prieſts—Nantua—Patriotic volunteers—Guard—Prieſts undiſguiſable—Rencontre—Engliſh character reſpected—Arrival—Reflection upon events, &c. 342

LETTER CLV.
Tour into Germany projected—Attack upon Savoy rumoured—Effect upon Geneva—Arrival at Berne—Deſerter—Generous patriot—Embarras—Dulneſs of Berne.
349

LETTER CLVI.

Military festivities—Swiss officers—Precis Historique—Aaraw—Broug—Dilemma.

Page 354

LETTER CLVII.

Route from Broug—Postilion vanquished—Postilion victor—Cascade of Schaffhause reviewed—Table d'Hôte—Swiss politics—Religious œconomy. - 359

LETTER CLVIII.

Swiss towns, their character—German language — Little analogy with other languages—Plan of tour—Decision—French travellers—Swiss phlegm—English impatience. - - 365

LETTER CLIX.

Departure from Schaffhause—German waggon—Company—German character—Accident—Embarrassment. 370

LETTER CLX.

Simile—Embarrassment renewed—Route continued — Post-house — Eclaircissement — Dinner—Journey resumed. Page 375

LETTER CLXI.

Society—Further difficulties in German language—Riedlingen—Pleasant discovery—Journey to Ulm continued—Ulm described, &c. - - - 381

LETTER CLXII.

Embarking for Vienna—Frenchmen obnoxious—Passengers, &c.*—Landing—French character in youth and age—Inquisitiveness—Table d'Hôte when agreeable.* 387

LETTER CLXIII.

Departure from Gunsburg—Mode of passing the day—Character of passengers—Basle merchant—Hungarian teacher—Madame Vogel—Darmstadt lieutenant — Swiss — Issue from barge. - 392

LETTER CLXIV.

Battle of Blenheim—Scene depicted—Marquisate of Baden—Donavert—Neuberg—Bavarian troops—Adventure—Passing under bridge. - - Page 397

LETTER CLXV.

Forcible current—Ingolstadt—Errors in German character corrected—Diversions of evening—Arrangement of day's voyage—Amusements. - - 402

LETTER CLXVI.

Majestic course of Danube—Military sensibility—Ratisbon—Jealousy of French—Reflection—Comedy of dogs—Departure. 408

LETTER CLXVII.

Village misery—Delicate arrangement—Viltzhofen—Apology for trivial details—Chance of greater adventures. - 413

LETTER CLXVIII.

View of Passau—Nature undescribable—Dresses of females—Scrutiny—Engelhartzel—Austrian officer—Inscription. 417

LETTER CLXIX.

Course to Lintz—Lintz—Interesting scenes—Strudels—Enchanting picture—Pilgrimage of Morbach—Religious salute—Crems—Vienna. - Page 422

LETTER CLXX.

*Entrance upon Vienna—*Caernerthore *theatre described—*Wiedner *theatre, its species of amusement—Remark on German serious song—Theatre in Josephstadt.* 428

LETTER CLXXI.

The Emperor described—Hetz, or combat of wild beasts—Departure of the Hessian.
433

LETTER CLXXII.

Change of residence—German hauteur exhibited in language-masters—Manner of living at Vienna—Diverting embarrassment. - - - 438

CONTENTS.

LETTER CLXXIII.

Knowledge of life how obtained—Italians at Vienna—Independence maintained by a reformation in dress—By avoiding three sorts of characters—Adventurers, good sort of people, Englishmen—Rule illustrated. - - Page 444

LETTER CLXXIV.

Contrast of Sunday in England and in Vienna—Summer rendezvous—Prater—Augarten—Dancing—Humours of a Tanzsaal described. - - 450

LETTER CLXXV.

Streets of Vienna—Squares—Platz Graben —Platz of the Hof—Reception of the Emperor and Empress at the Opera—General freedom of manners in this city. 457

LETTER CLXXVI.

Pleasure of unobserved speculation—Dining-houses, &c. described—Music—Debate—Political orator. - - 463

LETTER CLXXVII.

Situation of Vienna—Extent—Promenades—Climate—Use of ofens—*State of streets—Houses—Lights—Hackney coaches—Order of city—Police of Berne reprobated.*
Page 469

LETTER CLXXVIII.

Singular rencontre—Discovery of Madame V——— —Reflection upon the character of the Hessian, - - 475

LETTER CLXXIX.

Public buildings—Court—University—Academy—Lombard—Liberal institutions.—Churches—Cathedral—St. Peter's—Hof, or Court Church—Tomb of Mareschal Laudohn—Reflections upon sepulchral trophies. - - 479

LETTER CLXXX.

Church of the Reformed—Curious epitaph—Intention of departure—Custom of Angedencken—*Proposed route.* - 484

LETTER CLXXXI.

Pride of office—Entrance upon Bohemia— Particulars respecting the country—Bohemian beauty—Grievances of Wagen-travelling. - - Page 488.

LETTER CLXXXII.

Travelling philosophy, what—Vexatious début—Prague described—Reflections on its history—Alliance of cruelty and religion.

492

LETTER CLXXXIII.

Character of the inhabitants—French politics—Language of Bohemia—Union with Prussian in scheme of travel. 495

LETTER CLXXXIV.

Departure from Prague—Carriage described—Price of travelling—Dangers of the night—Arrival at Peterswalda. 498

LETTER CLXXXV.

Village post-house—Route to Dresden—Dresden described—Gallery—Theatre—Appearance

CONTENTS. lxxiii

pearance of the Elector at the theatre compared with that of the Emperor—Fair sex—Political landlord.   Page 504

LETTER CLXXXVI.

Route to Leipsig—Leipsig described—Population—University—Church—Promenade—Character of the inhabitants.   509

LETTER CLXXXVII.

Free discussion at Leipsig—Departure for Berlin—Adventure—Injury repaired—Arrival at Potzdam.   -   512

LETTER CLXXXVIII.

Advance of posting progressive—Visit to Sans-Souci—Parade at Potzdam—Prussian sensibility.   -   -   517

LETTER CLXXXIX.

Journalière—The search—Berlin described—Houses contrasted with the inhabitants—Opera, &c.—Absence of the King, its effect—Probable change in system.   522

LETTER CXC.

Landlord, &c.—Attendants on stranger—Living costly—Mode of life amongst the natives—Caffés—School of speculation.

Page 526

LETTER CXCI.

Society—Language—Accent of Berlin and Vienna contrasted—Eulogium on the language—Libraries—Manners of people—Humours of a dance—English *rule of fashion—Pipes—Question of trade.* 530

LETTER CXCII.

Severity of climate—Schloss—Prussian Count—Assimilation of German and English character—Study of government neglected.

536

LETTER CXCIII.

Diversions—Theatre—Rotunda—Thüregarten—Charlottenburg—Fashionable ball—Splendor—Project of departure—Morals of city—German acuteness. - 539

LETTER CXCIV.

Courage defined—Retreat from Berlin accounted for—Entrance of Poſt-wagen—Wagen deſcribed—Inconveniences of route—Conductors—Arrival at Hamburg—Table d'Hôte. - **Page 543**

LETTER CXCV.

Society defined—Members of Table d'Hôte deſcribed—Miniſter—Heſſian officer—Lubecker—Hamburg officer—Violent Antigallicaniſm of Heſſian—Baron Trenck—Anecdotes of Joſeph II. and laſt Frederic—Heſſian Royaliſm. - **548**

LETTER CXCVI.

Pleaſures of a commercial town—Storms—Route projected—Poſition, &c. of city—Mode of life—Military—Burleſque diſtich—Fête of Chriſtmas—Anxiety for French and Engliſh intelligence. **554**

LETTER CXCVII.

Sequel of adventures—Travelling ſtock—Paſſage of Elbe—Haarburg—Waggon, &c.

&c.—*Luxuries of Bremen—Journey resumed—Rencontre—English pilot—The contract.* - - Page 559

LETTER CXCVIII.

Route to Leer—Pilot's harangue—Scrutiny—Varieties on way to Neueskans—Gala—Panic in Friesland—Passage to Gröningen—Country described—Costume—Landlord and pilot—Strobusch—Lemmer—Passage of Zuyder See—Residue of stock.
564

LETTER CXCIX.

Sensations on prospect of port—Calculations—Dialogue—Compact—Result—Political aspect of country—Route to Rotterdam—Event at entrance—Finances strengthened—Adventures on route to Helvoet—Embarkation—View of Harwich—Apostrophe of emigrant—Landing—Exit pilot—Arrival at metropolis—Change of costume—Final reflection. - - 570

LETTER I.

Bruffels, April 21, 1791.

MY engagement with you on leaving England ſtands full in my recollection. The delay, be aſſured, has not ariſen from any change of inclination or purpoſe, but ſolely from circumſtances of accidental embarraſſment. The channel is now opened, and you ſhall have no reaſon to charge me with a want of punctuality.

That your expectations may not however be unreaſonably elevated, I will juſt ſtate the ſort of entertainment I undertake to furniſh. The track of Europe, which we are to purſue, is already explored: all that could create wonder or afford

afford delight, has been fo often and fo fully difplayed in the volumes of ancient and modern travel, that curiofity feems nearly exhaufted. What in ages paft were marvels, are now *bagatelles;* and if aftonifhment yet remains to be excited, Mandeville and Munchaufen have written in vain.

I undertake not to unlock the cabinets of princes, or to difentangle the intrigues of courts: tranfient obfervation muft ill fucceed in developing the myfteries of political fyftems. Mine will neither be the voyage of the connoiffeur, nor the journal of the naturalift: I can neither pretend to throw light upon the fchools of painting, nor the fcience of phyfics. If I climb the mountain, it will not be to gauge the atmofphere, to analife the foil, or to clafs the pebbles: if I range among the vallies, it will not be to gather the lilies, or catch the butterflies. But to human nature in all her varieties, to the manners of men and the temper of the times, to the habits of life and the state of opinions, my attention will be directed; and my observations will be delivered, with only so much of order or ornament as may happen to suggest itself at the moment of impression.

Apprized therefore of my plan, you will not, if I depart from the strict line of gravity or criticism, censure me as volatile, nor condemn me as superficial. I appeal from your judgment, to your candour; from the critic, to the friend: and if, after all, the merit of *originality* be wholly wanting; you may at least derive a sort of pleasure from that *variety*, under which the most exhausted subjects rarely want success. Fashions the most obsolete are daily advanced by some new colourings; and an old play seldom wants attractions, when revived with new scenes and dresses.

LETTER II.

THERE is something very peculiar in the first sensations of a man who finds himself transferred to a foreign clime, whose aspect exhibits a groupe of novel images. This sensation is perhaps felt with additional force by the inhabitant of an island who has been accustomed to regard himself as " penitus toto divisus orbe." The country he leaves, seems explored in every recess, though he may not have traversed half its provinces: all before him forms a mighty vista, which he contemplates with eager anxiety.

I confess the first sight of the French coast operated upon me like enchantment. With it seemed associated all the images which bore relation to the history of this wide extended empire—the magnificence of its kings, and the lustre of its heroes; its celebrity

celebrity in arts, in letters, and in arms. When I confidered that this gallant nation, once the admiration and the dread of Europe, was become the feat of internal diftraction and the theatre of political experiment, I fighed over the recollection of its departed grandeur. But when I traced with deeper reflection the foundation of thefe divifions, and the objects of this experiment—when I viewed in impartial retrofpect, the ambition and perfidy which fo remarkably characterized the government of that nation; how incompatible its wars with the principles of reafon or humanity, how formidable a rival it had ever proved to the power, how determined an enemy to the repofe, of Britain—when I reflected how the cabals of this court had perpetuated diffenfion in the kingdoms of Europe, to gratify the paffions and aggrandize the power of its princes; and in how many inftances the blood of nations had been facrificed to the caprice of a miftrefs, a miſtreſs, or the intrigues of a confeſſor, I could not but exult in the changes effected by the united energies of philoſophy and patriotiſm.

The diſorders which accompany every revolution of political moment, are the indiſpenſable terms upon which ſuch felicity is to be obtained; torrents of blood have been deemed not wantonly ſpent, to procure a leſs good: and I could not but anticipate the coming æra, when the laſt touches ſhall be put to a revolution, which has aſtoniſhed, and may inſtruct mankind: —when out of the ruins of tyranny and ſervitude, ſhall ariſe a government, flouriſhing in all the luſtre of reaſonable authority and juſt ſubordination; a government whoſe *internal* policy ſhall exhibit a king ruling by law, and a people obeying by choice; whoſe *external* policy ſhall diſplay the happy effects of an unambitious and equitable ſyſtem of conduct, in the permanent tranquillity of Europe.

The

LETTER II.

The ancient prejudices of this nation acknowledged no heroifm but that of the fword, and applauded no atchievements but thofe of conqueft. It was referved for a later æra, and a more enlightened legiflature, to eftablifh the dominion of reafon on the ruins of prejudice; to annex to the life of each individual, an importance hitherto unfelt; to convert the laurels of war into civic wreaths; and decree thofe triumphs to the defenders of liberty, which had been prefcriptively appropriated to the defolators of their country, and the deftroyers of mankind.

LETTER III.

WE landed at Ostend, and took the route by Ghent to Brussels. This gave us an opportunity of seeing a town, which has occupied an important place in the history of Europe. Ghent, or Gand, possessed in ancient times a population far superior to its present numbers; and was of such extent as to occasion a humorous boast of Charles V., that he could put all Paris in his glove, " dans son Gand." This town, the capital of Austrian Flanders, was long the seat of commerce in time of peace, and the bulwark of defence in time of war; no place has acquired more military fame, nor been witness to more heroic acts.

The early records of its history report the spirit and intrepidity of the Gantois. The

LETTER III.

The pacification of Ghent forms a great epoch in their history. This was formed in 1576, by a union of the estates for the establishment of their religious and civil privileges, and ratified by Philip II. Famed for revolt and sedition of old, it became again the seat of tumult in 1787. Ghent had till that moment taken no decided part, but the entrance of the Brabanters in military force, joined to the insolence of the Austrian soldiery, drew the citizens to the party of the insurgents, and the Austrian army quitted the place with disgrace. If we may credit the accounts given of this defeat, it redounds infinitely to the discredit of the Austrians, who, to the amount of several thousand disciplined troops, abandoned the town, citadel, and magazine, to the depredations of three or four hundred vagabonds, " flying," as a writer expresses it, " devant quelques malheureux de la po-" pulace, sans chefs, sans armes, and sans " culottes."

The

LETTER III.

The issue of these revolutional tumults had cast a gloom over the place. It wore the aspect of war, though in a state of actual tranquillity. The majority of its inhabitants seem composed of soldiers and ecclesiastics; and promenades, streets, and avenues were thronged with hussars, priests, and beggars.

The churches are the grand ornament of Ghent, as of every country under the influence of superstition. These sacred edifices are adorned with all that art and riches can contribute to constitute splendour; but what renders them most the object of a traveller's attention is, that they are the grand repositories of the chefs d'œuvres of the Flemish school.

The cathedral of St. Gédule is a magnificent building, and crowded with paintings of the Flemish masters. Though it was passion week, and the priests were constantly upon duty, the altars were not as usual thronged with devotees. The population of a Catholic town may be easily inferred

inferred from the aspect of its churches at this sacred season. Some few miserable wretches only were to be found engaged in their devotions, and bowing round the deserted shrines. I shall not enter into a detail of the works of the admirable artists which embellish this place, nor attempt to describe the sensations created by them. I suffered my sensibilities to be spontaneously excited, and probably often felt emotions at variance with academical law. Criticism may decree what *ought* to please; but in painting, as in poetry, an appeal will not fail to be made from the understanding to the heart. Shakespeare has charmed, not only *without*, but even *against* rule: and yet the English nation would rather sacrifice the laws that control, and the critics that censure, than yield to oblivion and obscurity one drama of the immortal bard.

A town in the circumstances of Ghent, could not long find amusement for a traveller; the ferocious aspect of the military,

whose

LETTER III.

whose numbers and discipline are scarcely sufficient to retain in subjection the turbulent malcontents, added to the gloom of evacuated houses and a deserted theatre, induced us to quit Ghent on the following day, and pursue our route to Brussels. I could not leave the town without lamenting the evils which have defaced and depopulated a place, that once possessed such strength, splendour, and opulence. The miseries of unsuccessful revolt are here accumulated upon the head of the laborious and peaceful citizen.

Political grievances when extended to an enormous height demand political reform; and this can, in certain cases, only be effected by popular opposition. That there existed circumstances sufficiently aggravating, and sufficiently oppressive, to warrant the remonstrances preferred by the Brabanters, cannot be disputed. The cabals of his ministers and agents, rather than the disposition of the Emperor, prevented the equitable

LETTER III.

equitable arrangements at firſt required; till the ſpirits of either party became heated, and ineffectual remonſtrance was ſucceeded by outrageous revolt. The knavery and miſconduct of thoſe who headed the refractory Belgians, were the cauſes of thoſe diſtreſſes and diſtractions which afterwards attended them.

The conceſſions of Leopold are a demonſtrative proof of the injuſtice of Joſeph. Had Belgiojaſo poſſeſſed the conciliating talents of Merci d'Argenteau, the ſword probably had never been drawn; and had there been prudence and patriotiſm in the leaders of the revolt, had the poſts of Vandernoot and Van Eupen been ſupplied by a Mirabeau and a Fayette, the ſword had not been ſheathed till Belgic independence had been eſtabliſhed.

I have ever commiſerated the lot of a country, which by conqueſt or ceſſion has become the appendage of a great empire. An arbitrary monarch may poſſeſs in ſome happy moments the feelings of a man, and all that lies within the compafs of his own adminiftration comes more or lefs under his own infpection; but a government by agent, fuffragan, or viceroy, is furely a government moft formidable to the liberties of a people. How are they to prefs through that phalanx of minifters, penfioners, and courtiers, which fill up all the avenues of appeal? The diftance from the fountain of authority extinguifhes hope of redrefs, and urges them to remedies the moft violent and defperate.

LETTER IV.

WE find Bruſſels inveſted with the ſame military terrors, and deformed by the ſame melancholy rites, as Ghent. That part of the town in which the people of faſhion reſide, is of modern date; the houſes are built of ſtone, the apartments ſpacious, and the general aſpect of the place is magnificent. The gloomy ceremonies of the holy week have thrown a veil over the uſual gaieties of this capital, and interrupt for the preſent the tide of amuſement. Even active occupation is in great part ſuſpended; and the church has ſupplanted the theatre, the ball-room, and the exchange. The avenues of the cathedral are crowded from morning to night. All ranks and conditions ſeem unanimous in the celebration of the ſacred ſeaſon.

The

LETTER IV.

The carnival, which I underſtand was uncommonly brilliant, has left behind it the memory of ſome irregularities; but if the moſt aſſiduous and uninterrupted attendance upon the ceremonies of the church can avail, there will not remain a folly to bluſh for, or a crime to repent of. It is really amuſing to ſee the multitudes that throng around the ſacred porticoes, and the ardour of the devotional penance which they diſcover. Not content with worſhipping at one ſhrine, and making intereſt with one ſaint, they fly from altar to altar, ſeek an intereſt in every ſacrifice, and mingle their devotions with the incenſe of every order. In England, it is deemed unneceſſary for the great to interfere in the ſervices of religion; faſhion and convenience are there paramount to reaſon and duty; but here the greateſt blend with the meaneſt in all the ſervices which are called religious, however jealous of rank and ſuperiority in civil and ſocial life.

A card-

LETTER IV.

A card-party was formed on Friday evening, being the Vendredi Saint, the singular object of which induces me to mention it. It was held at the apartments of the Comtesse de Choiseul, and attended by most of the fashionable people. Agreeably to the law of the assembly, the gains of the evening were to be disposed of, at the discretion of the lady of the house, in purposes of charity. This is a custom of ancient establishment.

An assembly of this nature, where pleasure and religion are combined, must give birth to many singular impressions. No day in the calendar can wear a more gloomy face, or excite more devotional sentiments in the breast of a catholic, than the day of the crucifixion. Every means are employed to excite superstitious horror, and recal to the mind the memory of that darkness which enveloped the face of the earth. All that breathes the air of dissipation must be entirely banished, and amusement so qualified by motive, and so chastised by austerity, as to receive the serious cast of religious exercise. To-morrow is, I understand, the concluding day of this severe penance: consolation will then be administered to the consciences of the devotees, who will emerge, fully acquitted of all past guilt, and at liberty to commence a fresh account. The streets, parade, and promenades will resume their brilliancy: at present, they exhibit a striking picture of spiritual indolence. Superstition has long since consecrated this week to purposes which are deemed incompatible with secular occupation. The days being too sacred for labour, and too long for devotion, a great part of time is yawned away in listless *ennui*.

The consecration of days* is a custom of barbarous origin; and the pious enthusiasm of the first christians gave it the sanction of their own observance. The church of England,

---

* This is only to be understood in reference to days consecrated to *particular persons*.

land, which has had the merit of reſtoring to ſociety the days and weeks hallowed by bigotry, ſtill retains ſome few, which ſhe refuſes to ſecularize, and which ſerve, like the ancient hangings in a modernized manſion, to mark the date of the edifice, and perpetuate the taſte of thoſe who undertook its reform. It is plain, the contract between prieſt and people in thoſe regions of ſuperſtition, is very much in favour of the former, though equally to the ſatisfaction of each. The latter ſurrender without reluctance the fruits of their labour to the uſe of the former, who only engage for an undefined retribution—a bright reverſion in the ſky—at ſome future and diſtant period.

LETTER V.

Bruffels, April 24, 1791.

I AM juft returned from affifting at a ceremony, in which I appeared to myfelf to make no very refpectable figure. A proclamation, pofted in a public fpot near the Hotel de Ville, announced the return of a celebrity, in which all pious catholics take great intereft, and from which, agreeably to the tenor of the advertifement, every devout chriftian might derive great advantage. It was the celebration of an event moft important to the caufe of religion, in the prefervation of the Image of the Virgin Mary, from the anti-catholic zeal of the reformers of Scotland. The attachment of her friends induced them to hazard much for her fafety. They fled beyond fea with her, and after a thoufand thousand miracles, and experiencing numerous vicissitudes, " per varios fluctus et " tot discrimina rerum," they auspiciously reached Brussels. Many honours were paid her upon her arrival on the Continent, and particularly at the ceremony of her solemn reception among the Augustine monks. Successive popes concurred in granting plenary pardons to all who would commemorate the anniversary of her happy deliverance. The Image was placed in the centre of the church, and illuminated with numberless tapers. High mass was sung, to which succeeded a variety of religious *divertisements*, intended to represent the *hair-breadth escapes* the Virgin had experienced, and the efficacy which this wonderful Image still possessed. All seemed eager to croud around her, and some never quitted her feet. A splendid procession concluded the service: and the holy fathers chaunted their lays, preceded by all kinds of mysterious insignia, from their own to the church of St. Gedule.

LETTER V.

As I was not so deeply interested in the ceremonies as the rest of the congregation, I had more leisure to comment on the drama. The devotion of the people was unquestionably sincere. They bowed, and prostrated themselves, with an energy and fervour, which indicated the most unsuspicious faith in her more than magnetical virtue. I observed several walking round the shrine, and bowing with the utmost inconvenience to themselves, lest they should accidentally turn their backs upon her. As I had disposed myself in the middle of the aisle, the procession passed me, and gave me an opportunity of admiring the happy influence of a religious life upon these holy fathers, who seemed to have profited much from the residence of the Virgin among them. Countenances more expressive of pleasure and festivity could not be found, even in the paradise of Mahomet. It was not a little surprising to see so great a multitude assisting at those services, considering the recent

LETTER V.

recent penance performed in the holy week.

It should seem that the people of Bruffels muſt be deſperate ſinners, or exemplary ſaints. The quantum of holineſs, including all the beads that are counted, and the *Ave-Marias* that are ſaid, bears certainly, if any allowance be made for human frailty, more than a juſt proportion to the ordinary *quantum* of ſin. But here mankind are, perſuaded that none of thoſe pious duties will be loſt. When ſufficient has been done to cancel their own crimes, all ſupernumerary acts become a ſort of clear gain, which reſts entirely at their own diſpoſal. The canons of the church allow the tranſfer of this, with the ſame eaſe as any other ſpecies of alienable property. If a man die inteſtate, it naturally reverts to the church, and becomes a part of the eccleſiaſtical fund. This commerce, in paſt ages ſo productive to the proprietors, has ſuffered conſiderably in its revenues. A great part

part of Europe, however, continues pioufly attached to the old traffic, and multitudes yet facrifice folid poffeffions for this imaginary property; convinced, it fhould feem, that the exchange is decidedly in their favour.

LETTER VI.

Bruffels, April 27, 1791.

THE gloom is diffipated, the curtain is drawn up, and the gay orgies of pleafure fucceed to the melancholy folemnities of penance. The theatre is opened, the artificers refume their occupations, and the circles of the fafhionable world their amufements. If I read aright the countenances of thofe who are emerged from religious aufterity to pleafurable relaxation, they are not a little gratified by the change. The torrent of feftivity, which is now opened,

appears

LETTER VI.

appears to infinuate, that religious aufterity has had its effect; that its devout fubjects have amply cancelled all paft guilt, and made, as it were, Heaven their creditor for future fins.

The theatre is under very bad management. The edifice itfelf is fufficiently large and commodious, but the fcenery and the performers are much below mediocrity; though the enormous price paid for the boxes, which are engaged by particular perfons, brings in a revenue fully adequate to its fupport. The fociety here is numerous and brilliant; regular evenings are appropriated to thofe ladies who lead the *ton*.

In addition to thofe which are eftablifhed, and of ordinary recurrence, concerts and dances are occafionally given. An introduction once effected, and the regular ceremonies of etiquette performed, the whole field of amufement is opened, and wherever you hear mention of feftivities, you are at liberty to participate them. The

Comtesse de Choiseul is at the head of these parties; at a very advanced period of life, she possesses found health and hilarity of spirits. The duties and the pleasures of life occupy the whole of her attention, and her time is divided between amusement and devotion. The dignity of her age and station, and the courteousness of her manners, give her the highest importance in the fashionable assemblies.

The modern champion of chivalry has expressed in terms of brilliant lamentation, his sorrow for the extinction of the ancient gallantry of France. But this I assure you, that, however expatriated, and rooted from its native soil, gallantry flourishes here with increasing vigour: and in no part of Europe, perhaps, is the empire of the fair sex so firmly established. All who would move in the sphere of polite life, must pass the ordeal of female scrutiny.

The " Ladies club," is by far the most brilliant society here, and this club disposes of

LETTER VI.

of the fates of every stranger, who solicits a part in the amusements of the place. The ladies who compose it have their regular times of meeting, and of settling business. The stranger who sues for initiation must in due form be proposed; and, under the direction of the lady president, the club proceeds to a ballot. Nor is this always an ineffective form.

The club gave a ball lately at the hotel " Prince de Galles." Each female member has the privilege of introducing a gentleman for the evening, and it was in virtue of this privilege that I obtained admittance. The company were numerous, and exhibited a splendid show of beauty and rank. The greater part was formed by the fugitive noblesse of France. Here were rallied the scattered members of the dis-embodied phalanx; and, in defiance of decrees and spoliations, gave brilliancy and hilarity to the assembly.

LETTER VII.

Bruffels, May 1, 1791.

POLITENESS is a term with all mankind of familiar and continual ufe; all fuppofe they underftand it; and to requeft a definition, would be to offer an affront. I had an opportunity a few evenings paft, of feeing it exemplified, at leaft in a manner very entertaining, by the Marquis de ———, who has lately purchafed an eftate in the vicinity of Bruffels, upon the excellence of which, he was enlarging to fome Englifh ladies—the convenience of his houfe, and the elegance of his gardens, in which he had exactly copied the Englifh ftile. He had ftored his cellars with excellent wine, and nothing was wanting to his felicity, but the honour of their opinion upon the tafte and
execution

LETTER VII.

execution of the whole. The ladies gave him to underſtand, that his deſcription had ſo faſcinated them, that they would certainly not loſe ſo fair an opportunity of being amuſed.

This was what the Marquis neither intended nor expected, yet the embarraſſment cauſed no viſible interruption of his converſation. Nothing could indeed charm him more than the honour the ladies intended him, but he muſt not at the ſame time neglect to inform them that his houſe had ſuffered conſiderably in the late tumults—his ground had been ravaged—his plantations deſtroyed—his cellars robbed—and, in a word, ſuch diſorders committed, that the preſent ſituation of his villa would not recompenſe the ladies for the trouble they would be at in viſiting him; and, concluding with a turn of pleaſantry and a handſome bow, left the room with an air " *par* " *faitement bien.*"

I was

I was forcibly ſtruck by the *addreſſe* with which the Marquis extricated himſelf from this delicate diſtreſs, without any ſymptom of alarm, or violation of gallantry. His advance and retreat were equally finiſhed in their kind; and we were compelled to acknowledge, that no man could make an offer with more politeneſs, than a Frenchman; and no man could relieve himſelf from the pain of fulfilling it, with a better grace.

LETTER VIII.

Bruſſels, April 29, 1791.

THERE is a philoſophy which can triumph over the accidents of life, which can ſmile in the face of the moſt calamitous events, and blunt the ſhafts of the moſt adverſe fortune. It is the philoſophy of the heart, and has no connection with the fabricated ſyſtems of the ſchools. No nation upon earth exemplify ſo ſtrongly the truth

truth of this maxim, nor give such evidence of the operation of its principle, as the French. Expelled a country which gave them birth—divested of all that gave them importance—stript of their hereditary honours and patrimonial fortunes, they retain what gold or titles could never give, and what no decree can take away, " *la* " *gaieté de cœur.*" Brussels, at this moment, proves an asylum to almost all the expatriated noblesse of France. Every hour announces some new arrival, and hotels and promenades are thronged to excess.

The accumulated evils which pursue these splendid fugitives, the fatal dislodgment they have experienced from the seats which their ancestors had occupied for ages, and which the sanction of government, the prescription of time, and the temper of their vassals, seemed to augur eternal, would be sufficient to depress a people less insensible of calamity. The morning is however occupied in councils, the evening in cards; the pressing exigencies of business have not weakened in them the thirst of pleasure; though plots, assassinations, and all the horrid machinations of defeated aristocracy fill the hours of cabal, they find no place in the circles of society. Counter revolutions fall before " *La bagatelle.*" No plots are agitated beyond intrigue; and no assassinations meditated but of time and spleen.

No man who mixes with the evening parties would imagine that the countenances he beholds on those occasions, are worn by men who are bankrupts in fortune and in title. The charms of song, the movements of the dance, and the evolutions of Faro equally interest the whole: the same gesture, the same volubility, the same enchanting vivacity animate the assemblies, that prevailed in days of better fortune.

The most vigilant observer would not discover a moment in which the memory of annihilated grandeur induces a transient gloom. If reports transpire of any new
patriotic

LETTER VIII.

patriotic ravages, an involuntary figh efcapes, which is inftantly replaced by returning gaiety; and neither air nor feature are fuffered to betray the moft diftant fymptoms of dejection or defpair. An Englifhman in fimilar circumftances would fly for refuge to folitude, perhaps to fuicide.

The character of a Frenchman is to be found in his language. A *moderate* man can fcarcely fatisfy himfelf with the terms fuited to the temper of his mind. All is exaggerated and exceffive. If you attempt to be natural, you will yet be figurative; and can fcarcely make yourfelf comprehended, without a metaphor.

Such is the tone of this language, that praife and blame, pleafure and pain, joy and forrow, admit of no mediums. *Charmant* and *fuperbe* is the leaft you can fay of what is recommended to your approbation: if you fay lefs than *vilaine* of what you diflike, you will be deemed phlegmatic;—if you are pleafed, you muft be *ravi*;—if you are vexed,

vexed, you muft be *defolé*;—if you are not in extacies, you muft be *au defefpoir*. All thefe you may heighten by a thoufand arts, and you will do the language very little juftice without thefe augmentatives. If *charmant* is not fufficient, repeat it, and you will talk more like a Frenchman. There are a million little prefixes which you may employ to great advantage, *très, fort, infiniment,* &c. which ferve to colour your fenfations, and raife your expreffions as far beyond nature as imagination extends.

The genius of the people accords exactly with their language. The moft lively forrow or rapturous joy is excited by the moft trivial incident: but lively fenfations, like vivid colours, are not made for permanence. Thus the man endued with this temper of mind, will triumph over all the efforts of malice or misfortune. He is poffeffed of refources, which will illumine the darkeft fcenes of mifery. He will combat with undiminifhed confidence, though thoufands fall; and continue to hope, where all others would defpair.

LETTER IX.

Bruffels, April 30, 1791.

NATIONAL varieties form the grand fource of entertainment to a traveller: nor is it of confequence to him, whether the manners and cuftoms of the people he vifits, claim any manifeft fuperiority over thofe of his own country; it is fufficient for the purpofes of his curiofity that they *differ*. Novelty is the charm which commends them to his attention, and the merit of the difference is a fubject of fubfequent reflection.

A celebrated moral philofopher has affigned three laws for the government of man, and as the rules of human conduct—the law of honour, the law of the land, and the divine law. Thefe are certainly very competent to the decifion of any queftion

in morals, but had he chosen to have been more universal, he might have added a fourth law—I mean, the law of etiquette; for the law of honour, in which some might suppose it included, only prohibits the perpetration of any act which would degrade the gentleman, or interrupt the offices of social harmony. This, therefore, applies only to the more prominent parts of conduct, and those actions which border upon morality. The law of etiquette confines itself wholly to those minutiæ of deportment, which have as little connection with morals as with physics. A word, a look, or a motion, contrary to etiquette, fixes upon you the stain of culpability. And then, though you had observed the other three with the spirit of a man, the fidelity of a citizen, and the virtue of a saint; you would stand no fairer chance of maintaining your rank in polished society, than a Hottentot. And so various are the character and sentiments of the people of different countries, that a man
might

LETTER IX.

might as well attempt to find the reasonings of Newton in the system of Des Cartes, and deduce the doctrines of the Koran from the writings of Voltaire, as to determine from the general principles of politesse the maxims of national etiquette.

I was led to these reflections by a circumstance which took place the evening of the ball given by the ladies club. An English gentleman, who had been introduced as a stranger, and whose ignorance of French etiquette might seem to plead his excuse, was actually observed holding conversation with his partner when the dance was ended. Had she been a married lady, this would have attracted no notice. The circumstance would have been imputed to gallantry, or intrigue, in either of which cases, the lady is subject to no authority, and the gentleman responsible to no tribunal—but that of her husband. *He* is in all probability engaged in too many similar intrigues, to find leisure for so irksome a business. Thus a *tête-a-tête* of this nature would neither have been

deemed

deemed criminal nor dangerous. But the lady was *unmarried*, and the extraordinary conduct of the gentleman was referred to the sudden influence of a soft attachment. The eyes of the company were upon him. " Le pauvre homme! il est amoureux," was circulated in whispers. This sudden passion filled up the chasm of conversation in the morning circles; and my friend, who had hitherto continued unsuspicious, was surprised the following evening, by finding the eyes of the company pointedly fixed upon him. He received with astonishment the congratulations of some, the condolences of others, and the assurances of all—that he was really in love. It was in vain that he denied the charge, and persisted against the existence of the passion; it was in vain that he urged the shortness of the conversation, and the innocence of its object; all were unanimous in deciding against him: and it was resolved *nem. con.* that when a gentleman holds conversation with an unmarried

married lady, love muft be either the caufe or the confequence.

I fhould perhaps intreat your indulgence, when I record thofe trivial details. But though the bold and prominent lines of character are to be found in acts of higher importance; though heroifm is moft fuccefsfully traced in the field, and fagacity in the cabinet; manners are only to be deciphered in the leffer incidents of focial intercourfe. It is the zephyr and the fhower which difclofe the foliage of the rofe or the myrtle, though ftorms and tempefts may be neceffary to prove the ftrength of the oak or the cedar.

LETTER X.

THE park at Bruffels is a very charming promenade. The walks are indeed for the moft part ftraight, cutting each other at right angles, and ornamented with ftatues. There are, however, fome varieties in thofe walks, not ufual in continental gardens.

The buildings which face the park on each side, appear very magnificent from the different avenues. In addition to the amusement of walking, you may retire into some rooms, which are to be found in the recesses of the gardens, to drink *coffee*, *liqueurs*, &c. and read the papers of the day. The fashionable people are to be seen upon the walks usually from twelve to one, and mixed ranks of people in great numbers promenade here in the evening.

I have been to visit a place in the environs of Brussels, which is esteemed one of the most striking beauties of the vicinity; it is the palace of the arch-duchess, and built of a beautiful stone. It merits well the eulogium that has been passed upon it. The apartments are large and well finished, and the situation commands a very charming and extensive prospect. The grounds are, agreeable to the reigning fashion on the continent, laid out à l'Angloise, and discover

cover some taste. The furniture of the Palace, which is said to be uncommonly elegant, was removed, in consequence of the outrages committed during the late troubles. It is now about to be replaced, and the arch-duchess is daily expected to resume her court at Brussels.

All the accounts I have received here, respecting the *dernier coup* of the revolutionists, are filled with the tragical horrors experienced by the inhabitants of Brussels and its environs. Public men and public measures were at first the sole objects of the popular indignation; but upon the ill success of the Brabanters, and the triumphs of the Austrians, the face of affairs changed, and private property fell a sacrifice to the madness of the multitude. Abandoned by their leaders and pursued by their enemies, these unhappy wretches formed the desperate resolution of restoring their ruined hopes and fortunes by a general pillage. The ravages committed on this occasion
were

were unparalleled in number and enormity. Not bounding their infolence to the public roads and ftreets, they entered private houfes, and committed all the outrageous acts of an unprincipled banditti. The entrance of the Auftrian troops terminated thofe depredations, and reftored to the difordered town the appearance of tranquillity.—I fay, *the appearance,* for I cannot reconcile myfelf to the afpect of a place in the fituation of Bruffels at this moment. The ftern countenances of the huzzars, who are ftationed in all poffible avenues—who eye all our motions with the moft favage jealoufy—and who are authorized to fire upon us at their difcretion, ftrike me with a horror which I fhould fcarcely have felt in the tumults which preceded their entrance.

The diforders of a mob are hideous, yet if property is to be fecured at the expence of liberty, and perfonal fafety to be bartered for general protection, I cannot conceive

the

the situation greatly meliorated. For my own part, I can as easily imagine misery to prevail in a free government, as enjoyment to exist under the control of military law.

LETTER XI.

Brussels, May 2, 1791.

OUR resolution is formed for quitting Brussels to-morrow, and entering upon the tour of Holland. I leave with regret this court of amusement, though the objects which lie before me most warmly interest my curiosity. A traveller should not long rest at one place. He may reside with safety the period necessary for observation; but if he pass that limit, curiosity ripens into attachment: he strikes his roots into the soil, and is not torn away without reluctance. A longer residence at Brussels might produce this effect.

If

LETTER XI.

If I have framed juft fentiments of the character of a modern Fleming, this people have fuffered confiderable degeneracy. In the higher ranks of life, the intercourfe of nations has very much affimilated the external characters of men, and the genuine traits of nature are only to be developed, where neither force nor fafhion have been employed to new-model or refine.

The opinions which I have eftablifhed, from my beft inveftigation, are very difadvantageous to the prefent race. The moft prominent features in their character are ignorance, dulnefs, and obftinacy. A more provoking trio of evil properties cannot be imagined. It was our misfortune, in more than one inftance, to be the victims of them. In the high road between Ghent and Bruffels, we efcaped by a miracle, from the accidental fracture of the fhaft of the carriage, the confequences of an overthrow. The alarm occafioned by this cataftrophe foon brought around us

the

LETTER XI.

the boors of the adjoining village, who, with folded arms and vacant countenances, encircled the chaife, offering no affiftance, and talking, as if each were emulous to out-croak his fellow in their horrid guttural jargon. At length the arrival of the poft-mafter was announced. Scraps of cordage were immediately employed, and this expert veteran, having ended his job, bade the poftilion lead forward. " Allez," faid he, and turning to me, " Soyez tranquilles " meffieurs—tout ira bien, vous ne rifquerez " rien; J'en reponds." Thefe words were fcarcely uttered, when every knot gave up its hold, with an explofion which induced us to difmount with all convenient fpeed; the carriage was then dragged to the neareft town, and put into the hands of a profeffed artificer. It was difficult, among the multitude of workmen, to diftinguifh who was principal, not fewer than fifteen or twenty being employed in this paltry bufinefs. We foon perceived that this Herculean tafk furpaffed

their

LETTER XI.

their talents, and urged to them the inefficiency of their contrivances; but our advice and directions were treated with equal contempt, and the consequence was, that the shaft broke from its hold before we had lost sight of the town.

The inhabitants of the Belgic provinces were always a brave and a hardy people, but never famed for quickness or penetration. The pillars of their fame are monuments rather of industry than of genius. They have acquired the praise of agricultural skill, for the patient labour which they bestowed upon the improvement of their marshy lands. Their tapestries were the admiration of Europe, before the reign of good taste commenced; and if their school of painters be excepted, they have, I believe, little else to boast. As to their moral qualities, they rank, if possible, still lower than their intellectual. Imposition and extortion circumvent you on all sides—no vigilance of your own will avail you;

LETTER XII.

you; and no magiftrate will attend to your complaint. Againft fraud and difhonefty there are no laws, or the laws have no energy. You even frequently become the victim of rapacity to the very organ of juftice; and the man whom you would punifh, is the judge to whom you muft appeal.

LETTER XII.

Spa, May 17, 1791.

THE fcenes which have intervened fince my laft, are fo numerous, and their fucceffion fo rapid, that I feem to have made a vifionary journey. In thirteen days we have defcribed a courfe which might well have occupied thrice the number. Our route lay by Antwerp, where we paffed the firft day after quitting Bruffels. No town has been more celebrated for its fplendour and its importance than

LETTER XII.

Antwerp. Entering it with expectations raised to no common height, my disappointment was proportionably severe. Its buildings are, indeed, formed upon a bold model, and exhibit fine specimens of ancient architecture.

The church of Nôtre Dame is a cabinet of rare workmanship and exquisite paintings. It has not the polished elegance of St. Bavon at Ghent, but it is in my opinion more majestic and venerable. The grand altar piece by Rubens, however, made me regard all other objects with comparative indifference. This celebrated painting is a descent from the cross, and possesses an energy, a beauty, and an expression, which entitle it to rank with the first productions of this master. I believe it is generally allowed of this painting, that it has the united excellencies of design and colouring in a very eminent degree, and connoisseurs give it a place in the highest class of crucifixion pieces.

The

LETTER XII.

The churches and convents are so numerous at Antwerp, that no one but an amateur of the fine arts, of the most exhaustless patience, could attend to a particular investigation of the whole. For my own part, I could scarcely resolve upon undertaking the routine, such a melancholy aspect clouded the face of every thing—the streets appeared depopulated—the best houses cleared of the inhabitants—neither the bustle of trade, nor the rattle of amusement, were to be heard. The channel of commerce has been diverted, and pleasure flown to other climes: six thousand Austrian troops were in possession of this town, the fanaticism and violence of which made so conspicuous a figure in the late Belgic revolution. Though Leopold's clemency passed an act of amnesty and oblivion, numbers refused to return, either from obstinacy or distrust.

We went to the theatre in the evening, which exhibited a melancholy picture of desertion.

desertion. The only amusement which attracts at present, is derived from the evolutions of the parade, which are performed in the Place de Mer. Here you may observe a motley assemblage, of which Abbés compose the greater part, ranged on the several sides, and with folded arms seeking some occupation for the heavy hours. Scarcely any provisions are to be purchased in the town, and the small market which has survived holds up a price beyond the capacities of all but the rich.

The storm, though hushed, is not dissipated. Many unquiet spirits remain, whom neither force nor favour have yet subdued. Secret combinations still exist; the cap of liberty is occasionally exhibited, and the name of VANDERNOODT devoutly invoked. A convivial meeting had, some few evenings past, expanded the hearts of some old rebels; and the orgies of Bacchus having rekindled the flames of freedom, this sally of intemperance was not terminated
without

LETTER XII.

without the intervention of the military. Dangers more serious may be apprehended from the ambition of the Prussian court, which will doubtless lose no opportunity of re-animating the Belgic discontents; nor is it quite clear that the House of Orange will hold itself bound by the faith of the last treaty to continue neuter.

The manœuvres of the House of Brandenburg are generally known in the late revolution, and the negotiations of Vandernoodt with the House of Orange have not lost their impression. The fate of Belgia is not yet decided, and Leopold holds on a very unsure tenure this part of his dominions.

The general temper of the people may be inferred from the general aspect of the country, in which nothing is to be read but dejection or discontent. Were the overtures of the Emperor cordially embraced, cheerfulness would have relumined the countenance; industry and amusement would have been prosecuted as usual, and

every

every thing ere now·have recovered its tone. But, when all ſtagnates—when trade has no vigour, and pleaſure no attraction—a juſt foundation exiſts for ſuſpicion, that the wound is not yet healed;—that though quelled by terror, the ſpirit of ſedition yet rages in ſecret; and only wants a favourable moment for breaking forth with aggravated fury.

LETTER XIII.

ANTWERP is one among thoſe numerous cities which have experienced the viciſſitudes of fortune. For near two centuries it aſtoniſhed Europe by the magnitude of its riches, and the extent of its commerce. Equally celebrated for the arts of war and peace, it ſuſtained with firmneſs the attacks of its enemies. The obſtinate reſiſtance made by this city to the Duke of Parma, and the ten months ſiege it suftained in 1585, form a very honourable part of its hiftory. In common with the other Belgic towns, it has repeatedly changed its mafters, and been repeatedly the fubject of war and pillage. Rubens and Vandyke, Cramage, Plantin, and Muretus, are among the number of thofe who have diftinguifhed Antwerp as a mother of the fine arts, and a nurfe of literature.

Weakened by fucceffive affaults from its neighbours, and its tyrants, Antwerp experienced its laft and moft decifive blow from the Hollanders, by the treaty of Munfter. This treaty, configning to Holland the exclufive navigation of the Scheld, cut off the refources of commercial wealth, and precipitated the declining grandeur of this ancient city, the gloomy and deferted edifices of which ftill remain the monuments of its paft fplendour. One *trait* which ever diftinguifhed this city, is ftill to be found in its decayed and fallen ftate. Fanaticifm has fuffered no diminution, nor have

have any of those rude assaults which subverted its wealth and its commerce, weakened or impaired its rooted attachment to the Catholic faith.

No place in Europe is so immediately under the influence of every religious absurdity. All the long series of monkish iniquities has not convinced these people of the possibility of error in ecclesiastics; and their consciences, their faith, and their purses, are still at the disposal of priests and prelates. The late revolution owed much of its energy to the religious prejudices of this deluded people; and Antwerp and Malines discovered the genuine fury of fanaticism. The notorious Van Eupen, who acted so principal a part in that political drama, was originally a canon of this place; and if we may credit the intelligence received in those parts, and the universal tone of the writings of that time, his history is not greatly to the credit of ecclesiastical purity. In the capacity of Grand Peniten-

LETTER XIII.

Penitentiary, to which he was exalted by the liberal patronage of the Bishop of Antwerp, his province comprehended all spiritual jurisdiction over the numerous inhabitants of this great see. All cases of conscience, doubts of faith, and religious embarrassments, came under his review, and were determined by his decisions. The duties of his office introduced him into the closets of all, and the illapses of the spirit were sometimes made subservient to the impulses of the flesh. * * * * *

Such was the man who moved the principal springs in those tumults, which so lately shook the Belgic states. Vandernoodt, though foremost in name, was but the organ of this arch-politician; who, expatriated by crimes which insult heaven and earth, had no hope of recovering his forfeited fortunes, but by entering his country sword in hand. To compass his re-establishment, he practised all the arts of political hypocrisy. He is naturally cool, subtle, and enterprising—

under the garb of sanctity, he has a heart capable of any crime. Patriotism was the lure he held out, and by his address he contrived to obtain credit, till he was detected in embroiling, by insidious artifices, the several parties of the state; aspersing by his emissaries the intentions of those, who from principle espoused the cause of the Belgians—covering with the mantle of religion the machinations of rebellion;—and labouring to establish the empire of the church and the noblesse, upon the blended ruins of imperial authority and democratic freedom. The conciliatory measures of Leopold were very ill calculated to serve the ends of this arch-hypocrite. He therefore employed every sinister engine to prevent a union. The reconciliation which took place between the contending parties defeated his designs of personal aggrandizement, and compelled him to fly from justice into some distant clime, where his hypocrisy may hereafter play a more successful game upon the credulity of mankind.

LETTER XIV.

WE took the route by Breda into Holland, and for a few leagues rolled along a good *pavée*, and then entered upon a road, which, had we not actually passed it, might very fairly have been deemed impassable. A deep sand formed the soil, elevated into mounds on one side, sunk into hollow pits on the other, and in many places completely buried in water of considerable extent; every step the horses took required great exertion, and their utmost efforts could never accelerate them beyond a foot-pace. It was near ten o'clock when we entered Breda, and it was fortunate for us that the gates do not finally close before that time.

All the country between Antwerp and Breda, for many miles, exhibits a melancholy

choly scene—vast wilds and deserts which seem to defy the hand of culture, and upon which the most laborious industry would operate in vain. The lateness of the evening concealed from our view the change of country which takes place as you approach Breda, which is a neat and well fortified town.

We experienced a very striking change in every object around us; the houses and streets had neither the awkwardness nor the filthiness of the Brabant towns. An air of ease, vivacity, and content pervaded the countenances of all—the soldiers wore a less hostile aspect—neither folded arms nor sauntering paces were to be seen; activity, vigour, and industry seemed to prevail; and each appeared emulous to perform the duties of his occupation.

Breda may claim no inconsiderable merit from the public places which adorn it. The palace of the Prince of Orange is delightfully situated, and the gardens which surround

LETTER XIV.

round it are a great ornament to the town. The church of the Proteſtants is a very noble edifice—it is hung with eſcutcheons, which diffuſe a gloom around the ſacred walls, and are but an indifferent ſuccedaneum to the maſterly paintings which fill the Romiſh churches. The monuments which are raiſed againſt the walls in the Engliſh churches oftener deface than adorn the buildings; but the numerous eſcutcheons which inveſt the walls of the beſt churches in Holland give them more the air of mauſoleums, than of places of worſhip. There is a very ancient tomb of marble in one of the receſſes, now crumbling into ruins. What remains is however a curious monument of early taſte and primitive ſculpture.

Breda was diſtinguiſhed as the head-quarters of the late revolutionary intrigues. It was here that the firſt committee was formed under the joint conduct of Vander-noodt

noodt and Van Eupen. This committee, at which the factious nobles of Brabant attended, declared Vander-Merfch general of the troops which they refolved to raife; and publifhed a manifefto, dated at Hoogftraten, in the name of the people of Brabant. This manifefto was, by a decree of the Auftrian government, deftroyed at Bruffels, and feveral members of the fecret committee taken into cuftody. Three thoufand infurgents upon this attacked and captured the forts of Lillo and Liefhenfhoek. This was the firft blow ftruck by them, and the government diftracted by internal divifions now loft all energy. The defeat of Chroeder at Turnhout foon followed, which gave fpirit to the revolutionifts, and excited the higheft alarm at the court of Bruffels. The entry of the rebels into Ghent, and the difhonourable retreat of D'Arbers with his four thoufand troops, gave to the revolution a force and a refpecta-

LETTER XIV.

respectability, which proselyted those who, averse to its principle, would yet profit from its success.

The impolitic measure of concluding an armistice at Tirlemont by D'Alton, at the head of an army fully competent to annihilate the rebels, was the finishing stroke of this ill-judging infatuated ministry. The armistice opened a channel for communication between the regular troops and the vagrant rebels; and the glow of patriotism being thus disseminated, not less than 500 men deserted at once—filling the air with the most outrageous shouts of liberty and revolution. These were of the regiment of Murray; their example operated upon others---desertions took place from all quarters, and every part of Brussels resounded with the popular cry of " Vivent " les Patriotes! Au Diable les Royalistes!" This was shortly after succeeded by the departure of the Austrian troops from Brussels, which Vandernoodt on the 18th December

LETTER XIV.

cember 1789 entered with all the triumphal honours of a proud victor; was hailed with the loudest acclamations as the subverter of tyranny, and the author of Belgic independence.

I must entreat your pardon for the frequent reflections with which I trouble you on the Belgic affairs. Every part of Brabant bears the vestiges of the late commotions, and interests by its melancholy aspect our pity and indignation. The court of Berlin had doubtless some objects of profound policy to compass in fomenting the discontents of the Belgians against the Austrian government. The transfer of the Belgic provinces to the Prussian sovereignty would have furnished that power with a vast ascendant, and enabled it to assume a tone with the Emperor very much to the advantage of its authority. Holland, ever attentive to the main point, contemplated with a feeling beyond indifference the apprehended disunion of the Belgic states from the Austrian government---

ment—regardlefs who fways the fceptre, provided they occupy the market, thefe prudent fpeculators promifed themfelves an augmentation of their commercial advantages. This is the notorious object of Dutch intrigue, and their neighbours, who experience its effects, were not at a lofs to account for the fecret fuel added to the flames of rebellion. " Le feul avantage " qu'ils en veulent tirer," faid the Brabanters; " c'eft de vendre aux Belges " de mauvaifes munitions a très-haut " prix."

LETTER XV.

HOLLAND is certainly a very convenient country to travel through, provided a man will make up his mind to difpenfe with the fplendour of equipage. All the roads which communicate with its environs are intolerably bad, but a carriage of the country will roll over them without difficulty, yet not always without alarm to the traveller. Had we availed ourfelves of the precaution given before we quitted Bruffels, of leaving our carriage at Antwerp, we fhould have experienced lefs difficulty in paffing the moor between that place and Breda. The grand advantage in making the tour of Holland arifes from the canals which pierce the country, and form an agreeable mode of communication between the feveral places.

We

LETTER XV.

We had been led into an error by the inftructions furnifhed us at Breda, and had entered a veffel for Rotterdam, which we foon found ill-adapted for the conveyance of paffengers. Our fituation in it became irkfome—the veffel was dirty—the cabin filled with children. The air without was extremely cold, and the Captain could only reply to our complaints in a language we did not underftand. Thefe difagreeables, added to the apprehenfions of a long paffage, the wind blowing hard and contrary, induced us to form a refolution of abandoning the veffel the firft opportunity, and trying our fortune by land.

Shortly after our forming this determination the veffel came to a mooring in the vicinity of fome few houfes, from which we promifed ourfelves information refpecting the route to Rotterdam by land. We difembarked, to reconnoitre; and after many fruitlefs experiments, had the good fortune to difcover a fchool-mafter, who underftanding French, acquainted

quainted us with the particulars which we wifhed to learn.

Inftructed by him that we could procure a cabriolet in the adjacent village, we returned to the veffel, in order to fettle with our Captain. It was a work of no fmall difficulty to make him comprehend our intentions. We endeavoured, by figns, to teftify that we were completely *ennuied* of this mode of travelling. Every motion we made embarraffed him, till paying him the whole fare of our paffage, we threw our luggage over our fhoulders, and left him to meditate on the fingularity of our conduct, at which he had little reafon to repine. By the good offices of the village fchool-mafter we obtained a carriage, and traverfed upon a wretched road, through the moft wild, fwampy, and defert country, for more than a league and a half. In our driver we had the firft picture of a real Dutchman. In his figure he was fhort, with broad hips, and fpherical fhoulders: his features were fharp, yet

yet steady—a two-inch pipe issued from his mouth, and completed his profile.

One of the *agrémens* of travelling in these cabriolets, which are the only carriages that can run over the heavy roads, is, that if the wind should set against you, it always comes strongly impregnated with tobacco. It was our fate, whenever we travelled, in those carriages, to receive the incense which those amateurs of the pipe are constantly offering to those who sit behind them. Our situation reminded me of the inhabitants of the upper regions, who are usually represented as riding in cabriolets, invested with circumambient clouds.

By eight o'clock in the evening, we arrived at the extreme limit of our journey by land. Mynheer transferred us to the *commissaire*, who was to answer for our conveyance over the Biesbock, usually stiled the Moerdyke. There are no harlequins in Holland. There may be such a thing as *dispatch*, in the warehouses and manufactures; but I question if the language con-

tains

tains an expreffion fynonimous to the English word *hafte*.

All I mean by this, is, that though the evening was fo far advanced, and we had fo much water to crofs, thefe fteady-pacing wights would not accelerate their movements in arranging the few preliminaries neceffary to embarkation. At length we entered the boat, and caught a breeze, which continued in our favour but a fhort time; then veered and blew a head, and in the third and laft place funk into a dead calm. Night had now thrown a gloomy veil over heaven and earth—a pale and ill-formed moon afforded a few faint glimmerings, which opened our eyes to the tracks which furrounded us. A mighty wafte of water, whofe boundaries were only to be difcerned on one fide, prefented a moft chilling fcene; and the defolate fwamps, which furrounded it, fcarcely wore a lefs melancholy afpect. A man and a boy were all who compofed the crew of the veffel conveying us over this melan-

LETTER XV.

melancholy lake. We were barbarians to each other: we could neither animate them to activity, nor question them of our danger. How often have I deplored in my tour through this country, the fatal ambition of those proud architects, who, by their rash designs upon heaven, provoked the division of tongues, and the annihilation of universal language.

Not to aggravate our perils by water, I shall remark that all was perfectly calm—that, if you except the extreme cold that prevailed, the little prospect of coming to an anchor in any reasonable time, the apprehension natural to a situation of the most dreary description, at the mercy, and under the direction of two strangers, whom we could neither soften by promises, nor alarm by threats; if you except these, and some trifling concomitant inconveniences, we encountered no evil of moment. But I must tell you, that our perils, which appeared at their zenith on the water, were considerably augmented

augmented when we gained the land; for, wearied with their exertions, our conductors brought us to a mooring, which suited their convenience, but was very little to our accommodation. No vestige of a house, or habitable spot, appeared. Our guides pointed to us that we were to use our feet; and one preceding, and one bringing up the rear, we traversed a region of the most doleful appearance. Like the fiend that bewilders the lorn traveller, our pilot carried us over marshes and fens, where we could with difficulty find ground sufficiently firm to bear our feet.

The facility with which our leader surmounted those embarrassments, was an aggravation of our distress. It was important to our safety that we kept close: we could not check him, because we could not explain; and some part of the track over which he hurried us, was piled into heaps of swashy clay, and, at numerous intervals, divided by streams that broke from the adjoining

joining canal. At length a gleam of light darted upon us, and preſſing with anxious exertion we arrived at a *cabaret*, where it was deſtined we ſhould paſs the remainder of the night.

If you tell me that I have drawn a melancholy picture of theſe pigmy perils, I aſſure you that they appeared to us in gigantic forms. Though I guarded you againſt the expectation of prodigious events, I did not intend to encounter danger, or combat terrors, without making you a party in our adventures. If it ſuit the mournful temper of your ſoul, you may commiſerate our painful ſenſations. If, on the contrary, this finds you in the moment of gaiety, you are welcome to laugh at our embarraſſments, provided you triumph in our ſucceſs,

LETTER XVI.

THE Dutch are represented as very trickish and imposing. This character applies in the great towns, but I have a better opinion of the villagers. They have all the marks of honesty, and certainly all the *agrémens* of cleanliness. An old woman opened the door to us, after having satisfied herself by questions to our guides of our good intentions. She conducted us into a chamber, which, from its situation, I should rather style a cellar. We were thoroughly wetted by, what an Hibernian alone would call, our land expedition; and a very few signs made the old matron comprehend that we wished for a fire, which, by her industrious attentions, soon blazed before us.
She

LETTER XVI.

She then opened, what appeared to us, a cupboard-door, full three feet from the ground;—when a voice from within addressed us in French. We held a short dialogue, in which the invisible person engaged to furnish us a carriage in the morning, when, wishing us a good night, the old woman closed the door upon him.

The Dutch are very industrious, and rise very early—men of all ranks drink coffee in great abundance. The labourers sip their coffee before they go out to their toils, and appear to eat very little. This may, in all probability, be owing to the quantities of spirits which they are accustomed to swallow. I have repeatedly seen the most robust men taking their morning's meal, previous to the fatigues of the field, and this has consisted in two or three cups of weak coffee, a glass or two of Hollands—then the pipe is kindled, and with *one*, scarcely square inch of bread, these laborious hinds are equipped for the most sturdy services. Our old hostess had kindled

LETTER XVI.

kindled a fire, and boiled our coffee by five o'clock; and notwithstanding the late hour at which we entered, all were up and active, and by six o'clock we were seated in a cabriolet, and took leave of this curious company.

A great change of scenery takes place as you proceed to Rotterdam. The country is still open, but less deformed with wild wastes, or marshy grounds. The roads also improve, and you have an agreeable variety of villages and rivers. The Old Maese, which we first passed, exhibited a noble view. This is navigable for vessels of considerable burden. Numbers of these were lying in the river, and gave a very commercial appearance to the country. Our route after this lay through some villages, whose extreme neatness attracted our particular attention. Nothing can equal the purity of these cottages. The excessive labour they bestow on every article of the most minute importance, leaves nothing to offend the

eye,

LETTER XVI.

eye, and gives the humbleſt cot that air of elegant ſimplicity which palaces do not always poſſeſs.

Rotterdam is a fine object for many miles before you reach it. The country is quite open, and the road purſues a very ſerpentine courſe, which gives you ſufficient time to meditate on the ſingular beauties of that celebrated city. Rotterdam will ſtrike the traveller with wonder; perhaps no town in Europe poſſeſſes objects ſo expreſſive of commercial importance. The canals are numerous and large; crouded with veſſels in all parts, and covered with numerous draw-bridges, they exhibit a magnificent ſcene. All theſe canals are bordered with trees and *promenades*. Wherever the eye turns, objects of commercial grandeur ſtrike it with aſtoniſhment. The public buildings are all conſecrated to the ſame purpoſes. The churches are heavy and taſteleſs. There are cabinets of paintings in the poſſeſſion of ſome private individuals; but the only public

lic monument of letters and the fine arts, is a statue to the memory of Erasmus, who was a native of this place, and among the few luminaries of science which this country has produced. The artist has inspired the countenance with wonderfully fine intelligence.

The different degrees of zeal with which the memory of Erasmus was cherished, bespoke in past times a growing taste for literature. The statue first raised in honour of this great scholar, A. D. 1540, was of wood. Seventeen years refined their feelings, and blushing for the little respect they had shewn to the memory of the man who had immortalized their city, the statue of *wood* was exchanged for a statue of *stone*. A succeeding age, emulous of its predecessors, gave to the Apotheosis of Erasmus the last touch, and raised this statue of *bronze*. Doubtless this œconomical people had at the first well calculated the extent of the future expenditure, if literary characters should

should abound in the republic; but finding this swampy soil unpropitious to genius, and productive only of dull commentators and sombrous logicians, they converted the image of *wood* into a statue of *stone*, without risquing, in consequence of this precedent, any material diminution of the public revenue. In the sixty-five years which succeeded, no rival Erasmuses yet appearing, the utmost extravagance of civic honours was exhausted upon him, and a statue of *bronze* erected, all apprehension of future claim being at length entirely dissipated.

LETTER XVII.

WHAT Rome is to the antiquary, and Florence to the connoisseur, that is Rotterdam to the merchant. The manœuvres of a Prussian army are grand and striking; but the strength there displayed excites reflections,

reflections, at which the heart revolts. When the olive is exchanged for the laurel, though the eye may be dazzled with military splendor, the heart sickens with grief. Commerce is the only art of national aggrandizement which reason sanctions, and humanity approves. This increases the strength, and extends the limits of an empire, without abridging the liberties, or shedding the blood of mankind.

Regarded in this view Rotterdam claims a distinguished rank among the objects of curiosity. Streets, markets, and quays, are crouded with the sons of active industry. Every coffee-house is a *bourse*, and all the society that is there cultivated, refers to bargains, transfers, and contracts. Here are no theatres, but warehouses; no routs, but on the Change; no amusements, but counting of gains. They have little deference for a stranger, particularly if he appears to take no interest in their commercial transactions. You may dine in company

LETTER XVII.

company with them, yet scarcely obtain the interchange of a minute's conversation: this being with them usually taken up by topics of infinitely higher moment, than those which the vague curiosity of a traveller would start. Their language, it must be owned, seems formed for them, and they for their language. Rude, harsh, and guttural—it never was intended for the polite intercourse of society, nor the soft effusions of an amorous passion. But gallantry and politeness are playthings to tare and trett; and all the courtly graces of language are baubles, compared with those sinewy terms that tie and untie with effect the knots of trade.

We soon satisfied ourselves with the rarities of Rotterdam, and as we did not enter feelingly into the sublime speculations of these, we could not help regretting the dearth of public entertainments. The objects which struck us at first, soon lost their energy. Familiarized in a few hours to their

their canals and their warehouses, we panted to find some new scene; and parting from this mart of traffic, this depositary of commercial wealth, we entered a passage-boat at the close of the Saturday evening, and made the best of our way to the Hague.

LETTER XVIII.

THE lateness of the evening obliged us to pass between Rotterdam and the Hague, more rapidly than we wished. On our way we scarcely stopped at Delft, which is a pretty town of no great extent, but distinguished by two churches, in one of which is the monument raised to the memory of the famous Admiral Van Tromp. The china manufacture has been long celebrated throughout Europe, and still preserves its vigor and reputation. The town is charmingly situated, and the canal runs by it.

We

LETTER XVIII.

We quitted the barge at Delft, and took carriage, in order to reach the Hague before the gates should shut. Here a new scene opened upon us. The Hague exhibits a striking contrast to Rotterdam. It is a town built in a stile of uncommon elegance, with all the air of fashionable residence. It has not the bustle, the population, nor the crouded objects of Rotterdam, yet it has the aspect of cheerfulness, and combines the vivacity of trade with the polish of pleasure. The *promenade* towards Scheveling is one of the finest things in Holland, and perhaps in Europe. It extends more than two English miles in length, and is kept in the most delightful order. The village at Scheveling, which terminates it, forms a very agreeable boundary, and the ocean rising above the land closes the vista, and gives to the whole a wonderful sublimity. Scheveling is a fishing town, and is situated on a fine sand—the view of the sea from this sand is beautiful and extensive. As to the gardens of Count Bentinck and other *maisons de plaisance*, they are certainly curiosities in Holland, where the moſt uncouth diſtribution of grounds prevails, but merit little the attention of an Engliſh traveller, who will have ſeen in his own country more taſte diſplayed in the green which ſurrounds the cottage, than in the moſt admired villas * of Holland.

When I remarked that the houſes were built in a ſtile of elegance and grandeur, I did not mean to applaud the taſte of the architects, as many of them wear a heavy and ſombrous aſpect; but the general effect is ſtriking. The palace of the Stadtholder is more celebrated for the paintings and cabinets which adorn it within, than the face it exhibits without. The churches are ſpacious, but not numerous: the whole town poſſeſſes but *three;* of which one is the church of the reformed,

* Mr. Hope's manſion at Haerlem is a known exception to this general character.

the

LETTER XVIII.

the second the Lutheran, and the third Romish. The first is the handsomest, and was, at the time I saw it, filled with a splendid audience. The preachers here preserve those immense wigs, which in England ornament only the heads of the judges. Thus accoutred, and with only a small bible before them, they wear a very oratorical appearance—resort to an action by no means ungraceful, and appear animated and energetic. The still silence which prevailed throughout the hallowed edifice, convinced me that the impressive ardor of the preacher was not without its desired effect.

We were fortunate in being at the Hague during the fair. This began on the Sunday afternoon, agreeable to the practice in these countries, which, if it does not enjoin Sunday as the beginning, usually includes it within the number. This fair may possibly have given us a more cheerful idea of this place, than it would ordinarily excite. Theatres, reviews, public breakfasts, and every species of amusement, took place; all the public roads were filled with carriages, passing and repassing, and the streets were crouded with puppet-shews, mountebanks, and wild beasts. What amused me beyond other novelties, was the singular dress of the Dutch girls. Any one would have imagined, that the figures which appeared on these occasions were masques, or designed as caricatures; but the numbers which crouded all the public ways, and the winning airs they affected, convinced me, that nothing but my want of taste resisted the influence of such singular attractions. Imagine a short figure, with more breadth than goes to the proportion of elegance, and with very little alteration in the width downwards to the waist, the petticoats descending half way only below the knee.— Imagine further, a round face, usually small, covered with a hat of near three feet in diameter, perfectly circular, and applied to the head in a part contiguous to the circumference.

cumference. You will readily perceive, that the hat, thus difpofed, will project before the face, nearly the fpace of the whole diameter, touching the head, agreeably to the property of fpheres, only in one point. Now you have nothing to do but to conceive a number of thefe figures in motion, brandifhing their horizontal hats, rolling their diminutive eyes, and affecting a thoufand ridiculous graces, under cover of this extenfive canopy. The *tout enfemble* brought to my recollection thofe fculptural vagaries, in which a human figure is often made the prop of a cathedral feat, the fupport of a wainfcot pulpit, or the ftand of a mahogany table. If you deem my obfervations fomewhat fatirical, I muft, in my own vindication, fay, that this is a country in which few objects are to be found for panegyric or applaufe. The fingularity of its fituation, and the extent of its commerce, are almoft the only topics on which curiofity would dwell, without terminating in cenfure: and our daily obfervation evinces, that a nation, great in the arts of commerce, and poffeffed of all the refources of fplendor and affluence, may yet be ignorant of the arts of refinement, and yield to nations lefs important, and lefs opulent, in the more fafcinating attainments of elegance and good tafte.

LETTER XIX.

THE paffage by water from the Hague to Amfterdam exhibits fome pleafant fcenery, and the boats are under fo dextrous management, that you never travel flower than four miles an hour. They will pretend to greater fpeed, but I never found the motion exceed this. People are ufually counfelled to engage the *ruffle*, which is the name diftinguifhing the beft cabbin; and for thofe who are averfe to mixing with a promifcuous fociety, and have a decided antipathy to fmoke, it is certainly a very wife precau-

LETTER XIX.

precaution. Motives of curiofity always determined us to prefer the oppofite meafure; and we had many opportunities, by this means, of commenting upon the manners of this fingular people.

Every man who enters the boat, whatever be his condition, either brings a pipe in his mouth or his hand. A flight touch of the hat, upon entering the cabbin, franks him for the whole time of his ftay; and the laws of etiquette allow him to fmoke in filence to the end of the paffage. We fee, as at a meeting of quakers, fixed features and changelefs poftures; the whole vifage myfterious, and folemn, but betraying, it muft be confeffed, more of abfence than intelligence. Hours will pafs, and no mouth expand, but to whiff the fmoke; nor any limb be put in motion, except to rekindle the pipe. The *coutume* of thofe focieties, in the liberal ufe of the *crachoir*, does not preferve that attention to delicacy which fome conftitutions would require.

On our way to Amsterdam we had an opportunity of taking a tranfient view of Leyden, and of Haerlem. The Dutch towns have fo clofe a refemblance to each other, in their canals, their bridges, and their buildings, that a traveller's curiofity is foon fatiated. The univerfity of Leyden owes its celebrity more to the talents of its profeffors, than the fplendor or magnitude of its edifices. The oil painting by Jean de Leyde, is the only attraction which the Hotel-de-Ville poffeffes. Haerlem boafts Laurentius Cofter, one of the inventors of printing, as a native. The great church, and the fuperb organ which it contains, are known throughout Europe.

A fhort time fuffices to examine all the objects of curiofity in thofe towns, which are a perpetual repetition of the firft impreffion. The banks of the canals are ornamented with various gardens and pleafure grounds, which the mafters of the veffels are induftrious to difplay. I fhall fufpend my

LETTER XIX.

my obfervations upon this clafs of curiofities till a future occafion. The firft coup-d'œil, as we approched Amfterdam, was fingular. I counted between 70 and 80 windmills, as we were coming down the canal. A grander object foon prefented itfelf—the harbour crouded with veffels, and exhibiting all the apparatus of commercial opulence.

We entered this city at the clofe of the evening, and took up our quarters at Young's Hotel, which is ufually efteemed the beft, but for fituation and convenience does little credit to a city of fuch magnitude.

I fhall indulge you with the privilege of recreating your fpirits, and recovering from the *ennui* which this uninterefting recital muft have occafioned, before I venture my remarks upon Amfterdam. If the paffage has appeared dull and heavy in the relation, I affure you it was not lefs fo in the performance. The equable motion of the

barge,

barge, the uniform solemnity of our society, and the unvaried face of the country, gave birth to a sombrous depression, dissipated only by the change of scene, which took place in the great and populous town of Amsterdam. We quickly perceived, that Amsterdam had few attractions for *delicate* curiosity. Amusement, however, we could not fail to derive from the novel scenes it inclosed, though they were usually deformed by some offensive appendages: satisfaction was, in most instances, lowered by disgust, and one sense generally gratified at the expence of another.

LETTER XX.

THE city of Amsterdam is renowned throughout Europe for its population, its traffic, and its opulence. Nothing can equal the grandeur of its port, which is thronged

thronged with veffels of all magnitudes. Wherever the eye ranges, mafts and fails appear, covering the whole fphere of vifion, and exhibiting the proud triumphs of commercial enterprize. It is contended of this harbour, that it wants depth ; and that veffels of great burden, which enter the Texel, are reduced to numerous inconveniences: yet the toiling induftry, and the perfevering talents of this laborious people, have baffled all the oppofition, and furmounted all the difficulties of nature and fituation. They have ftripped the furrounding nations of their refources, and concentrated the rays of commerce in their own republic. Not content with barricadoeing their realms againft the rude affaults of Neptune, carrying off his waves by artificial channels, and preferving, by daily efforts, their empire from diluvian deftruction—they have fought a good beyond the narrow pittance which their chill and cheerlefs foil produces, have emulated the greateft powers in navigating the ocean,

and

and in importing from distant parts of the globe the luxuries of happier climes.

While I viewed this harbour, and ruminated on the succeffive advances of this people to the highest pinnacle of national prosperity *, I turned my eye to that city which once disputed the palm of commerce with this republic, and which, by the growing importance of this neighbouring power, had been reduced to insignificance. The treaty of Westphalia raised the grandeur of Holland upon the ruins of Antwerp. The forts of Lillo and Liefenshoek determined the fate of that unfortunate city, and the antient majesty of the Scheld now bows to the usurped authority and furtive honours of the Texel.

The ardour, the activity, the croud, and the bustle, which prevail in all quarters of the

* The trade of Amsterdam has of late years been very much on the decline, and now consists chiefly in the negociation of bills of exchange. The real imports and exports do not probably much exceed one half of what they were some years past.

port, are inconceivable. Bells are founding, and veffels parting, at all hours. Piles of merchandize, and throngs of paffengers, fill all the avenues. It appears the mart of exhauftlefs plenty, and the grand depofitary of Europe. The ftreets of Amfterdam are narrow and filthy—the whole city pierced by an infinity of canals, which cut each other in every poffible direction. The Bourfe is convenient, and not inelegant. The Maifon de Ville, or Stadthoufe, is fpacious and magnificent—encumbered neverthelefs with fanciful ornaments, and ill-proportioned in its feveral parts; but the fcale on which it is built is immenfe, and the general effect ftupendous. The churches are raifed after no very fuperior model, and can boaft of few attractive ornaments. I entered three the fecond evening of our ftay, where fervice was performed; numerous congregations hung attentive on the preacher's accents, and zeal on the one part was returned by correfponding emotion on the other.

It

LETTER XX.

It requires no small perseverance to run over the objects most deserving attention at Amsterdam. The uniformity of the streets, and the uncleanness incident to a crouded population, offend the eye, while the action of the sun upon the stagnant waters increases in a high degree the difficulties of being pleased.

Nothing can wear a more aukward appearance than the carriages, the bodies of which are placed on low sledges, and drawn by one horse. The driver is on foot; and in addition to the concern of the horse, he is obliged to watch every movement of the sledge, that the carriage may not be overset. The origin of this custom is well known to be founded in the apprehension of danger to the houses by the violence of wheel-carriages, and all the *fiacres* are therefore, by authority of the government, constructed upon sledges. Some few years past, no four-wheel carriages were to be seen. Later refinements have at length introduced

LETTER XX.

troduced them, and this inelegant and inexpeditious mode of vifiting and airing is abandoned to perfons, whofe fortune or frugality admit not a more coftly equipage.

The bridge over the Amftel is confidered as a choice *morceau* of antient architecture, and is a great ornament to the river, which rolls beneath its arches.

I faw nothing beyond thefe, which merits a moment's difcuffion; and I haften from thofe fcenes of uncleanly afpect, this compound of villanous fmells, as Falftaff would call it, to one of the moft charming vifions that ever feafted my eyes—where all that prefented itfelf gave birth to oppofite fenfations, and banifhed for a moment every obnoxious image this city had excited. But I muft referve this account for a fubfequent letter. Your nerves might fuffer by too fudden a tranfition, and fome interval may be neceffary to purify the channel of thofe ideas which have fo long dwelt upon polluted

luted objects. The scenes to which I shall conduct you, will repay the penance of a short delay. They are curious, on the score of singularity, if not upon the principle of taste. They boast a neatness unexampled in courts or palaces, and in a certain mode of ornament have no parallel in Europe.

LETTER XXI.

In my last I engaged to furnish you with a relation of a little excursion made into North Holland, for the purpose of visiting the village of Broek. It was early in the morning, that, curious to examine a place of which report had spoken so loudly, we entered a vessel for Buyk-sloodt. This passage took up an hour, and gave us a very gratifying view of the scenes which most adorn Amsterdam.—Parting from the port, we turned our eyes to contemplate the mighty

mart

LETTER XXI.

mart of commerce we had quitted—the objects were crouded, and the groupe sublime.

The city appeared invested with numerous flotas, which reared their towering masts, like forest-trees, into the air. All that offends the eye, and deforms the aspect of this celebrated city, was obscured and concealed by the more prominent objects which form its grandeur. The opening scenes of North Holland presented a beautiful contrast to the country behind. All was soft, still, and flourishing—the houses exhibited the appearance of ease, affluence, and neatness: the lands, highly cultured, displayed the marks of laborious industry, and growing fertility.

From Buyksloodt, which is charmingly, situated, at an equal distance from Amsterdam and Broek, we entered a second boat, which was to convey us to the latter—the canal ran along a most pleasing country—the banks were occasionally crowned by some neat villa of private residence, or some beautiful rendezvous of public resort.

We were gradually prepared by the different cottages on the banks of this canal, for the scenes to which our ardent curiosity tended. Broek at length caught our eye. It is a village of no great extent, situate on the western side of the canal, and forming the most ravishing landscape. As we eyed it from the boat, it resembled a finished picture, and appeared to exist only in imagination, or upon canvas. We landed with anxious curiosity, and pursued some winding-paths, in order to examine, with more minute attention, this enchanting vision. Placed within the bosom of these surrounding beauties, I fancied myself in that Elysium, which poets have described, where all that meets the senses is creative of pleasurable tranquillity. The houses were painted with the most vivid and varied colours. The windows were transparent as chrystal; and the tiles which roofed these pure abodes, adorned

LETTER XXI.

adorned with varnished surfaces, reflected a thousand hues from the rays of a meridian sun. The gardens were framed with singular art and ingenuity, and were distributed into the most fanciful divisions. Each several department exhibited a groupe of fantastic forms. The shrubs, which had shot their roots deep into the soil, were sculptured into all the forms of real and imaginary nature. Birds, beasts, and reptiles of every description, were here congregated in peaceful union, as in the ark of old: all wore the same livery, and derived their nutriment from the same elements. The church, however, was excepted from the law of universal decoration. The only ornaments of this sacred building were finished simplicity, and spotless purity—happy emblems of those sacrifices which alone adorn the altar of religious adoration. Wherever the eye could penetrate, or the feet could stray, throughout this fascinating village, all was completely correspondent.

The

LETTER XXI.

The areas which furrounded the houfes—the winding walks, alleys, and avenues, were equally correct.

Nor is it alone exterior elegance to which thefe people afpire—the infides of many houfes are richly decorated, and finifhed with the moft coftly ornaments. We obtained admittance into one, and were aftonifhed at the polifhed furfaces which every article of the moft minute defcription poffeffed. One apartment, which we entered, was paved with fmall fquare tiles, put together without any cement, and prefenting the moft pleafing afpect. The furniture of a chamber in the fame houfe was very fumptuous, compofed of filken ornaments, richly embroidered. This is, agreeably to antient prefcription, bequeathed from father to fon, and preferved as an offering to Hymen—fuch is the cuftom of thefe Arcadian villagers—from generation to generation. There is alfo a practice prevailing here, common, I believe, to all the natives of North Holland:

LETTER XXI.

land: To every houfe, of whatever quality, there is an artificial door, elevated near three feet above the level of the ground, and never opened but upon two occafions. When any part of the family marries, the bride and bridegroom enter the houfe by this door; and when either of the parties die, the corpfe is carried out by the fame door. Immediately after the due ceremonies are performed in either of thofe cafes, this door is faftened up, never to turn on its hinges again, till fome new event of a fimilar nature demand its fervices. The extraordinary neatnefs which prevails throughout the whole is a prodigy.

On a vifit which the late Emperor Jofeph made to this village, he is faid to have experienced the rigour of thofe injunctions, which are laid upon all who view the Orphan Houfe; and before he was admitted to tread the facred floor, he conformed to the ceremony of taking off his fhoes. That care and attention may preferve the
feveral

LETTER XXI.

several apartments in a state of internal neatness, is readily conceivable; but that the outsides of their houses, roofs, and fronts,—their gravelled grounds, and open paths, should exhibit no marks of occasional violence, should betray no symptoms injurious to their systematic correctness, is a mystery for which I cannot account. The natural action of the elements—the blowing storm, and the driving shower, might well be deemed, too strong opponents of art and nature: yet, exposed to all the vicissitudes of the seasons, not a vestige of injury could be traced. How patient must be that assiduity, which watches those accidents, which imperceptibly repairs their ravages, and gives to those unexampled productions of industry, uniformity and permanence.

I quitted this singular spot with reluctance. As the barge moved slowly along, my eyes feasted upon the parting fairy landscape. I could not govern my sensations.

tions.—Did ever poet image aught so fair?

> Dreaming in whispering groves, by the hoarse brook,
> Or prophet, to whose vision heaven descends!

The picture gradually disappeared, as the colours faded, and was at length ravished from my sight. The vulgar scenes of Amsterdam reduced my ideas to a less rapturous standard. Were I to measure existence with the antediluvian antients, I should never be able to erase those scenes from my mind, nor entirely convince myself, that the whole was not a delightful illusion of the fancy.

LETTER XXII.

I WAS so extremely delighted with the little I saw of North Holland, that I could, with great pleasure, have penetrated farther; but our time did not admit of any extension of the tour. At a very short distance

tance from Broek lies Saardam, a village in many refpects fimilar to that we vifited, but more particularly celebrated for the temporary refidence of the Czar Peter the Great, who fpent a confiderable time here; and *Peterfhoff*, or Peter's houfe, is fhewn to the prefent day. We contented ourfelves with viewing it as we paffed, and quitted Amfterdam the following day. We continued to travel by water, and the paffage between Amfterdam and Utrecht difplayed a greater variety of fcenery, than we had yet met with in any part of Holland. The country wore a more fertile afpect, and the banks of the canal were covered with gardens.

Utrecht is built very much upon the model of the towns we had before feen. Its public buildings poffefs no particular beauty. Its univerfity owes none of its celebrity to the magnificence of its ftructures. The great tower of St. Martin is indeed a very noble remnant of antient art. The view from

LETTER XXII.

from the summit of this tower is very extensive. Near twenty cities may be discovered by the eye, within a very bounded space. I ascended the tower with great eagerness, and was impatient to reach the point of observation. But, when arrived at a certain height I took a survey of the country—my situation was not perfectly to my satisfaction: the stone, mouldered by the finger of time, and apparently loosened by decay, wore a tremendous aspect. Having climbed within a few paces of the summit, I descended, with a sober determination to take in future my views from some less aspiring eminence, where, if I saw objects to less advantage, I should also see them with less trepidation. I took little pains to examine the town. It wore a very dull appearance, and was animated only by the images it revived, of its political importance. This city was distinguished in 1572, for the union of the provinces, which was there formed. And the celebrated Congress of 1712,

1712, has interwoven the name of Utrecht, with the hiftory of the greateft ftates in Europe. Duclos's Hiftorical Records of thofe Times, have fome particulars of a very interefting nature, refpecting the conduct of the Dutch in this Congrefs. One anecdote related by him, I will tranfcribe. Villars, you recollect, had gained an important victory over the allies at Denain. The Dutch minifters ftill however prefumed, notwithftanding this difafter, and the armiftice concluded between England and France, to talk in a ftyle of great haughtinefs, But the Cardinal de Polignac arofe and filenced them, by declaring in a firm and decifive manner, that the period for haughty and imperious language was paft. " Meffrs." faid he, " les circonftances " font changées—il faut changer du ton. " Nous traiterons chez vous, de vous, & " fans vous."

From Utrecht we took cabriolets for Bois-le-duc, or, as the Dutch call it, Hertzogenbofche.

bofche. This occupied a night, and part of the following day. The route we purfued is not very frequently travelled. It gave us however an opportunity of feeing another part of the country. It was between ten and eleven o'clock when we reached the banks of the Leck, and the latenefs of the hour was pleaded as an excufe for not paffing the river; fo we flept in our clothes till morning, and paffed the river at fun-rife. We then proceeded to Bommel, croffing that arm of the Rhine which bears the name of the Waal.

From Bommel to Bois-le-duc, we had to encounter a road worfe than any yet feen, and which admonifhed us momentarily to prepare for the chance of an overthrow. The country around was wretched, barren, and fwampy. After croffing the Maefe, we arrived fafe in the middle of the day at Bois-le-duc, where the carriage waited for us. It had been our plan, previous to commencing the expedition, to take this courfe,
and

and issue by Bois-le-duc, which formed a more extensive tour than is usually made. The customary track is to quit Holland by way of Gorcum and Breda, on which side the country is more fertile, and the roads infinitely better, than by the route we took; and I know of no advantages which can be mentioned, to counterbalance those inconveniences, except that of traversing more extensively the country, and making ourselves acquainted with some of its worst parts.

Bois-le-duc had nothing to attract us; but for the purposes of refreshment, we determined to continue there the day. We had travelled very hard for a week past, and had seldom rested night or day. The inn at which we were lodged, offered us comfortable quarters, had we resolved to spend a longer time; but, impatient to enter upon the pressing parts of our tour, we settled every preliminary for our journey to Maestricht, and held ourselves in readiness for an early departure.

LETTER XXIII.

THE Dutch are univerſally celebrated for their attention to cleanlineſs; and *artifice* is not more proverbial of this nation, than *neatneſs*. I have before remarked, how well this obſervation is founded with reſpect to the villages: here, indeed, it prevails in every poſſible ſhape, and pervades all ranks. No labour is ſpared to give ornaments and luſtre to the meaneſt cottage, nor is it in the power of the painter to do more than juſtice to thoſe poliſhed ſcenes. But this extraordinary attention to neatneſs has a nearer connection with neceſſity than choice. The moiſt exhalations which ariſe from the ſwampy ſoil they inhabit, would be an over-match for inferior induſtry; and without thoſe repeated exertions, their health and their property muſt be deſolated

by

by their invariable foes, Damp and Mildew. What was firſt their irkſome duty, is now become their pleaſure and their pride.

In many houſes the beſt chambers are kept conſtantly cloſed. Suites of apartments are in many inſtances reſerved for the ſingle purpoſe of oſtentatious neatneſs, while the rich poſſeſſor himſelf inhabits a garret, or a cellar. A Dutchman is not remarkable for perſonal cleanlineſs, and the crachoir, of which they make ſo general a uſe, demonſtrates that they have at leaſt a ſet of feelings not ſtrictly in uniſon with delicacy.

It is univerſally remarked of this people, that they are knaviſh and extortionate—their trading avarice would ſeem to render this charge not wholly undeſerving of credit. The extreme paſſion for wealth which actuates them, and the credit attached to extended poſſeſſions, are not very favourable to the cultivation of uncorrupt integrity. The mind abſorbed in the adoration

of

LETTER XXIII.

of such an idol, is often found slipping: the darling pursuit will not suffer check from slight obstacles, and the progress from one stage of avarice to another, is imperceptibly rapid. The tender feelings of honour and honesty once repulsed, become less obtrusive in their monitions, till at length the most essential principles of morality are regarded as shadowy distinctions.

That such reasonings are strictly applicable to the Hollanders, I shall neither pretend to affirm or deny.—Such is at least the turn of general opinion; but I think, however, that justice has not always been done to those laborious people. The character they may have merited in the great towns, and the most notorious places of resort, is ill-applied to the hardy inhabitants of the humble cot: and a numerous class undoubtedly exists, who, secluded from the crouded mart, have not yet become tinctured with the national foible. Were I to pronounce upon these, agreeably to the experience I have

had

had of some, and the observation I made upon others, I should rank them with the more meritorious part of mankind, over whom honesty, virtue, and content, maintain an equal influence. There was an expression in the countenance of those toiling villagers, which disarmed fear in the most perilous situation.

When we entered the dark abode, after crossing the Biesboch, and found ourselves surrounded with men whose language we could not speak—the solitary and desert situation inspired alarm; but a few moments interview with those uncouth cottagers discovered how groundless had been such terrors. The language of nature spake in their looks the integrity of their hearts, and we passed the evening with less dependence upon the arms we carried, than the unsuspicious honesty we found. The little apartment which we occupied, exhibited a circumstance rarely found in houses appropriated to the purposes of a *cabaret*. In one

LETTER XXIII.

one corner of the chamber was a book, apparently deftined for general ufe. One of our guides had taken up the volume, and was occupied great part of the night in ftudying its contents. Curious to know the object of his amufement, I intreated his permiffion to view the book, and found that the lad was regaling himfelf with fcripture hiftory, and though nearly exhaufted with the fatigues of the voyage, he fpent great part of the night in reading the Bible.

Our paffage between Leyden and Haerlem gave me an opportunity of remarking another circumftance of fimilar report to their religious character. The mafter of the veffel had prepared his dinner, which confifted of fome potatoes, boiled to a powder over the little fire-pan which kindled the pipes. He had placed his little difh upon a bench—when, taking up his hat, he held it before his eyes for fome moments; and having confecrated by this act of devotion the provifion before him, he devoured it without

without apprehenfion or delay. I obferved his partner, who fucceeded him, perform the fame facred rite upon beginning his fimple meal.

Thofe circumftances made me decide, that great refpect was paid to religious obligations, fince the prefence of ftrangers did not interrupt the order of duty. An equal curiofity induced me to take up a book which lay open upon a table at the *cabaret* on the banks of the Maefe, of which I confefs I could not report fo favourably. The balance, however, yet ftands on the better fide; and if I were to draw any conclufions from my own obfervations in relation to religion and morals, it would certainly contain an encomium upon their virtue, which I am willing to believe the Hollanders deferve in a higher degree than is confiftent with general opinion.

LETTER XXIV.

I KNOW not any thing which strikes a traveller more, in entering upon Holland, than the nature and general face of the country, pressed by the rising ocean, whose mighty waves are elevated beyond the level of the land. It appears the country of art, wrested by the industry of its natives from the realms of Neptune, and guarded by eternal toils against his irruptions. Nothing can equal the impression excited by a view of the distant waves, whose swelling surges seem ready to swallow up lands, cities, and hamlets, in primæval ruin. Goldsmith's accurate picture of this country recurred to my memory, as I meditated upon its miraculous existence:

> To men of other minds my fancy flies,
> Embosom'd in the deep, where Holland lies:
> Methinks her patient sons before me stand,
> Where the broad ocean leans against the land,

> And sedulous to stop the coming tide,
> Lift the tall rampire's artificial pride;
> Onward, methinks, and diligently flow,
> The firm compacted bulwark seems to grow,
> Spreads its long arms amidst the watery roar,
> Scoops out an empire, and usurps the shore:
> While the pent ocean, rising o'er the pile,
> Sees an amphibious world beneath him smile,
> The slow canal, the yellow-blossom'd vale,
> The willow tufted bank, the gliding sail,
> The crouded mart, the cultivated plain,
> A new creation—rescued from his reign.

It will naturally be imagined, that a country under such circumstances, can boast little beauty. Flat, swampy, and open, it exhibits no variety to the eye—the soil appears coarse, the prospects dreary, and the atmosphere chilled, and impregnated with constant exhalations.

But if no pleasing varieties exist in the general aspect of the country, a still greater uniformity appears in the best and most populous towns. Divided and sub-divided by an equal multiplicity of canals—pierced by streets, and crouded by buildings in the same mercantile stile of tasteless grandeur, they

LETTER XXIV.

they afford only a perpetual repetition of the same impression. The water, which usually contributes to variety, here adds to the uniformity, and is indeed its grand source, conducted, as it invariably is, in those channels which best suit the purposes of commodious navigation. The gardens are only so far estimable, as they exhibit at one period of the year a show of beautiful flowers, and serve to convince the traveller that vegetation *actually exists*, amidst the profusion of water, which overspreads the face of the country. In all other respects, the Dutch gardens are proverbially at variance with every principle of taste and elegance.

I dwelt with rapture on those which ornamented the village of Broek, because they pretended to no magnitude or stile. They were consistent with every other part of the system, and contributed essentially to the decoration of that artificial scene. They had a merit in that situation, which they would

would have wanted in another, where any thing beyond neatness and singularity were attempted. But to examine those mangled grounds which cover the banks of their canals, and which are denominated gardens, is only to see how far depraved taste can extend. Nature is, in those regions, wholly out of repute. From some secret suspicions of her awkwardness, they impose a code of vegetative laws, agreeably to which it should seem she *must* act, and condemn all deviations from it as inelegant luxuriances. Hence the pruning knives, and a thousand instruments, are perpetually in hand to keep her in order. They think that trees ought to grow like animals—like door-posts—like walls—or in short like any thing but what they were intended for. Hence you see what these people call a garden, is often a range of parapets, a string of alleys, or a very menagerie. They seem to have found out the art of effecting what the elder sages thought impracticable, and weakened

LETTER XXIV.

weakened my faith in that maxim of Horace, which I before deemed univerfal:—

" Naturam expellas furcâ, tamen ufque recurret."

A more complete victory of art over nature never exifted. Proftrate, enchained, expiring, the latter feems now to fubmit without a ftruggle to the tyranny of the former, refolving to wage no longer a war upon fuch unequal terms. Moft of the gardens, I faw, led to thofe reflections: they were adorned with the trophies of victorious art. Shaped into the fantaftic forms of dragons, griffins, or dolphins—the defpairing fhrubs feemed to meditate no further irregularities, but conformed their vigorous fhoots to thofe arbitrary laws by which they had been difciplined. A garden *a l'Angloife*, is not without its imitators in Holland, yet almoft the whole country is ftill over-run with thofe Gothic devices. They are ftill held in fecret refpect, and cultivated with unwearied attention. They are

are esteemed the precious monuments of *antient* art—the invaluable bequests of their industrious ancestors, and the chief ornaments of their country.

There is certainly a consistency in this predilection: it is very much in character with the air, the dress, and the habits of life, which those people cultivate in themselves. Moulded personally on no principle of elegance, they borrow no improvements from their dresses, which are equally at war with convenience and beauty. Nature seems to have hewn them with a rough chisel, and formed them upon a plan of business. All their pursuits bear reference to the same principle: taste is industriously excluded from all their designs, to whatever they apply; and their buildings and gardens are not more grotesque and uncouth, than their habits and manners. Any man, however, who sees the intenseness with which they pursue their plans of traffic, will cease to wonder that so wealthy a nation should yet
be

LETTER XXIV.

be fo far removed from refinement. The elegancies of life have fcarcely a name in their vernacular tongue; the vortex of trade ingulphs all confiderations; and wealth is fufficiently refpectable, to atone for the abfence of every other quality. Thefe maxims, which are here reverenced by all ranks, are fufficient to preclude the introduction of thofe improvements which adorn fociety, and give a luftre to ftates. It would indeed be a novel event in the hiftory of mankind, if any thing great in arts or refinements fhould arife from a nation, whofe fole talent is induftry, and whofe ruling paffion is the love of gain.

LETTER XXV.

The kings of Spain, from the time they became masters of the mines of Mexico and Peru, have been considered as the cashiers of Europe; and it was well said by Boccalini, that Spain is to Europe, what the mouth is to the body, " tout y passe, et rien n'y reste." However Holland may stand in the same predicament in one respect, it certainly differs very widely in the other. The Dutch are at this moment the cashiers of Europe, and the bankers of every state; but with a policy peculiar to themselves, they convert the weaknesses of other nations, into the instruments of their own aggrandizement. Their speculations are usually formed upon solid principles; and though they appear to hazard much, they seldom sustain loss. So completely are they occupied

LETTER XXV.

occupied by the predominant concerns of negotiation, that they appear indifferent about their government. Naturally they are bold, steady, and enamoured of liberty, Europe has witnessed their courage when provoked. Few nations have entered the lists of war with more reluctance, or quitted them with more renown. A slight injury will not arouse, nor a slight revenge appease them. Inveigled into treaties by hope or fear, never by choice, they usually relieve themselves from such obligations. They hold them no farther binding, than their interest dictates, and never scruple to traffic with the declared enemies of their allies—provided it can be done with secrecy and safety. Considering themselves rather in the capacity of a commercial association, than a state of Europe, they regard the cabals of cabinets, and the revolutions of empires, with political indifference. Unambitious of those laurels for which monarchs too often interrupt the peace of mankind,

they

LETTER XXV.

they calmly cultivate the arts of induftry, and ftudy to fill their coffers; while kingdoms, inflamed by trivial animofities, are exhaufting their treafures to equalize dominion, and preferve the balance of power. The fame phlegmatic inattention is apparent to the political movements which take place in the bofom of their own country. Conftitutionally averfe to monarchical authority, and inheriting from their anceftors a rooted attachment to republican government, they yet fubmit to forms which fhadow forth a fubjection that their forefathers had blufhed to acknowledge. We were under the neceffity of wearing the orange cockade, throughout every part of Holland. All ranks of people continue to wear this badge of princely authority. Formerly it marked the diftinction of parties—at prefent it covers thofe divifions, familiarizes thefe tame defcendants of a hardy race to a yoke at which they fecretly revolt, and tends to eftablifh the authority of a power

LETTER XXV.

whose existence at one moment appeared equivocal.

The reasonings which determine the Hollanders to such passive measures, are not founded on the extinction of antient prejudices, or the forfeiture of original spirit; but the inconveniences which would result to *trade* from an opposition to the victorious power. The grand wheels and springs must be for a period neglected—revolutions would generate confusion, and arrest for a time the tide of commerce: nor can plans of revolt be successfully supported, without great expence of time, labour, and manufactures.

It is evident, that considerations of this nature must influence the Dutch to their present conduct, as they are by no means reconciled to the authority of the Stadtholder. Personal safety was pleaded as the reason for assuming thus universally this badge of servitude, yet discontents are numerous, and the *throne* of the Stadtholder

appears

appears but ill-secured. The government which exists at this moment is certainly ill-suited to the temper and genius of a people whose reigning prejudice is an aversion to princes. It is a government, whose parts do not well assimilate, and which never have accorded. The superaddition of an hereditary Prince to the pre-established authority of the state, has counteracted their antient labours—has destroyed the uniformity, the purity, the correctness of their republic, and opened a channel for political interference from the Powers of Europe. Louis the XIV. and XV. by turns, gave them a Stadtholder; and the late commotions, which shook the House of Orange, were not viewed with political indifference by the Powers of Europe.

What will be the issue of those discontents, which, though quelled, are not composed, time can alone decide; but certain it is, that the temper of the Hollander is not the most placable, nor the most disposed to forgiveness.

nefs. Princes are, in general, obnoxious to this people, who acknowledge no diftinctions but thofe of property; and if a Hollander has ever imagined the reigning Prince tinctured with principles of tyranny—if he has at any period detected him in defigns to aggrandize his own authority, and contract the public liberties, he will ever regard him with fufpicion, and no after-acts can purge the memory of this delinquency.

Louis XV. experienced in this ftubborn people, the lafting effects of firft impreffions. Mafter of Flanders, and in poffeffion of 35,000 Dutch prifoners, he preffed them to accept a peace, which their fituation would have rendered a more proper requeft on their part; but they obftinately refufed to attend to his offers. Impreffed with the *hauteur* of Louis XIV. in 1672, they could not confider a fucceffor of the fame *name*, as divefted of the fame *qualities*. Deeming that what a prince could offer, a republic fhould not accept, they viewed with a fufpicious spicious eye all his overtures—referring his most specious declarations to artifice or necessity, and deeming every effort to effect a conciliation, a symptom of weakness, or a snare for their seduction.

Voltaire has remarked this conduct in the Dutch with his usual animation: " L'ir-
" ruption de Louis XIV. & l'année
" 1672, etoient encore dans leurs cœurs,
" et j'ose dire que je me suis apperçu plus
" d'une fois que leur esprit frappé de la
" hauteur de Louis XIV. ne pouvant conce-
" voir la moderation de Louis XV. ils ne
" la crurent jamais sincere. On regardoit
" toutes ses demarches pacifiques, et tous ses
" ménagemens, tantôt comme des preuves
" de faiblesse, tantôt commes des pieges."

LETTER XXVI.

THE journey from Bois-le-duc to Maestricht was very laborious for the horses, and very irksome to ourselves. The road continued to exhibit numberless difficulties; it was almost the whole way composed of a sandy soil, ploughed into deep and dangerous furrows; and we had the mortification to be dragged for two days, at a foot pace, over a country which wore the most desolate aspect. The only objects which rose out of this barren soil were some scattered gibbets, which well assorted with the murderous face of the country.

Our first night was, however, passed at a very pretty village, whose name was so guttural, that I could not divine how many consonants went to the formation of it; for you know, both in Dutch and Flemish lore, a few vowels go a great way. I must content myself, therefore, with telling you, that it was about half way between Bois-le-duc and Maeſtricht—was ſurrounded in its immediate precinɛts by ſome charming village ſcenery, and wore a very piɛtureſque appearance: and this will, I hope, compenſate for the omiſſion of a hoarſe name, " quod verſu dicere non eſt."

Our ſecond day's journey was equally forlorn, and equally diſguſting, till our eyes caught the banks of the Meuſe, and the lofty bulwarks of Macſtricht. It was fair-time when we entered it. All were dreſſed in their holiday attire—the ſtreets were crowded with old and young, and the air was filled with the ſounds of mirth, interrupted by the diſſonant braying of trumpets. We ſaw nothing in Maeſtricht beyond the ordinary run of towns. Its fortifications are, indeed, poſſeſſed of immenſe ſtrength, and exhibit an impregnable ſyſtem of defence. There is a cave into which the curious ſometimes venture; but the circumſtances accompanying it did not induce us to add to that number.

Our

LETTER XXVI.

Our next day was taken up in the journey from Maeftricht to Spa, which gave us an opportunity of feeing Liege. I have before remarked, that Amfterdam was the moft uncleanly town I ever faw. I fhall now except Liege. I never could have imagined a town in fuch a fituation deformed by fo much filth. The ftreets were paved, the buildings faced, and the houfes lined with dirt of the blackeft colouring. In addition to this, the whole town was in uproar. Huffars, with naked fabres, were ftationed at regular intervals throughout every avenue of the town; and the favage countenances of thefe rude barbarians, were to be encountered at every ftep. The cathedral is noble, the *bourfe* fpacious and commodious. We were not a little rejoiced to quit this town in the afternoon, and I think we left behind us the aggregate of every thing that is dark, tremendous, and offenfive.

Our route then lay upon a good *pavée*, with no inconfiderable hills, to Spa, and we entered this fingular place in the dufk of the evening. The great charm of Spa consists in the blended society, which is there found from various motives. The country is romantic, and the *promenades* pleasant. The places of usual residence are embosomed by hills of no great magnitude, but whose relative situation to the town gives a picturesque air to the spot. The salubrity of the springs first formed the importance of this place: but as mankind are oftener afflicted with *imaginary* than *real* complaints, as the disorders of the spirits are more numerous than the maladies of the body, Spa is less in repute for its medicinal nostrums than its more potent attractions—the ball-rooms, the concerts, and the galas.

If one may judge from the exorbitant charges here made, health is not purchased upon moderate terms; and though the springs gush unbribed from the soil, their waters do not continue to flow with equal liberality. A Spa residence, of the shortest duration, is not made without considerable expence. Were a palace to be converted

into

LETTER XXVI.

into a caravanſera, ſcarcely would an higher price be fixed upon the apartments than is here demanded. Yet our kind landlords aſſure us, that the price of our apartments will increaſe in, what appears to me, a geometric progreſſion with the advancement of the ſeaſon.

One would imagine, that in a place which nature deſtined as an aſylum for the ſick, as a kind of grand hoſpital of invalids,—wine would be a ſuperfluous article, and ſcarcely fetch any price. The contrary is the faƈt: the afflicted multitude who crowd here, ſeem to ſwallow down—no doubt by the advice of their phyſicians—larger potions of this favourite beverage than even of the pure and unadulterated element: by which judicious medical arrangement, this place maintains its reputation, as the grand continental mart, not only of health, but of feſtivity and pleaſure.

LETTER XXVII.

Spa, May 20, 1791.

MANKIND have almost uniformly converted necessity into a virtue, and what has been originally submitted to with reluctance has usually terminated in choice. The swampy soil of Holland, and the numerous nervous fevers which arose from this circumstance, gave birth to those black patches upon each temple, which, by the superstition of antient times, were deemed specifics against nervous affections. These are now become a part of the Dutch dress. In vain does " La petite Hollandoise" put on her broad orbicular bonnet, or coiff herself in uncouth lustre; till the large black patches are affixed, she can expect to make no conquest. She may display her rounded shoulder, and exhibit her slip-shod heel; yet

will

LETTER XXVII.

will her artillery prove ineffectual without the aid of these proud ornaments.

Something similar has taken place in the numerous springs and baths throughout Europe. Accident discovered their salubrious effects in remedying disorders, and restoring shattered constitutions. Amusements are deemed necessary to the dissipation of that languor, which ill health and medicinal regimen are apt to engender. The colours of pleasure are never displayed in vain. The votaries of amusement soon crowded to that standard, where the banners of their goddess were exalted, and the empire thus became divided between the valetudinarian and the voluptuary.

This commerce is not without its advantages. Doubtless the associated supplicants of Esculapius had formed a ghastly band, and might have passed a miserable *séjour* in the society of each other. The pallid face, the leaden eye, the hollow cheek, and the emaciated frame required the introduction of some more cheerful countenances; the commixture of those in whom the tide of blood is not chilled by age, nor tainted by malady, would enliven the scenes thus deformed, and tend to accelerate the salutary effects of the springs. But mankind know no medium; at present the rivulets of health are swallowed up in the torrents of pleasure, the severity of regimen relaxes into the luxury of debauch, and the medicinal potion is supplanted by the Bacchanalian draught. Nor is this all—the harpies of fortune are disposed in every quarter of this Circean Elysium. The young and the incautious are inveigled by the specious appearances of personal splendor and titled consequence. Fortunes are thus committed, not to the mercy of a card, or the chance of a die,—but to the artifice of those, whose sole talent is imposture, and whose sole property is vested in the funds of human weakness.

The anecdotes which are here circulated, and the estimates here formed upon the issue of

LETTER-XXVII.

of former seasons, render it more than probable, that the vast influx of company in the present, will exhibit various revolutions of fortune in the gaming circle. Charmed, as I am, with the aspect of its hills, and the fame of its waters, I cannot but consider Spa as first amongst those places of general resort, which swell the tide of human corruption. I cannot but believe, that more morals are debauched by the contagion of its vices, than nerves braced by the vigour of its air; and that more fortunes are ruined by the fascination of its amusements, than constitutions restored by the salubrity of its springs.

LETTER XXVIII.

Duffeldorf, May 25, 1791.

THE man who travels for higher purposes than those of pleasure, will not make a long residence at Spa. We left it after having bestowed a whole week upon contemplating its deserted springs, and strolling amongst its silent promenades. I glanced on the Sunday over the tablets which decorate the church; and found, that superstition has *once* enjoyed as great dominion here as pleasure *now* does. I could not forbear remarking one in particular, which held out a variety of indulgences to the *confrères* of the holy sacrament. One of those grants purported, that if any one of this fraternity visit the sick with the holy sacrament; or, if indisposed, write " Pater " Noster," and " Ave Maria," five times, he shall be entitled to indulgence for sixty days
next

LETTER XXVIII.

next enfuing. This appears a very reafonable purchafe, and is, I imagine, the only article at Spa, which has not advanced in price. Aix-la-Chapelle finifhed our journey of Monday. The road paffed for the greater part through a hilly country, and ill-announced, by its vaft inequalities in the neighbourhood of Aix, the entrance to an afylum of invalids.

Aix is, indeed, a grand infirmary; the baths are falubrious and convenient; they are deemed highly reftorative of decayed conftitutions; and are, therefore, frequented by numbers, whofe debaucheries have fcarcely left them the ftrength to complain. That quarter of the town in which the hotels ftand, is alfo the fituation of the baths, and for the moft part, the refidence of the invalids. There is an air of vivacity in the fhops, the porticoes, and the affembly rooms; and the general exterior is not without a pleafant and cheerful effect. But fo many ghaftly figures are perpetually moving

ing before you, wrapped in sedans, or crawling from seat to seat, that cheerfulness is crossed by a thousand painful emotions; and amusement in such a scene would scarcely have upon me a better effect, than a dance in a dungeon, or a concert in a lazaretto.

The cathedral of this town is a very noble monument of antient times, and stands in high repute for the regalia of Charlemagne, and other precious toys, which it is known to contain. The greatest curiosity it had for me, was the groupe of worshippers, which was planted round one of its altars. An old Franciscan was conducting the religious ceremonies; and the people, who were of various qualities and conditions, had thrown themselves for the most part into the attitude resembling a cross. They extended their arms as they knelt, and preserved both these and their countenance immoveably fixed,—notwithstanding the interruption they might be supposed to
experience

LETTER XXVIII.

experience from the paffing and repaffing of ftrangers.. An equal fervor of devotion prefented itfelf at Juliers, to which we paffed in the evening of yefterday. The rain was falling inceffantly; yet this did not deter a number of people from repairing to an altar erected in the open ftreet, facing the window of our hotel, in order to perform their vefpers. For nearly an hour they fucceeded each other in thefe facred fervices,—kneeling upon the naked ftones, without the leaft precaution, in contempt of the frowns of weather, or the fmiles of the rude fpectator.

I confefs I feel rebuked, rather than diverted, by fuch examples; nor can I withhold my refpect from thofe, who, after the way which *we* call fuperftition, fo fervently worfhip the God of their fathers. We left Juliers this morning by fun-rife, and taking a breakfaft with an honeft German, three leagues on our way, obtained from him inftructions for our route; and having croffed the

the Rhine; in face of Duſſeldorf, find ourſelves agreeably accommodated by the good offices of Zimmerman, at the Hotel de Deux Ponts.

LETTER XXIX.

May 26, 1791.

I KNOW not how others may feel, but I muſt confeſs very little pleaſure is by me derivable from the *ſolitary* contemplation of works of art. When the eye has feaſted upon the charming tints of a captivating picture, and is called to gaze upon others in fucceſſion,—it appears as though ſome difcuſſion of the firſt, and ſome communication upon its excellencies were indiſpenſable. Such at leaſt was the temper of my mind in viewing the gallery of Duſſeldorf; and as we are now houſed under the roof of an honeſt poſt-maſter, five leagues on our way to Cologne, I am impatient to diſcloſe

LETTER XXIX.

to you the impreffions I received from the invaluable collection that place contains.

You muft not expect *as yet* much fcience in my defcriptions; for I have not yet learnt the technical phrafeology. From fome motive which has efcaped me, I chofe to invert the ufual order of obfervation, and intreated to fee the chamber of Rubens firft. The three principal paintings in this department were the Adoration of the Shepherds, the Death of Seneca, and the Laft Judgment. In the firft of thefe the countenance of the Virgin was wonderfully expreffive of folemnity and joy—the looks of the fhepherds of furprize and congratulation. The Death of Seneca made me fhudder. Of the Laft Judgment, I *ought* to fpeak in raptures, but fhall refer you to thofe, whofe optics are better qualified to do juftice to this vaft and fublime groupe.

The fecond chamber was that of Vander-Werf. The paintings of this mafter, whofe polifhed pencil defies the ftrictnefs of criticifm,

cifm, prefent little that can move the heart. I gave him but a fhort trial, and haftened to the third, or Italian chamber. Where Raphael formed his gay and youthful idea of St. John the Baptift, I know not,—but I fhould rather have expected to find this great preacher of repentance in the Hermit of Salvator Rofa, which hangs in the fame apartment.

Two admirable productions of Carlo Dolci, of very different characters, fhared my next attention. The firft prefented our Saviour bearing his crofs. I was particularly ftruck with the delicacy of execution in the livid hue, which the burden of a crofs, and the anguifh of a crown of thorns muft naturally induce. The fecond was a St. Agnes the Martyr, in whofe countenance the painter had contrived to introduce fuch touches of fweetnefs, that I could have gazed upon it for ever.

Two paintings of Schalken interefted me greatly. The firft reprefented " la lumiere
" vraiement

LETTER XXIX.

"vraiement soufflée," or "the candle actually blown out.", This is one of the pleasantest things I ever saw. A girl is pictured as holding in her hand a lighted candle, which a boy endeavours to blow out, and she—by a counter-action of breath—to recover. The boy's lungs are, however, too strong for the girl's resistance: he gives a steady blast, and the candle is seen upon the point of losing its flame. All these circumstances and effects, with the corresponding fluctuations of light and shade, are rendered with inimitable accuracy.

The second of this master was of a more serious description, and represented " the " wise and foolish virgins." The painter has chosen the moment, when the call is heard of, " Behold the Bridegroom cometh! " Go ye out to meet him."—The wise virgins are described, as obeying with promptitude the summons; their countenances wear the air of confidence, and speak the language of preparation. Their lamps are trimmed,

trimmed, the lights are brilliant, and they appear to have heard the sudden call without fear or surprize. On the other hand, a greater scene of confusion and derangement cannot be imagined, than that in which the foolish virgins are found. Their air is that of persons perplexed and disconcerted: some of their lamps are already out, in others the light is expiring. They are busied in fruitless endeavours to preserve the fading, or rekindle the extinguished flame. The agitation, with which they supplicate a supply of oil from their wiser companions, is extreme. Those latter regard their ill-timed petitions with looks expressive of astonishment at their improvidence, and inability to supply them. This is surely a master-piece of painting for the artful disposition of lights, and the strong delineation of circumstance and character.

The beauteous groupe of the Holy Family, by Raphael, came unfortunately too late to produce its perfect effect. Schalken had

had full poffeffion of me,—and while diligent to ftudy the chafter lights of that perfect mafter, the flafhes of the Dutchman danced like a meteor before my eyes. Such is the influence of firft impreffions on future habits; and—to indulge a tranfient moral reflection—he has ill ftudied life and nature, who fhall think it indifferent, which of two oppofing principles fhall have been the *firft* inculcated.

LETTER XXX.

Coblentz, May 30, 1791.

COLOGNE was the firft town we entered after leaving the poft-houfe from which I laft wrote. It is a very antient and dignified city. The Romans knew it by the diftinction of Colonia Agrippina; and it has been befieged and plundered as often as its rank and dignity demanded. Would you wifh for more honours? It is an Hanfe town,

town, poſſeſſes an univerſity, boaſts an archbiſhopric, a principality, and a thouſand other important appendages. The city is of wide extent; its churches are numerous and ſplendid, its fortifications ſtrong, and its inhabitants civil and obliging. You will, by this time, aſſuredly allow, that I have not made a bad uſe of my time, in learning ſo much of the hiſtory and manners of a town, in which I paſſed *four hours.*

Before we entered Cologne, we had to paſs the Rhine. Ourſelves and equipage were embarked in a large ferry-boat, and quickly whirled acroſs. The inn, where we ſtopped, abounded in German barons and French counts: a peep at the cathedral, and a ſtroll about the ſtreets, were all the actual obſervations I had opportunity to make.

We paſſed the night, and a conſiderable portion of the following day at Bonn, which, in reſpect of ſituation, far ſurpaſſes Cologne. The palace of the Elector commands

LETTER XXX.

mands a very fine landscape of mountainous country, and, at the time I entered the gardens, a groupe of velvet suits—retired from the *ennui* of the drawing-room—were cooling themselves with a *promenade*. I attended the mummery of the cathedral—a mixed emotion of indignation and respect possessed me; and I knew not whether most to despise the absurdity of the worship, or admire the devotion of the worshippers.

The village where we passed last night is called Remangen, between four and five leagues distant from Bonn. The country now begins to wear an interesting appearance, and the road which conducted us from Bonn to Remangen was distinguished by beauties of a peculiar nature—mountains on the one hand clothed with vineyards, the Rhine flowing in silent majesty on the other.

The approach to Remangen was marked with circumstances of singular sublimity. The road passed under a rock, upon whose bosom

bosom were thrown, as it were in rude confusion, houses and vineyards; and from whose shady summit glittered the spire of a church. This mass of rock over-arched the road, which was here very narrow; and the whole appeared to project in formidable magnificence over the Rhine that rolled below. I strolled in the evening over these picturesque scenes; and, seated upon the heights, was charmed with the landscape softened by the last tints of the setting sun, and the harmony of three rustic voices, which sung a *trio* upon the rocks below me—a practice very frequent among the Germans.

We left Remangen the ensuing morning, and passed through a continuation of that scenery I have described, but still improving in beauty. The mountains to our right were of considerable magnitude, and shaped in various forms; yet all appeared in an high state of fertility and culture. Andernach, where we breakfasted, is a curious

remnant

remnant of antient ſtrength. It is ſurrounded by ramparts mounted with a covert way, by which one can make the tour of the whole place, and view from a ſufficient eminence the houſes beneath. I know not the hiſtory of this place, but judge, from the magnitude of its fortifications, that it has once been of conſiderable note, and not unfrequently the ſeat of war. My mind was occupied by ſerious reflections, when I trod among its ruins, and counted its dilapidated towers. " And ſuch, ſaid I, is hu-
" man grandeur, and ſuch the boaſted
" monuments of arms and heroiſm—" I had continued my reverie, but the crack of the whip announced the moment of departure; and I was dragged in ſullen ſilence to the place from which I now write.

LETTER XXXI.

Mayence, June 2, 1791.

SITUATED at the confluence of the Rhine and Moselle, and flanked with mountains overspread with shrubs and ruins, Coblentz presents a very charming picture to the traveller's eye. I have kept a tolerable look-out upon the countenances of the fair sex as I ascended the Rhine, and have found their beauty upon the increase as I advanced into the country.

The dresses of the men are stiff, formal, gothic. It is truly ridiculous to look from the window upon the bag-wigs, swords, and chapeaus-bras that pass. I told you above of mountains and ruins that entered into the scenery of Coblentz; but crossing the Rhine to the opposite vineyards,

yards, the fairy vifions faded, the objects grew lefs interefting in proportion as they were more nearly viewed; and my difficulties increafed, when I had flattered myfelf with the idea of conquering them. After encountering much heat and fatigue, I relinquifhed my project, and retired to my old ftation. Thus, like the greater part of human profpects, thefe diftant delights appeared to advantage only in the expectation.

There are two evils in travelling, for which a man muft prepare himfelf with fortitude,—a change of language, and of money. This latter is extremely perplexing in running through the different Electorates and Principalities. Every tranfition of half a dozen leagues has introduced us to a people—not indeed of a different fpeech—but of a different coin; and it would require profound fkill in calculation to pafs without detriment from Duffeldorf to Mayence.

I have

I have viewed the town of Coblentz, and read its hiftory; but as the firft has furnifhed me with nothing extraordinary, and the fecond would prefent to you nothing interefting—I fhall neither amufe you with the meafurement of its ftreets, or the detail of its revolutions; ftudious to avoid (though not always with fuccefs) the foible of thofe travellers, who, in the hope of giving importance to their temporary journals, forget themfelves into hiftorians—while the reader is left to murmur at being introduced to a people, not of modern, but of antient manners.

In the room, then, of erudite intelligence, I fhall relate to you two grievous evils, which we experienced at Coblentz,—in the extortion of our landlord, and the defertion of our coachman. The firft is an old and uninterefting complaint, the latter has fomething more of novelty and importance. Our coachman—he, alas! I mean, who once occupied the office—was known at Bruffels,

his

LETTER XXXI.

his native town, by the name of Antoine: all our intercourse with him discovered but one *fault* and one *virtue*. His fault was *obstinacy*—his virtue *universal language*. His obstinacy was cool, phlegmatic, and invincible. It shewed itself in a strict adherence to first habits; and, in defiance of advice and remonstrance, he to the last continued to carry his long green whip like a weeping willow bending solemnly over his right shoulder.

But justice must be done to his *virtue*. As an universal linguist, he served us for guide, interpreter, caterer—and in short, in every possible way of mediation. Such were the powers of his tongue, that he would argue with equal volubility in Dutch, Flemish, French, or German. He turned restive at Coblentz, where he seemed to have found a society he approved; and folding his arms, when summoned to his duty, peremptorily refused us the further services of his whip, and his tongue.

Thus

LETTER XXXII.

Thus disappointed, we continued our route, not without difficulty, to this place. We were amused, as we passed, with the varying views of a very fine country; visited some hot springs in our way, and arrived without accident before Mayence at the close of yesterday.

LETTER XXXII.

Spire, June 4, 1791.

MAYENCE, or, as it is stiled in German orthography, Mentz, is a very fine town. The approach to it from the bridge of boats here thrown across the Rhine is strikingly beautiful. It possesses a very noble quay, extending along the banks of the river; and is rendered, by its fortifications, capable of a strong defence.

The day after our arrival was the festival of the Ascension, and I attended the celebration of high mass at one of the principal churches.

churches. It was a grand folemnity, accompanied with very excellent mufic, and the audience very crowded. I was particularly ftruck with the beautiful countenances of a long range of children, who attended the performance. But what has furprized and diverted me, at this and fome other towns through which we have lately paffed, is, that boys eight or nine years of age walk the ftreets with queues literally reaching half way down their legs.

The table d'hôte where we dined was attended by a very brilliant circle of officers and Abbés. The latter appeared of more than ordinary confequence, were dreffed in very fhowy fuits, and wore half a dozen ftars, croffes, &c. Their hands were wrapped up in very wide ruffles, and their profeffion was only to be traced in the fhortnefs of their hair.

I have often been led to remark the very ftriking fuperiority in accommodation, which a ftranger finds in a French fociety, above that of every other nation. By whatever name it be called, and from whatever cause it proceed, the attention of a Frenchman to the embarrassment of a stranger is wonderful. I have witnessed on many occasions the exercise of this disposition. At a Dutch table d'hôte, one finds the reverse of this. Business swallows up all. The concerns of the change, the rate of merchandize, the rise and fall of the stocks, are the objects which take place of every consideration; and leave them neither leisure nor inclination to consult the ease, or relieve the embarrassment of a stranger. One is but little bettered at a German table: *themselves* are the parties whom they are anxious to oblige, and their attentions are excited to provide in the best manner for their own entertainment. I shall not draw the comparison between either of these, and what prevails at our public tables in England, lest my national vanity should be humbled by the conclusion.

I was

LETTER XXXII.

I was not at a lofs to account for the *hauteur* of the ecclefiaftics in this town; as the chapter is compofed of dignified characters; and no man can become a canon, till he has proved himfelf noble four generations deep. The wines drank here were exceedingly good. The richeft vineyards are to be found in the neighbourhood; and Hocheim, which has given name to the Hock, is at no great diftance from Mentz.

We employed the clofe of the day in making a journey of four leagues to Oppenheim, a town no longer of confequence. It ftands clofe upon the Rhine, and is furrounded with fcenery of no ordinary beauty. We paffed our night here, and advanced the following day through Worms to Manheim. You will not expect me to defcribe with minutenefs a town where I only took a breakfaft. I fhall content myfelf, therefore, with faying, that Worms is a pleafant town, fituated about five leagues from Mentz. As to its antient hiftory, you will

find

find it more celebrated in ecclefiaftical than civil records. Within this town, that intrepid champion of reformation, Martin Luther, made his celebrated defence before the ftates of the empire.

Our entrance into Manheim was obftructed by fome military formalities, and the treatment we received indicated much feverity and vigilance. I was very much ftruck with the beauty of Manheim, whofe appearance eclipfes, indeed, all the towns I have feen upon the Rhine. On entering the ftreets, we could difcover little befides French officers ftrolling arm in arm, bearing the white cockade. We very foon learnt, that this place is the rendezvous of the emigrants; that here they are fuffered to poffefs, not only an afylum againft danger, but a nurfery of vengeance; that here they are indulged with a particular fpecies of protection and countenance; and that hopes the moft fanguine are by them entertained of recovering their forfeited domains,

LETTER XXXII.

mains, and humbling in their turn thofe by whom they have been humbled. All the inns were crouded with thofe dignified Refugees; and the day after our arrival, great preparations were making to receive the Comte d'Artois.

I could not but reflect, when I faw them affembled on the parade, and confidered the impoffibility of their return,—how ftrikingly public juftice is executed upon them, as a body, in their profcription. A century paft, Germany received into its hofpitable bofom, Proteftants, exiled by the anceftors of thofe who are now paying the forfeit of ancient oppreffions. So true is it, that the ways of Providence are filled with equity; and the revolutions of empires refolve themfelves into fo many difpenfations of retributive juftice.

LETTER XXXIII.

Strasbourg, June 7, 1791.

I TOLD you in my laſt, that the diſcipline of Manheim appeared very ſtrict; and I found upon enquiry, that regulations of great ſeverity were enforced. I was cautioned, by the waiter at our inn, when proceeding to walk with my *ſword-ſtick*, to diſarm myſelf before I left the room; as orders the moſt rigorous had been iſſued on that ſubject. I muſt refer you, for particulars of this beautiful town, to thoſe who have ſeen more of it; and you will not have any great difficulty in finding deſcriptions of its palace, its gallery, its ſquares, and its fortifications. I paſſed but a day here, and ſlept at Spire the following evening. There is nothing very remarkable in Spire, excepting

LETTER XXXIII.

cepting its remote antiquity. It stands about six leagues from Manheim.

The following morning, we entered the province of Alsace. This was announced to us by an Office of the customs, bearing the inscription of "Bureau National," and superscribed "La Loi et Le Roi." We were commanded to halt, and the Officers inspected all our luggage. We were happy to be informed, that this is the sole inconvenience of this nature we shall experience till we quit the kingdom. This, therefore, is one of those improvements in the police of the country, for which we stand indebted to the wisdom of its Reformers. The recollection of what we experienced in Flanders, and of what was practised in France under the old system, disposed us to wish all possible prosperity to the new Government.

Passing the wood, which conducts to the town of Lauterbourg, we were incommoded with a deep and hot sand, and pursued by flies of an extraordinary magnitude. I was amufed with the very fudden change which I difcovered in the appearance, the drefs, and the air of the inhabitants, in paffing from the head-quarters of Ariftocracy. The people all wear, without exception, the national cockade; and each town has its *Garde Nationale.* I never faw people more at their eafe. They appear not yet to have recovered from thofe paroxyfms of tranfport, into which the Revolution firft threw them; and they are frolicking without apprehenfion, at a time when the exiled nobleffe are plotting fchemes for their deftruction, at the diftance of half a dozen leagues from their frontier.

The town of Lauterbourg was enlivened by the notes of military mufic; and the popular air of " Ça ira" refounded in every ftreet. The wine in this town was delicious, and appeared more abundant than we had yet feen it. We rofe at an early hour, and made a journey of twelve leagues, which brought us to Strafbourg. The heat
continued

continued to persecute us all this day, but we found relief by bathing in the Rhine.

Our entrance into Strasbourg was obstructed for a short time by the demand of a passport. Against this we stood out with some violence, perceiving the object of the officer was to obtain a fee, and were at length victorious. So difficult is it for the wisest and best regulations to defeat, in every instance, the attempts of corruption. The heavings of subdued oppression will occasion some temporary interruption; but truth, justice, and order will finally triumph.

I have, I believe, omitted in its place to mention, that our route from Coblentz was obstructed by a long religious procession. A very large cross was borne at the head of those devotees: priests in surplices succeeded; and a promiscuous throng of men, women, and children brought up the rear. They chaunted—as the procession moved—various services; and produced a very agreeable harmony. We had some difficulty to pafs them; and foon encountered a fecond fett, who were defcending the hill to meet them, and chaunting their matins with the fame mufical folemnity. The picturefque fcenes through which we were paffing, received an interefting colouring from thofe ceremonies of fuperftitious devotion.

My mind is, indeed, full of the varied imagery, which a rapid movement through fuch an extent of country has introduced. I have a thoufand pictures continually before me, of lofty mountains and level plains, of craggy rocks and cultured fields; but the fucceffion has been fo quick, that I can hardly review them with diftinctnefs. You will have much to fupply, as you travel with me, from the hiftories of thofe who have gone before. Such obfervations as circumftances fuggeft, fhall be duly regiftered as I pafs; and fo much fhall be recorded for your entertainment, as the current of thought may at that moment fupply; but I pretend to

answer

answer for no higher amusement than can be found in the imperfect colourings of a rapid pencil—faithful rather to the idea impressed, than to the subject which may give it birth.

LETTER XXXIV.

Basle, June 10, 1791.

WHAT a stupendous event is this Revolution! The evil which has baffled ages of resistance, and which seemed to know no limits of duration, has in a moment vanished. Surely, it is an interesting sight to contemplate upon the spot, those changes which have taken place upon a people, bound in the chain of immemorial tyranny. There is something so novel in the phraseology now employed, that the very language seems animated by the Revolutionary spirit. Liberty, Law, Constitution, Rights of men, are terms indeed of no new creation; but they had slept for ever in the cabinets of the learned, if the event—now the subject of univerſal celebration—had not awakened them into life and action.

I told you in my laſt, that we entered Straſbourg on the evening of the 6th. The following morning I amuſed myſelf in examining the different parts of the town. You have heard ſufficiently of the Cathedral, its brazen gates, its ſtupendous tower, its wonderful clock, &c. On thoſe ſubjects nothing can be added; but the temper of the people has aſſumed a new feature; and thoſe long converſant with the country, are alone competent to tell,—how great are the changes which have been introduced into the manners, the ſentiments, and converſation of the French.

For myſelf, who have not had that advantage,—I find it tolerably ſupplied by the intercourſe I held with the Emigrants at Bruſſels, upon whom no change whatever had

LETTER XXXIV.

had paffed, except a tranfient chagrin, which yielded to the firft occafion of merriment. I find a very ftriking contraft between the manners of the Revolutionifts and the Ariftocrats. The turn of politics which the firft have adopted has confolidated very greatly their natural vivacity, and reduced the buoyancy of their former levities to an agreeable humour.

All is political at Strafbourg. The corner of every ftreet is covered with *Programmas*, and the walls of every church decorated with Proclamations and Decrees. The greater part of the latter, advertife the fale of the national effects. It is very gratifying to fee, how rationally the language of the Preamble is worded; and what juft modifications of expreffion now convey the fanction of royal authority: " Louis XVI. " par la grace de Dieu et la loi conftitu-" tionelle de l'état, Roi de François, falut. " L'Affemblee Nationale a decretée, et nous " voulons et ordonnons," &c.——O Spirit of Louis XIV! what a contraft does this prefent present to the ancient form of the Royal decrees; and what a complete reformation of system does it bespeak, in those who *will*, and those who *obey !*—One scarcely walks twenty yards now, without meeting in places of public observation—a declaration of civil rights; and all the shops of music and prints, are hung with national ballads and political caricatures.

The counterpart to this, may be read in an extract from one of the late King's letters to Marechal Richelieu: " Je ne puis " plus differer à faire sentir à mon parle- " ment, que je suis *le maître absolu*,—et que " ma *puissance absolue* vient de Dieu,—et que " je n'en dois compte qu'à *lui*, le jour où il " me retirera de ce monde." And again, in another letter, he tells him : " Je leur ferai " voir, que je ne tiens mon pouvoir que " de Dieu,—que je n'ai de compte à rendre " qu'à *lui*,—et que personne dans mon roy- "aume ne doit s'opposer à ma volonté." It forms a very interesting speculation to

bring

bring together those sentiments of a few years past, and the patriotic declarations of the reigning sovereign. Louis XVI. is said to have expressed on every occasion the greatest readiness to accommodate his conduct to the wishes of the nation. " Je ne veux que " le bien de mon peuple," is a sentiment in which he has frequently indulged.

Moore was certainly no mean student of the French character. Perhaps no man ever caught with more accuracy, or rendered with more felicity, " the living man- " ners" of this nation. But he was not endued with the spirit of prophecy. The *steadiest* sight sees *distant* objects darkly and confusedly. Let him speak for himself: " If any of their kings were to behave in " such an imprudent and outrageous man- " ner as to occasion a revolt, and if the " insurgents actually got the better, I que- " stion if they would think of new-model- " ling the government, and limiting the " power of the crown, as was done in Bri-
" tain

" tain at the Revolution, so as to prevent
" the like abuses for the future. They never
" would think of going farther, I imagine,
" than placing another prince of the Bour-
" bon family upon the throne, with the
" same power that his predecessor had, and
" then quietly laying down their arms,
" satisfied with his royal word, or declara-
" tion, to govern with more equity." *Letter VI. on France.*——Upon such prediction, the events that have since happened are a sufficient commentary.

LETTER XXXV.

Basle, June 10, 1791.

THE general complaint at Strasbourg was want of money. Nothing is to be found in circulation, but paper and copper. " Tout iroit bien," said an old man, " si
" on avoit de l'argent." At all the shops, the greatest apprehensions are entertained

of

LETTER XXXV.

of being paid for their merchandize in paper. This, amongſt each other, they are obliged to admit; but in their intercourſe with ſtrangers, they ſtruggle very hard for ſpecie.

I turned into the ſhop of a *Marchande de modes* to purchaſe ſome articles. The bargain was ſtruck, the ſeveral particulars wrapped up, and I was ſearching in my pocket for the money; when obſerving me draw out ſome paper by accident, ſhe laid immediate hold upon the packet I had purchaſed, and demanded with haſte, " Allez-" vous me payer en papier, Monſieur?" " Si fait," ſaid I. " Eh bien donc," replied ſhe, "je garderai ma marchandiſe." I ſoon relieved her of the anxiety ſhe felt, and brought a glow upon her cheek, by counting out upon the table the ſum agreed. This is indeed the greateſt—I had almoſt ſaid the only—grievance that I have diſcovered among them; and they ſcruple not to predict, that the very favourable ſale of the national domains will raiſe the credit of

their

their paper, and give them as much money as they have liberty.

I must assure you, that I found the state of the people in this part of France very different from what it had been represented. At Manheim and Worms, reports prevailed of the most serious tumults now reigning in France; and we were more than once cautioned against trusting ourselves amongst a *canaille*, who would hang us up at the lamp-post for a word or a look. This statement has so little connection with truth, that every thing passes with the utmost order; and, so far as I can judge from observation and report, freedom of remark encounters less danger here than at the court of Manheim. Nothing could surpass the strictness which prevailed in every quarter where the fugitive nobility are received; and if I might draw conclusions respecting the country at large from what I see around me, restraint of opinion is exiled with those who owed to its existence their guilty pre-eminence.

The

LETTER XXXV.

The day after our arrival, was rendered festive by a new enrolment of National guards. This was formed out of the citizens over the age of eighteen years, and was effected without the least symptom of disorder. Beside the guard thus regularly embodied, the citizens are seen every evening in different parts of the town, learning, against an emergency, the use of arms. It certainly is animating to read, in a thousand conspicuous places, proclamations setting forth the right of private judgment; allowing to every man the free exercise of his opinion in matters of religion; and establishing to each individual the liberty of adopting that mode of worship he best approves.

This would, however, be nugatory and ridiculous, were the slightest encouragement given to contumacy and disorder. This has been said *out* of the country; but the contrary has appeared wherever I have enquired. I read upon the door of the cathedral at Strasbourg an advertisement, which stated, "That a young man having behaved improperly in the Cathedral during the performance of divine service; and, after admonition from the centinel, persisted in a conduct *unbecoming the so-lemnity of the place and occasion*, was, by the officers of the police, sentenced to imprisonment for this *insult offered to religious worship.*" This accords but ill with a toleration of disorder.

Before I left Strasbourg, I visited the mausoleum of Marechal Saxe, at the church of St. Thomas; and had an offer of seeing the National armoury, but it came too late to serve me. We reached Colmar in the evening, after a journey of sixteen leagues. Yesterday we made a very fatiguing one of fourteen leagues, and reached Basle in the evening. The heat and the dust were excessively troublesome. It was not without difficulty that we procured a bason of milk at a village where the horses were baited.

Coffee

LETTER XXXV.

Coffee is in general abundant in thefe parts of the country; and this is one of the firft inftances of diftrefs which we have experienced upon the article of breakfaft.

At the village of Mulhaufen, eight leagues from Colmar, we alighted to dine. The houfe was ordinary; and four travellers, wrapped in white night-caps, apparently of mean condition, were about to commence their meal. I enquired of the hoftefs, if we could be alfo accommodated with a dinner. She told me with an air of great unconcern, that we might dine with thofe gentlemen; or—if that did not pleafe us— we might take what they left; for that was the whole that her kitchen could produce. We did not long deliberate upon the choice which our landlady had given us. The dinner was indeed better than the company. They were Germans, except one,—who converfed with us in French, and afked me many queftions refpecting the opinions entertained abroad of their Revolution. I told him,

him, I had feen many Ariftocrats at Manheim. He afked me, if they had raifed any troops? I told him, No; there were none but Officers. " Ah, ma foi, Monfieur," faid he, " une armée d'officiers s'avancéra " peu." Another, with whom I afterwards converfed, declaimed with fome violence againft the propriety of Alface being continued under the French government: " On nous fait payer," faid he, " 80,000 " livres pour être François; et c'eft payer " affez cher, le *privilege* d'être gouverné par " des *etrangers*."

LETTER XXXVI.

Bafle, June 11, 1791.

WE entered Bafle at what would elfewhere be called eight, but what is here called nine, o'clock. I have never yet heard a fatisfactory account of this advance of an hour in the time of the day, or what

were

were the real circumstances that occasioned it. An old traveller, who passed this way near two hundred years ago, reports of it, that a conspiracy had been formed to betray the city, and that the false striking of the clock disconcerted the plot. He further says, that they preserved a certain stone, called the *Heisteine*, upon which the heads of the consuls and other conspirators were struck off; unluckily adding, however, that people were not agreed upon this piece of history,—and that some referred the advance of the clock to a design of hastening the proceedings of the council. It is, however, a curious circumstance, to see a whole city one complete hour in all their transactions before their neighbours; and to a stranger, it occasions some embarrassment, as the sun will neither rise nor set in conformity to the decrees of Basle.

The hotel of the Three Kings is that to which all the world goes; and I should suppose there is not a pleasanter Inn in Eu-rope.

rope. Situated on the weſtern banks of the Rhine, it commands a delightful view; and the ſaloon appropriated to the table d'hôte is the moſt cheerful apartment I ever was in. The walls are hung with various engravings, repreſenting ſome of the choiceſt ſcenery in Switzerland. The Rhine is here in its greateſt beauty, and fills a wider bed between this place and Straſbourg, than in any other part of its courſe. Nothing can ſurpaſs its colouring. The ſea, in all its azure and ſerenity, can alone furniſh a parallel to the cerulean tranſparency of its waters. It has conſiderable rapidity in its deſcent towards Straſbourg, and the boats which paſs thither are broke up and ſold. The ſame is done upon the Rhone and the Danube, it being impracticable, without infinite labour and coſt, to bring up a veſſel againſt ſo ſtrong a current.

The place and the people preſented to me an appearance particularly gratifying, by the ſtrong characters every where obſervable, of
ſimplicity,

LETTER XXXVI.

simplicity, cleanliness, and industry. Basle has been a place of no small dignity in the earlier periods of its history; though I question if it ever possessed, in the days of its Imperial grandeur, so solid a prosperity as it now derives from its union with the Cantons of Switzerland. Basle counts among its citizens, several men of eminence in arts and literature. Holben and Buxtorf were once, in their several departments, the ornaments of this town; and the great Erasmus is honoured with a monument in the Cathedral, upon the spot that contains his ashes. In addition to those distinctions, it claims the merit of having invented paper in the year 1417.

I took a walk in the evening through the different parts of the town, which are connected by a bridge over the Rhine. The shops appeared abundant in commodities: every one active in his occupation, and content with his condition. It was sun-set when I returned from my walk; and I found

found the shops shut, and the families seated upon benches at the doors of their houses. Here they enjoy the cool breeze of the evening, and relax from the fatigues of the day in cheerful conversation. I found this the case throughout all quarters of the town; and I seemed to myself passing through a saloon, the company in which was ranged in the highest order on both sides. This favours strongly of ancient and uncorrupt simplicity. Goldsmith has drawn the picture of it in his "Deserted Village." I had the images in my mind before I saw Basle, and was the more gratified in the revival of them, than I should have been by the first impression. Surely the noblest effect of the Muse is to learn to appreciate nature; and that Poetry is of the highest character, which conveys the faithfullest images of unadulterated life. It is on this principle that I consider Thomson and Goldsmith, as the oracles of genuine poetry, and the very best instructors of mo-

ral

ral sentiment. What volumes of verse have been written with uselefs elaboration!

" To me more dear, congenial to my heart,
" One native charm, than all the gloss of art."

LETTER XXXVII.

Berne, June 12, 1791.

THE dress of the women at Basle was very singular. Their hair was combed smooth back from the forehead—bound at the crown with a fillet—and brought behind into two plaits of considerable length. These are further lengthened by black ribbons appended to them, which descend almost to their heels. Their countenances, without much beauty, were very pleasant and cheerful. They appeared very affable and unreserved. The generality of them dress in black. This I had at first supposed to be particular to the Black Foresters, but I find it is not confined to them; and that the

LETTER XXXVII.

the univerfality of this ufage originates in œconomical reafons. The fhort petticoats— fo much the favourite of the *Hollandoife*— is here worn with much greater advantage; and difcovers a well-fhaped leg, ufually adorned with a fcarlet ftocking, forming—in the opinion of the females of Bafle—a fine contraft to the *fombre* fhades of their accuftomed habit.

I cannot difmifs the article of Bafle, without affuring you, that I was never more pleafed with a place which pretends to fo little. It owes all its beauties to nature and to induftry. Its only ornaments are, the landfcapes which furround it, and the fimple manners of thofe who inhabit it. Men, women, and children, all appeared engaged in the common caufe of enriching its markets, and fupporting its commerce. Here are no paftimes for the gay, no indulgences for the vicious: but the heart which can tafte of purer pleafures, and rejoice in the felicity of the human race, may here receive

LETTER XXXVII.

no common gratification, in contemplating a virtuous, a united, and a happy people.

We left Bafle in the morning of the 11th, and have arrived at Berne, after a journey of two days. I will endeavour to give you a faint fketch of the country through which we have paffed: but eloquent indeed muft be that pen, and animated that pencil, which can do adequate juftice to fuch fcenes of pre-eminent beauty. As we left Bafle, we gradually entered upon a mountainous country, with the Rhine flowing to the left of us. The road continued tolerable, excepting that in different parts it was fcattered with loofe and inconvenient fragments of ftone. The courfe is ferpentine, for the facility of afcent; and this gives a greater fcope for variety in the different landfcapes that prefent themfelves.

At Lieftal, where we refted during the heat of the day, the mountains appeared to gather round us. I was induced, by the fingular appearance of one of thefe, to

make

make an ineffectual attempt at reaching its summit, by catching at the roots, shrubs, and masses of stone which covered its surface. From Lieftal we entered upon a route which exhibited to our eyes the grandest pictures imaginable. Mountains piled on mountains seemed to inclose us on all hands. These were of various forms and complexions. Some rose in conical beauty; others presented aspects more rude and majestic. Some were clothed with verdure; others with dusky umbrage; and others, displaying their bosoms of naked flint, seemed to set vegetation and culture at defiance. The road in many parts pierces these rocks; among which, as you pass, you hear the roar of waters—descending from precipice to precipice; and trace, among the stupendous scenery, the hut that protects the peasant from the storm. The approach of Bieftal passes over a mountain, esteemed a league in ascent. The entrance to this place was particularly striking. On our
right,

right, were mountains of uncouth form and prodigious height — on our left, vallies clothed with verdure, and scattered with human habitations. It was dusk when we entered, and the sun had given place to the softer shades of twilight.

This morning we left Bieftal, and passed through Soleure to Berne. The scenery increased in beauty and magnificence as we advanced. Soleure is a town of very pleasant appearance, and the Church is a very elegant building. This place is the capital of the Canton which bears its name; is of the Catholic religion, and the ordinary residence of the French ambassador to the Helvetic Union. It being Sunday, all the villagers and inhabitants of the town were parading in groups, with their short cloaths and their scarlet stockings. At the table d'hôte there were many Emigrants; but no articles of intelligence transpired. Our object was to reach Berne in the evening, which we effected; and the necessity of

some

some repose, must plead my excuse for withdrawing myself thus abruptly from your society.

LETTER XXXVIII.

Geneva, June 17, 1791.

THE night of our arrival at Berne we supped at the table d'hôte, and met some agreeable company. Among others, was a Frenchman, who appeared a well-bred man. We asked him some questions respecting Berne. He pictured it in most deplorable colours. "Ah mon Dieu! tout "est tranquille ici: il n'y a point de spec- "tacles, ni de caffé, ni de societé." His countenance interpreted very fully the calamitous situation in which he found himself. "Je me mourai!" was his conclusion. He was particularly complimentary upon the English nation as a nation of splendor and

LETTER XXXVIII.

and amufements. "On y trouve tant de "belles chofes," faid he; and then began enumerating Bath, Vauxhall, &c. I could not help reflecting on this principle, which feems to enter fo univerfally into the character of a Frenchman. This man was, to appearance, a well-educated man—at leaft upon the fyftem of French Education;—and he was an exile from his country: yet the *gout* for amufements ftill continued to prevail over every other feeling; and the Revolution of his country, appeared to him only fo far inconvenient,—as it had robbed him of his amufements and his rank.

The fituation of Berne is extremely fine. The fcenery around it is indeed magnificent. The town is almoft encircled by the river Aar; the houfes are remarkably well built with Arcades; and the utmoft neatnefs is kept up in every quarter. Berne is not entirely without its amufements. Thefe are principally the pleafures of the Promenade; and perhaps no city in Europe can
boaft

LETTER XXXVIII.

boast a terrace whose view commands a more sublime collection of natural objects. Our table d'hôte was enlivened, the day after our arrival, by a political disputation upon the interests of Europe; and it was warmly contended, *à l'unanime*, that England should unite with Spain, and strike a blow at the Empress of Russia.

We encountered at table, in the evening, one of those inquisitive characters who offer no small annoyance to strangers. He was a man of a certain age, but of a most voluble tongue. He attacked us the moment we were seated, with a succession of interrogatories, of " What place we came " from?—Which way we were going?— " Whether we had made the tour of Swit- " zerland, or whether we intended it?" and then began, unasked, to give us his advice. He insisted upon it, we *must* make an excursion in the neighbourhood of Berne—that we must *not* content ourselves with a direct route to Geneva—and enumerated

merated a variety of objects to which we *ought* to attend. Finding the anfwers we gave, were not likely to filence him—we began to be more laconic in our replies. This induced a calm of a few minutes; when, turning his head from us, he broke out aloud with, " D'où venez-vous, Monfieur?" to an officer at the further end of the room. A Frenchman makes great allowance for frivolous enquiry—The officer replied with the utmoft readinefs to this firft queftion, and to thofe which fucceeded; and thus we became perfectly acquainted with his hiftory. " Où allez-vous ?—Quand par-" tez-vous ?—Etes-vous marié ?—Madame " doit être malheureufe pendant vôtre ab-" fence." Such was the nature of his attack upon the officer.

I feared the arrival of fupper would bring our affairs again into play : and it happened juft as I had furmifed. He took his chair by me, and renewed the charge, with the fame perfevering curiofity, during

the whole of the seſſion. "Eh bien, vous
" allez à Geneve. Il faut, cependant, faire
" des petites tours ; ou bien, il faut revenir
" à Berne. Comptez-vous reſter à Geneve?
" J'y ferai en quinze jours-moi. Je ſerai
" mortifié de ne pas vous trouver." Such
were the perſecutions I experienced during
ſupper. Fortunately for me, he recollected
that a gentleman, who ſat oppoſite him,
had not yet been catechized. He opened
the trenches againſt him, and drew out in
a few ſeconds the whole of his hiſtory.
We took advantage of this diverſion made
in our favour, and withdrew ourſelves
from his farther importunities. I had Ho‑
race full in my recollection, during this
adventure; and when he opened his at‑
tack upon me, with "Comment vous va‑
" t-il, mon cher?" I thought I heard,
" Quid agis dulciſſime rerum?"

We left Berne the following morning;
and dining at the charming town of Morat,
paſſed in the evening to Paliere; where we

LETTER XXXVIII.

had some difficulty to find accommodations—such were the numbers of French emigrants who are on their way to Worms and Manheim. From Paliere we proceeded early the next day, and arrived by the setting of the sun at Lausanne. It was not our intention to make any stay at Lausanne; and as the journey from Brussels had been long and fatiguing, we hastened to the place of our destination. Reposing therefore the night at Lausanne, we made our last day's journey, in the finest weather and upon such a road as we have not before witnessed, and arrived yesterday evening at Geneva. Here we fix for some time our residence, and such is the general aspect of the country, that I think we may promise ourselves a very agreeable *séjour*.

LETTER XXXIX.

Geneva, June 28, 1791.

I HAVE now been near a fortnight at Geneva, and have little more to report to you than the state of the weather. Our mode of life is perfectly recluse. The scenery with which we are surrounded is the object of our constant contemplation, and our evenings are invariably passed in sauntering upon the banks of the Lake.

Here let me indulge for a moment in drawing some faint outline of this magnificent country. The Lake, which in magnitude is rivalled only by that of Constance, is situated in a valley between the Alps and the Jura, which runs through Switzerland as the Appenine through Italy. The width of this Lake is well proportioned to the height of those mountains which inclose it;

and

and the form of its bed is such as to give scope for all the varieties of scenery. Its waters are deliciously pure, and exhibit—particularly at their issue—the most enchanting transparency.

At the head of this Lake is situated Villeneuve, at the rectilinear distance of fifteen leagues. Along the banks of the Lake, on either side, are scattered towns and villages, whose magnitude is so reduced by the stupendous mountains which tower behind them, that they appear but clusters of diminutive sheds, and scarcely seem to rise out of the waters. The mountains of which I speak, are those which stand on the side of Savoy, and form a part of the Alps. These present a very noble range of bold and majestic objects: their forms, their magnitude, and their aspect, have every variety necessary to the harmony of the scene. The grand Saleve is the first in order, proceeding from Geneva, which it flanks. This is a mountain of no pre-eminent

nent height. Its furface is covered with an agreeable verdure, and fcattered with fome cottages in thofe declivities which approach the town. Its fummit exhibits the form of a wedge whofe angle is rounded off. Next to this ftands the Petit Saleve, which bears a more pointed form, and whofe roots approach more nearly the borders of the Lake. The Mole rifes next— of a very dufky hue, and conical figure, which contrafts well with the long and uniform appearance of the Voifons ftanding beyond it. The real figure of the Mole is faid to be by no means confonant with its apparent form, which is indeed conveyed to the eye in the ftrict character of the cone. Here are the mountains which ftand along the fouthern bank of the Lake, and which form to the imagination the rear-guard of the Alps.

Behind thefe darker maffes are ranged the Glaciers, which exhibit through the interftices of the former their lucid fummits.

This

LETTER XXXIX.

This chain of icy substances presents to the eye no uniform appearance: in some of its parts are glassy promontories discovered, shooting their silver points into the clouds. These are known by the name of *Aiguilles*, from the figure they represent. In others the blended snows and ice are swelled into unequal masses, and exhibit different configurations of the most transparent materials. Parent of all—the Mont Blanc—stands clothed in a robe of the purest white, and appears indeed sovereign of the surrounding scenes. The summit of this mountain rises much above the rest; and, though by no means so in reality, has the appearance of a conical figure rounded at its point. Such is the outline of those objects which form the back-ground of this majestic picture; and the softened light which beams at the setting of the sun, paints them to the eye in all the chastest colouring which fancy ever imagined.

LETTER XXXIX.

The Rhone issues from the Lake at Geneva. This noble river takes its course through the town, and its steep waters exhibit a colouring of the richest blue. The Arve, rolling down its torrent from the snowy Alps, forms its junction with the Rhone in the vicinity of Geneva; and at an angle, which occasions great turbulence to the commixing waters. Our house is situated at some little distance from the town, and our communication with it is not likely to be great. It participates, in common with all the states of Europe, of that political ferment to which France has given birth; and, though the aristocratic party administer the government at present, they are not without apprehensions from the restless activity of their democratic rivals.

LETTER XL.

Geneva, July 12, 1791.

SINCE I laſt wrote, very important intelligence has tranſpired. The news of the King's flight was very ſoon conveyed to this place, and every precaution was taken to prevent its operating any miſchief in this little republic. All the avenues were beſet with guards, to prevent a ſtranger's paſſing the territory; and patroles of horſe paraded the whole of the night. I heard ſome private letters from Paris read, which announced the moſt perfect unconcern, on the part of the Pariſians, at the departure of their king. The converſation in the public places of reſort was ſaid to have been, " Le " roi a pris la fuite."—" Eh bien !" ſaid the reſt, " on s'en paſſera."

LETTER XL.

This event, and the subsequent arrest, were variously received here, and in the *Pais de Vaud*. Many of the Genevese assembled every evening upon the promenades, comparing the separate accounts which each had privately received, as many had sons, cousins, or nephews in the national guard of Paris. " Le roi est parti," said one ;" " Tant mieux," said an old democrat, " on fera moins embarrassé." The evening after the retaking of the king, the promenade was in singular commotion; and the people were divided by sentiments of joy and sorrow. " On l'a repri," said one—" Tant pis pour eux," said another— " Apparemment on lui tranchera la tête," said a third. Such were the remarks upon the promenades of Geneva at this event.

At Lausanne, I understood, that political sentiment expressed itself in a more public manner. The news of the king's escape occasioned so great joy at this last place, that the aristocrates—who compose by far the majority

LETTER XL.

majority—indulged themselves in public illuminations. This triumph was however to undergo a mortification: the king was arrested, and the news was not long in making its way to Lausanne. The democrates would not lose so favourable an opportunity of disturbing their antagonists; they illuminated in their turn, and had the advantage of the laugh on their side.

I have mentioned the promenades at Geneva: they merit indeed more than a simple notice, at least those which are within the walls of the town. But as the gates are shut * irrevocably at half past eight o'clock—a time at which one scarcely begins to find the air sufficiently cool for respiration—I am obliged to confine myself to those walks which lie without the gates. These are frequented of an evening by large companies, with whom I am become in some degree familiarized, without the assistance of letters recommendatory. The grand

* The shutting of the gates is regulated by the hour of sunset.

enquiry

enquiry on the subject of politics relates to Paine and *Pierce*—by which they mean Price—a name they cannot pronounce. I told them all that I knew about them, *i. e.* just so much as they knew, and all the world knew before—that they were reputed champions of no mean strength in the field of politics.

Of this groupe is a veteran, less distinguished by his own character than by a very elegant daughter, whose personal charms and brilliant conversation have given her much celebrity. Expert in every subject of general interest, she is more particularly attached to political discussion, and has, by her beauty and her principles, acquired the appellation of " La belle democrate." She is very fond of enquiring into the character of the English ladies, for whom she has the highest respect. She wished to know, what particular system of politics the English women now defended. I told her, the ladies with us seldom interfered in political discussion.

cuſſion. She took it for a rebuke—" Ap-
" paramment Monſieur penſe que les dames
" ne doivent pas ſe meler de la politique."
" Pardonnez moi," ſaid I. Madamoiſelle
is often attended upon the promenade by
a German, who appears deeply captivated
with her 'charms, without however being
fortunate enough to excite a reciprocal paſſion. " Il ne fait que parler de la meta-
" phyſique," ſays ſhe—" L'amour ne
" s'ouvre pas ordinairement comme ça."
His accent offends her ear. " The Germans
" murder our language," ſhe ſays, " more
" than any people in Europe." I obſerved to
her, that the Engliſh ſeldom attained to a juſt-
neſs of pronunciation. " J'en conviens,"
ſays ſhe, " mais les Allemands travaillent a
" prononcer notre langue, au lieu que vous
" autres ne vous en embarraſſez point; et
" j'aime plutôt celui qui ne la prononce pas,
" que celui qui la prononce mal."

LETTER XLI.

Geneva, July 15, 1791.

THE dress of the Genevese is fashioned upon a very agreeable model. The generality of females of every condition are far removed from sickliness or deformity, and those of the higher classes are pleasing in their persons and their manners. Rousseau has indeed charged them with want of parental tenderness, in sending their infants to be nursed, or rather neglected, by the inhabitants of the mountains: but in this, as in other respects, modern Geneva bears little resemblance to the ancient.

The custom of taking a *gouté*, corresponding to our tea, I have not seen elsewhere; though I understand it is not peculiar to this place. I was invited to one of those

LETTER XLI.

repasts by the old patriot, and was surprized to find such variety of eatables at such an hour; it was five o'clock in the afternoon. The moment the company were seated, baskets of bread were handed about; these were followed by anchovies, and tarts of an extraordinary size. In the mean time, coffee, tea, wine, liqueurs, &c. were put in circulation; in so much that I, who had but just risen from dinner, made a very contemptible figure amongst them. " Il me " semble que les Anglois mangent peu," said one of the company. I replied in the affirmative, to avoid being further solicited. " Ils s'en tiennent beaucoup a leur *rosbeef*," exclaimed another of the party, who had destroyed a host of eatables. At the sound of *rosbeef*, Monsf. A. seemed suddenly struck; and apologizing for not having provided *rosbeef* for my *goûté*, insisted upon my consenting to dine with him at noon on the following Sunday. I waited on him the day appointed, and was much amused with

my

my entertainment. A variety of articles were ferved up; and I was urged to feaft upon foup, difhes of rice, &c. till I had quite loft fight of the grand defideratum. At length, when the defert fhould have come, enters a piece of roaft beef of an immoderate fize. It was diverting to fee the buftle it created among the company, whofe eyes were fixed alternately on *me* and the *beef*; and each appeared to wait with anxious curiofity the havoc my appetite was to make upon this huge mafs of flefh. Nothing but the very marked intention of gratifying me, prevented my refifting their intreaties *in toto*: and their difappointment was fo great at the very fmall progrefs I made, that I queftion if Monfieur will ever think it worth his while to confult again the palate of an Englifhman.

The great feftivities here are on the Sunday; and, notwithftanding the ftrict devotion which prevails during three parts of the day, the evening is celebrated with the moft most cheerful gaieties. The principal amusement is upon the Lake, which is usually covered with pleasure-boats, and affords a very delightful spectacle. Some of these boats are of a very considerable size, and are decorated with very brilliant ornaments. In these they amuse themselves with music, dancing, and playing off fireworks—principally those of a violent explosion. The reverberation of this, from the vast chain of mountains which surround the Lake, resembles very accurately the rolling of thunder, and is listened to with the most eager attention.

This little republic is not without its political ferments. It should seem, from their numerous precautions, that some great danger was apprehended. The orders of the Syndics are unusually strict. The vigilance of the magistrates and the bourgeois-guard is unremitting. For greater security, the gate, which formerly faced the Swifs quarter, has been within these two or three weeks,

weeks, with great labour and expence, turned towards the French territory: whence, it should seem, that hostilities were eventually expected. During the whole affair of the king's flight, every species of caution was employed; and the circumspection which this government thought necessary to exercise on that occasion, convinces me that they conceive much of their own security to depend upon the particular turn of French affairs. Their fortifications are undergoing repair; the inhabitants have lately been inrolled; and all the measures which vigilance can dictate, are now put in practice, with a view to guard against the designs of the democratic minority.

LETTER XLII.

Geneva, July 15, 1791.

I RECEIVED yesterday a very high degree of entertainment, and am anxious to report to you the journals of my proceedings. It was, as you will recollect, the commemoration of the French revolution; and, as agreeable to a decree of the National Assembly, the day was to be celebrated throughout France. Ferney, the ancient residence of Voltaire, was among the number of those towns which announced an intention of observing this anniversary. I had for some time past determined upon making a visit to Ferney, in order to view the mansion once occupied by this illustrious man; and my curiosity to witness this extraordinary festival, decided me to put my plan in execution on this day. I knew not the state of the place; nor could foresee, whether my person might be safe among a number of men,

men, assembled to celebrate the orgies of Liberty and Bacchus. I was unwilling therefore to be a solitary guest, and an order of council had been issued forbidding any subject of the Republic to be found at Ferney during this festival. I shortly however picked up an Englishman, of whom I had some slight knowledge; and who, though profoundly ignorant of the language, had as much curiosity as was necessary for my purpose. We placed severally a cockade in our hats, and drove to Ferney.

The village wore a very gay appearance: all the inhabitants, and many from the environs, were parading in numerous parties, dressed in all the trappings of their Sunday wardrobes. Having found with some difficulty a stand for our whiskey and horse, we repaired to a part of the town, which from the crowds assembled there seemed to be the place of rendezvous. We passed through many ranks of spectators, and came to a large area, in the centre of which was

elevated

LETTER XLII.

elevated the national ſtandard, and the colours inſcribed with—" Vivre libre, ou mou-" rir," were ſtreaming in the air. This ſpace was not incloſed with any fixed barrier, but preſerved for the company by the National guard; who acted alternately as centinels, and kept the line unbroken by the ſpectators. Within this area were two long tables, very nearly filled with company, and two ſmaller ones, occupied by ſelect parties. At the head of the *upper* table ſat the Commandant; and beſide him, the lady preſident. The reſt were for the moſt part officers of the guard, or, what is the ſame thing, volunteers; for the duties and the honours are taken in rotation. I underſtood from ſome of the attendants, that we ſhould find no difficulty in being admitted to the table. I therefore applied to a very genteel man, who was doing the duty of centinel, for permiſſion to ſit at the table. He aſſured me, it would do them ſingular honour. We therefore took our ſeats, and were served with some refreshment upon paying our quota.

The attention of the company was soon drawn upon us; and those nearest us at the table were solicitous to recommend themselves by drinking our healths. A band of military music regaled us during dinner. This ended, proclamation was made for silence: and the Commandant delivered an address upon the important advantages of the revolution. After commenting with some warmth upon these, and recommending as essential to their continuance, order and obedience to the constituted authorities,--he toasted the magistrates, the national assembly, &c. Every toast was drank with loud acclamations, and accompanied with the music of some popular air. When the Commandant had got through the toasts of office, he demanded silence, and begged leave to drink, " A la santée des Anglois, " nos meilleurs amis." This was received with the loudest bursts of applause. It was echoed

LETTER XLII.

echoed from every quarter, and the music struck up "ça ira;" which was sung by the greater part of the company. The nature of this toast turned the eyes of all upon us; and as my companion was not linguist enough to return the compliment, I mounted the bench. "Silence le plus profond," was called for on all hands; and I proclaimed aloud, "A la santée des François, "succes à la nouvelle constitution, fondée "sur des principes éternels, comme na-"turels." This had its effect: music, shouts, and songs, expressed their sense of gratitude: we were immediately handed by an officer to the upper table,—presented to the Lady President, who invited us to the ball. Ten thousand courtesies were now shewn us. They threw to the ground the burgundy we had purchased, and gave us in exchange some of the first quality. They spoke in terms of the warmest regard of the English nation, whose example they pretended only to follow; and commended that

generosity,

generosity, which declined to take advantage of their present distractions.

An officer now hurried us away to drink coffee. I was glad of the opportunity of being relieved from the superabundant civilities of the company. He conducted us to a house where liqueurs, &c. were served up, and many patriotic songs were sung by the different Officers. My friend, who was rather warmed by the burgundy and liqueurs, than enlightened by the conversation, desired me to express to these Frenchmen the respect he had for them: I interpreted his intentions, and all shook hands with him—shouting at the same time, " Bravo, le bon Anglois!" The liqueur was forcible, and the vivacity of the songs animating: these had a mechanical effect upon the humours of my companion. He desired me to assure these Frenchmen, that he loved liberty as much as they did, and that he had an estate in England, but that he would willingly sacrifice it all for the sake

of

of liberty. I again became his interpreter, and his hand was again demanded—with a repetition, in a still higher tone, of "Bravo, le bon Anglois!" The afternoon was indeed passed in the greatest hilarity, and without the least infringement of decorum. Never did I see men whose air, conversation, and gesture discovered more happiness. They harangued, they danced, and omitted no possible expression of gaiety. What particularly struck me in the midst of all this enthusiasm was, that not a term of reproach was used against the king; nor a sentiment of revenge breathed against those from whose yoke they had so recently escaped. Their feelings seemed to be engrossed by the single consideration of their present felicity, and not an evil passion was suffered to disturb the serenity of their pleasures. Upon the whole, no festival—which had for its object the commemoration of such an event,—could have been conducted with greater harmony, propriety, and good order.

LETTER XLII.

We contrived to withdraw ourselves from the company at the approach of evening, and made a visit to Voltaire's house. This was a gratification I could not refuse myself. The situation is fine; in the house itself there is nothing remarkable. We were shewn the apartment in which Voltaire usually passed his time. This is hung round with the portraits of eminent men, and adorned with the urn containing his heart, which he bequeathed, or pretended to bequeath, to this place. The church and theatre are still in existence,—but all around proclaims the master's fall. Upon returning from Voltaire's villa, we found the gaieties of the ball-room were commencing; but, adopting the prudence of the " conviva- " satur," we entered our whiskey for Geneva. As we drove through the town, we were received with shouts, and waving of hats. These compliments we returned in the best manner we could; and bade adieu to Ferney,—not a little satisfied with the adventures of the day.

LETTER XLIII.

Lausanne, July 20, 1791.

BY a change of syftem, our refidence at Geneva was fhortened by two months, and we are now at Laufanne—or rather in the environs, which are delicious beyond compare. The fcenery wants indeed that foftnefs and harmony which the Genevefe territory poffeffes; but then it has to boaft magnificence, boldnefs, and variety. The houfe we inhabit, is in the village of Ouchy, nearly a mile and half from the town. It is fmall and ruftic, fituated within a dozen yards of the Lake, and confronted by the mountains of Savoy, and the rocks of Millèrie. Since we have been here, the Lake —which is fubject to ebb and flow—has been more than once worked into a ftorm, and rifen to a confiderable height. This is a phenomenon for the folution of which

many

many hypotheses have been offered. That most approved is Mr. Bertrand's, who supposes, that electric clouds elevate the waters to various degrees of height, in proportion to the quantity of the electric fluid; and that the subsequent fall, or sinking of the waters—particularly in the narrow parts of the Lake, where these *seiches*, as they are called, are most violent—occasions these sudden storms.

Here is a good circulating library, and gazettes of every kind. But Lausanne is now so much frequented by foreigners, and particularly English,—that every thing peculiar and original is extirpated. In compliance with fashion and interest, every thing is *anglicised;* and you may now have the satisfaction of paying as much for the hire of a horse, a carriage, or a house,— as at the most splendid place of English resort.

Gibbon is the *grand monarque* of literature at Lausanne: I have seen, conversed,

and

LETTER XLIII.

and dined with him. Thefe are, I think, the three requifites, in order to know fomething of a man. His converfation is correct and eloquent; his periods are meafured, and his manner of delivering them folemn. He appears rather inditing to an amanuenfis, than holding converfation with a ftranger. But though he talks too oracularly,— he is at his table cheerful, frank, and convivial. His hofpitalities are however not ftrictly *patriotic:* his predilection for the Swifs is notorious; and, as a love of preeminence may not be claffed amongft the leaft of his failings, he feems to have decided well in the choice of his fociety.

The ftate of the weather here is remarkably fine, but hot to a degree of fuffocation. We purpofe taking advantage of this part of the feafon, and making in a few days a vifit to the Glaciers of Chamouni. I have now full in my recollection, the firft glimpfe I caught of thofe wonderful regions. It was on my way from Paliere to Laufanne,

and

LETTER XLIII.

and within about a league of this latter place. We had alighted from our carriage, while the horses ascended a hill;—and as we approached the summit, one of the most magnificent sights in nature presented itself on a sudden to our astonished eyes: it was a distant view of the Glaciers; and the unusual appearance they made, would not suffer me to suppose that they were of a solider texture than the fleecy and transparent cloud;— till the reports of those better acquainted with the country, rectified the errors of an indistinct vision. It was at the close of the day, and all the lustre of a setting sun was playing upon their spotless summits.—The scenery was at once novel, and sublime. I anticipate a thousand pleasures in visiting these singular regions, where an external conflict is kept up between heat and cold; and mountains of ice experience no sensible diminution from the scorching rays of a solstitial sun.

LETTER XLIV.

Lausanne, Aug. 10, 1791.

I AM now returned from a tour among the Glaciers; and what my recollection, aided by an occasional note made on the way, can supply, shall now be penned down for your amusement. It was on Thursday, July 28, that we left Lausanne on this expedition. We composed together a party of seven, not including servants. The morning of the 29th, we left Geneva, at an early hour; and crossing the brook at Chesne, little more than a mile from the town of Geneva, we entered the territory of Savoy. The road to Bonneville, the town where we first halted, became gradually mountainous, and we at length found ourselves at the foot of the Mole. Of this mountain I have before remarked, that its

appearance

appearance from Geneva prefents a conical form; but this vanifhed as we approached: and, agreeable to the teftimony of Mr. Sauffure, fome who have made an expedition to Bonneville in order to examine the Mole, have returned without feeing it—having miftaken for it fome other mountain whofe figure refembled moft nearly the form under which this appears at a diftance. We began, in this part of our journey, to enter the land of fprings, and the heat being immoderate, often regaled ourfelves with draughts from thefe icy waters. We were dreffed in the lighteft clothing, yet fuffered very much from the fcorching rays of the fun, and their reflection from the fides of the mountains. We took fome refrefhment at Bonneville, and found fhelter there for fome hours from the fervors of the day. I ftrolled to the church for amufement, and found it not behind its fellows in faintly dignity. Many cafkets were placed upon the different altars, containing *moft unqueftionable* fragments

ments of ancient worthies. I tranfcribed from one of thefe precious repofitories the following infcription—I leave the Monk who wrote it, to defend the purity of its concords.
" Reliquias Sanctæ Vincentiæ ritè cognitas
" in hoc capfulo inclufas generationi fide-
" lium Bonopolis in facello S^d Petri exponi
" permittuntur."

We left Bonneville after repofing two or three hours, and paffed by a very fingular and romantic route to Salenche. Every pof-fible diverfity of fcenery is to be found in this latter ftage. Springs and cafcades iffue from the roots of the rocks which inclofe the track, or fcatter their waters down the fhelving fides. The heat raged unabated, till the approach to Salenche gave us a diftant view of the Glaciers, whofe icy fummits afforded—to the imagination at leaft—fome relief. Salenche terminated our journey of the day, and the evening was employed in making the neceffary arrangements for our conveyance to Chamouni, and viewing a

cafcade

cascade at some little distance; I know not its name. The approach to it was over rough and loose stones, some of which lay so far under the water, that it was problematical whether the feet would alight upon them or not. The cataract gushed from a hollow rock, and was not without its grotesque ornaments; but when the difficulties of egress and regress are calculated, the balance of pleasure preponderates but little in its favour.

From a necessity—to which we were constrained to submit--we were not provided with *char-a-bancs* on the following day till near eleven o'clock. The char-a-banc is a small strong carriage, in which two or three may ride. Upon this you sit, with your feet near the ground, resting upon a swinging board, and are drawn sideways. It is surprizing how fast the mules trot with these vehicles at their heels, over some of the roughest and most craggy tracks; their feet are at once sure and invulnerable. Our char-a-bancs a-bancs halted at the village of Chede, and we were very greatly entertained with a view of the cascade. The water appeared to fall from a height of about 150 feet: as it descends it is very regularly scattered, till in the lower part of its descent it is dissipated in the gentlest distillation. There was much beauty in this fine cascade, the effect of which is not a little improved by the surrounding scenery. We had lost the hour at which it is viewed to the greatest advantage,—the guides assuring us that had we arrived somewhat sooner, we should have had the pleasure of seeing a rainbow formed upon this transparent shower.—Re-entering our char-a-bancs, we passed over a rough and broken track; blocked up in some parts by hideous masses of rock, intercepted in others by furious torrents that poured from the heights, till we entered upon a charming plain, in which was situated St. Gervais. Here all was gaudy. The Curé had given an entertainment:

mafs was juft over, and the villagers had commenced their dance. We partook under a tree of the refrefhments of the place, and diverted ourfelves with feeing thefe peafants perform the evolutions of the Valz. Shortly after this we entered the valley of Chamouni, and arrived by five o'clock at the foot of the Glacier de Boifons.

LETTER XLV.

THE Glacier de Boifons is the firft to which ftrangers are generally introduced. It makes fcarcely any figure from the valley, ftanding among many others of much greater magnitude. Being feverally furnifhed with a long ftick pointed with iron, we afcended with eafe the lower part of the mountain, which was covered with turf and not very fteep; but the approach towards the ice was difficult, and the fticks were eminently ufeful. Previous to our arrival

rival upon the level with the Mer-de-glace, we were stopped by the guides in order to view the magnificent prospect before us. It presented a range of icy pyramids of the purest complexion, and of the boldest forms: we were filled with astonishment at a spectacle which blended so perfectly the grand and the beautiful.

Arrived at the summit of the mountain, we entered upon the Glacier, but found great difficulty in keeping our feet. The sun had glossed the surface, and rendered it almost impossible to tread with any degree of security. In passing amongst these frozen tracts, we came to many wide chasms and gulphs of a formidable depth. We threw down flakes of ice or stones, whose fall returned a tremendous sound. It was curious to observe upon the highest parts many masses of stone ready to precipitate; and upon the mountains in descending we saw some of dreadful bulk, which had at different times been tumbled from the summit of the Glacier.

Pierre

Pierre Balmat, our principal guide, related to us, that he was witnefs to the fall of one of the largeft of thefe; and that it was attended with the moft tremendous circumftances. Indeed it appears extraordinary that men fhould be found to inhabit regions, where they are continually expofed to thefe impending dangers. All the way as we defcended, we obferved the ruins of trees whofe trunks had been fplit afunder, or their roots torn from the ground, by the violence of thefe *Avalanches*. We had fuffered but little fatigue by the whole of this expedition; the ice afforded us water of the moft refrefhing coolnefs, and ftrawberries abounded upon the mountain over which we paffed on leaving the ice. Evening was now advancing: we re-entered our chara-bancs, and fhortly arrived at the Priory of Chamouni.

Pierre Balmat undertook all the neceffary arrangements for the bufinefs of Montanvert, which we were next to undertake; and

and the following morning, after an early mass, came to announce that all was in readiness. We were but four who resolved on this expedition; and we began to ascend the mountain, having Pierre Balmat at our head, and another guide bringing up the rear, each charged with their portion of luggage, provision, &c. The first league, or hour as it is called, was rugged, but not steep. It is so much of the way as is usually made by the mules. We began from this boundary to experience some difficulties: the track, without being less rugged, became more steep; and we had occasionally to pass along a precipice, which could not be regarded without dizziness, and from which a false step must inevitably have terminated the journey. The prospect before us annihilated all sense of fear or fatigue; and, after an arduous struggle of about three hours, we gained the summit of the Montanvert, and had the glorious Mer-de-glace full in view.

LETTER XLV.

We had afcended the mountain very lightly clad, and had been much oppreffed by heat. The tranfition was inftantaneous to a chilling cold. The guides admonifhed us to wrap ourfelves up fpeedily, as the air from the Glacier might have a dangerous effect. The Mer-de-glace refembles exactly a billowy expanfe of water frozen while the waves were yet fwelling with the majefty of the ftorm. We defcended by a rugged path to the level of the ice; and by a proper union of courage and caution, afcended and defcended over the vaft columns of ice which covered this furface. Wherever the eye ranged, nothing prefented itfelf but objects of terrible grandeur;— precipices, over which hung the loofening rocks—gulphs, where the projected ftone could fcarcely find a bottom. The whole valley appeared, as ftill heaving with the tempeft. Before I quitted the ice, I caft a parting view at the vaft range of rocky fpires and columns that
inclofed

inclofed it. To the left, I faw the vale of Chamouni far below; and to the right, the Glacier extended more than twenty leagues among regions inacceffible to human difcovery. I felt an enthufiafm, which is revived in the narration—but which the moft elaborate defcription is ill calculated to communicate.

LETTER XLVI.

OUR repaft was prepared by the induftrious guides in a fhed known by the name of Blair's Cabin. It is principally formed by ftones, placed without cement upon each other; and the table is of one fingle ftone. It was, as Balmat reported, erected by a gentleman of the name of Blair, in confequence of a violent hail-ftorm—not unufual in thefe regions—from which himfelf and his friends had fuffered. The traveller owes Mr. Blair gratitude for this piece of philanthropy. The interior of this cabin is covered with a regifter of names engraved upon the walls by thofe who have vifited thefe fcenes.

Nothing can furpafs the intrepidity and zeal of the guides of Chamouni. There are no dangers, however formidable, that they will not face. When Mont Blanc was deemed inacceffible—an opinion which prevailed till within a few years—the exertions of the guides were neverthelefs indefatigable. An accident at length unfolded what the labour of years—perhaps of ages—might have explored in vain. The cafual wanderings of Jacques Balmat to a confiderable height opened to him a track, by which he deemed the afcent practicable. This fecret he communicated to Paccard, who had cured him of an illnefs contracted on the mountain. They agreed to make the attempt, in which they perfectly fucceeded Aug. 1786. Upon this M. Sauffure, whofe long refearches in that particular line had led him to offer rewards for any difcoveries of this nature,

repaired

LETTER XLVI.

repaired to Chamouni the following year; and, with eighteen guides furnished with a tent, provisions, and instruments of observation, ascended, with unparalleled hardihood and extreme danger, Mont Blanc Aug. 1787.

Having finished our repast, and allowed due time for our guides to refresh themselves, we began to descend. The beginning of the descent was not accompanied with any particular difficulties: but the latter part, which pursued a track different from that by which we ascended, was steep and hazardous. We were occasionally startled by the distant rumbling of those Avalanches, which are (particularly during the heats) detaching loose masses of ice or stone, and precipitating them with violent explosion. These mountains are not without their luxuries. We were presented in different stations of the descent with strawberries and goats-milk of delicious flavour. Those who have felt the heat can alone imagine how grateful these refreshments proved.

ed. Having at length effected our descent, we traversed a valley through which flowed the Arveron;—this, like all the bottoms in the neighbourhood of these mountains, was strewed with those fragments of stone, which once occupied a higher situation. Our guide now conducted us along this uncouth track to one of the noblest objects in nature —the source of the Arveron. It is a recess hollowed out by the hand of nature, and all the colours that enrich it are of her own pencilling. Imagine the openings of a mighty cavern—scooped in the centre—and over-arched by various masses of ice in forms the most wild, yet the most majestic.— Picture to yourself the purest tints, blending into each other with the most enchanting softness, and the most regular gradation. From the centre of this cave thus artfully formed,—thus sublimely coloured,—imagine a torrent issuing with violence, and tumultuously rolling among masses of rock, which obstruct the channel and spread its waters into foam. If the picture be not entire, throw into the canvas the furrounding fcenery;—the vale of Chamouni decorated in all the charms of induftry and culture;— the hoary magnificence of the Glaciers;—and the fombre majefty of thofe ftubborn rocks, which retain no trace of vegetation:—let the fetting fun throw his laft rays over this groupe;—and then tell me, whether it be enthufiafm to clafs this with the nobleft productions of nature.

I muft remark, from fome converfation I had this day,—that the Savoyards participate thofe difcontents, which feem to have become fo general in Europe. The yoke of the Catholic church is a caufe of great diffatiffaction, and they treat with ridicule the idea of papal fupremacy. They fpeak of the riches which the church amaffes, as an unmerited exaction from their labours; and even confider the *difme*, or tithe, as a very high price for occafional abfolution. This I was rather furprized to hear: but there is

another

another and very serious subject of discontent, in the preference given by the court to Piedmont, to the prejudice of Savoy. The Savoyards affirm, that they are treated with neglect; that their inferiority is marked by an exclusion from posts of distinction and emolument; and that in all cases where honour, profit, or authority are annexed to any places at the disposal of the government, they have the mortification to see a Piedmontese preferred. — The *greatest* ferment prevails in those parts which border on the lake, or connect with Geneva. The frequent communications which these have with the inhabitants of the Pays de Vaud—many of whom are strongly inclined to French principles—have contributed to the diffusion of that spirit of revolt, which reigns among them. At the mineral springs of Thonon and Evian there are occasional fetes, and this keeps up a perpetual intercourse between the Savoyards and the inhabitants of the other side of the lake; and *ça ira* has

has been trumpeted at their feftive meetings with no fmall fhare of applaufe. The clergy in the neighbourhood of Chamouni are by no means numerous; at Salenche and its environs they abound, and exhibit all the marks of fovereign pride.

. At firft entering Savoy, I was embarraffed to conceive how the land could be divided;. as it difcovered no vifible partitions. I was however told, that it is parcelled out with great accuracy, and preferved fufficiently diftinct;—though in many places by imaginary boundaries. Land is here preferred to every other fpecies of property; each man is emulous of acquiring a portion; and fuch are the happy manners of the valley —a ftick or ftone,—the moft *trifling* mark ferves to define the *meum* and *tuum;*—and, with few exceptions, his property is facred from violation.

LETTER XLVII.

THE evening after our descent from Montanvert, I amused myself with walking about in various parts of the valley, and gazing at the different surrounding objects of magnificence. It was within a quarter of an hour of sun-set that finding myself somewhat fatigued, I stretched along a bank, watching the decline of the sun—now about to retire among the Glaciers. The Aiguille de Midi, the Dome, and Mont Blanc were at that time richly illuminated; and I waited with anxious curiosity the issue. The rays of light gradually passed from the Dome and the Aiguille, till the former was enveloped in shadow, and the points of the latter glittered only at the extremities. All this time Mont Blanc possessed a large portion of solar lustre; and, after
the

LETTER XLVII.

the Aiguilles were enveloped in the gathering fhades of evening, the rays of the parting light ftill refted on the fuperior mountain.

It was this day determined by four of us to continue our expedition along the valley, and vifit as much as fhould be convenient of this extraordinary country. We were joined the following morning by two other gentlemen, whofe intentions co-incided with our own; and under the conduct of Pierre Balmat, feverally mounted upon mules, we began at an early hour to afcend the Col-de-Balme. This is a mountain which bounds the valley of Chamouni, and over which is the fhorteft paffage into the Pays de Valais. A more ufual, becaufe more practicable track is over the Tête Noire. The afcent of the Col-de-Balme is attended with little difficulty. The greater part is—and all may be—made upon mules. The defcent is hideoufly fteep; and, though the track is fufficiently ferpentine, yet it is not defcended without confiderable fatigue.

From

LETTER XLVII.

From the summit of this mountain we enjoyed a very noble and extended view. M. Sauſſure calculates that it riſes 1181 toiſes, or 7086 Engliſh feet, above the level of the Mediterranean. On completing our deſcent we found ourſelves in the valley of Trent, ſo called from a torrent of that name which iſſues from a contiguous Glacier. On the higheſt part of the Col-de-Balme there is a ſtone, defining the limits of Savoy; and from this land-mark commences the territory of Valais. We turned a little into the valley of Trent, in order to ſtop at the village of that name, and give ſome repoſe to our mules. Our guide conducted us to a ſmall hut, where the good folks did all in their power to entertain us. They ſucceeded better with the mules than with their riders; for all the effuſions of honeſt hoſpitality could not atone for the poverty of their fare. They ſet before us a diſh of honey and ſome bottles of meagre and acid wine.

This

LETTER XLVII.

This village is very curiously situated, at the bottom of immense and innumerable mountains,—and composed of an handful of diminutive huts. The largest of these were very little above the size of an ordinary stye, and constructed in a very grotesque style. They resembled a kind of wooden box, set upon four beams, which are laid upon a foundation of uncemented stones; and upon the roots are stones placed, as a provision against the violent winds, which are not unfrequent in these mountainous climes. The people did not appear unhealthy, nor did I see any *goitrous* persons here. The slopes of the mountains bore the marks of industry and fertility: all was simple, and primitive; and we felt our infirmity, when we saw our guides devour as a luxury—what revolted our palates. The shoes of our mules being repaired, and their stomachs replenished, we, passing from Trent over the Forclay, arrived at St. Blanchier in the evening.

LETTER XLVIII.

THE paſſage of the Forclay had nothing in it either formidable, or difficult. Wherever the track paſſes,—which it did in many places upon the edge of a precipice,— the imagination was amuſed with a ſlight fence; which was indeed rather a ſecurity againſt fear, than a protection from danger. The deſcent was extremely rough, and ſtrewed with a multitude of large and looſe ſtones. It took us up nearly two hours to deſcend into the valley of Martigny. From the Forclay we enjoyed a very fine view of the city of Sion, the Mont St. Gothard, and the Glaciers of Grindelwald. As our intention was to take Martigny in returning from St. Bernard, we purſued a courſe to the right from the Forclay; this track deſcribed a ſort of ſemi-circle round a hollow vale, watered by a river, or ruſhing torrent, over which clusters of trees hung in the most romantic forms.

We shortly after entered the valley of Entremont. The road by which we passed, ran along the steep declivities which flanked the valley to the right; and on either hand of us were mountains of correspondent height and magnificence. The Drance—a very powerful torrent which takes its rise from the Glaciers round St. Bernard—rolls down the valley with noisy impetuosity. It was between seven and eight o'clock when we entered the village of St. Blanchier. Our guides conducted us to a species of Inn, where we were to pass the night. We found our landlady very untractable: all our *toute-suites* were coolly returned with *tout-à-l'heures*. We had not however in the issue, reason to complain of any thing but the pertinacity and dilatoriness of our hostess; for in her own good time, an excellent and smoaking supper was introduced. Our night passed well, and the morning found us suf‑

ficiently

ficiently recovered to refume our march. We obtained fome bowlsof luscious milk of our landlady, who began to improve upon us by acquaintance; and having mounted our mules, we put ourfelves in motion for St. Bernard.

Very foon after iffuing from the village of St. Blanchier, we entered upon a part of the valley of Entremont, beautiful beyond defcription; and this continued with little variation to St. René, a courfe of three leagues. Between Martigny and St. Blanchier the whole fcenery was wild,—the mountains rocky and barren,—and the torrent below us obftructed by prodigious maffes of ftone. On the contrary, from St. Blanchier to St. Pierre all is fmooth, harmonious, fruitful. The mountains are ranged in the nobleft and moft beautiful forms, and connected with the utmoft regularity. Their fides are clothed with a charming verdure of various hues according to the different fpecies of cultivation. The Drance rolls
along

LETTER XLVIII.

along in one continued ftream of foam, and fills the valley with its echoes. I thought, as I beheld thefe fcenes, that the fables of Romance and the vifions of Arcadia were more than realized to my fenfes. My imagination feemed not to experience a want, nor could I figure to myfelf one abfent charm which could improve this wonderful valley. All the varieties of nature were here delicioufly blended. Here were viewed all the different fhades of verdure, and every artful diftribution of culture. Add to thefe, the finuous channel of the torrent,— its frothy furface,—its hollow roar,—and then fay what is there left for poetry to feign?

Between St. Blanchard and St. Pierre we paffed two villages—the firft of which is Orfieres, the laft Liddes. As we entered the firft of thefe, we paffed the Drance by a wooden bridge. They appeared in this part of the valley to be in a way of refinement. Some few houfes were undergoing repairs, and fitting up in—what I prefume may have been—the ſtile of a century paſt in the civilized parts of the world; and what may paſs for modern taſte, in a valley, where the viſits of the ſun are but juſt long enough for the purpoſes of exiſtence. It appeared much the faſhion along this valley to conſecrate the houſes by pious inſcriptions. I obſerved upon many doors, which had been lately painted, the names of ſaints inſcribed, or ſome religious motto. Juſt upon the part where in a mercantile town would have been advertiſed the name and occupation of the inhabitant, were inſcribed on many doors the three names *Jeſus—Marie— Joſeph.*

We now paſſed from Orſieres to Liddes, having the Drance to our right. Liddes is romantically ſituated in the narroweſt part of the valley, the mountains of which approach ſo near each other as almoſt to compreſs and entomb it. In paſſing through this place, we overtook one of thoſe good induſtrious Penitents who travel far for the benefit

nefit of their fouls. The pious pilgrim was in a garment refembling that which honeft Bunyan has defcribed his hero to have received from one of the *fhining ones*. It was variegated with the brighteft colours,—adorned with fhells, mottoes, and portraits of the moft fuccefsful interceffors in behalf of thofe who practife pilgrimage and penance. He bore a tall ftaff, his feet were bare,—that is to fay the upper parts,—and thus he was about to crofs the rugged flints of St. Bernard; in order to vifit the holy fhrine of Loretto, and—in the fpirit of antient fuperftition—" to feek him dead who lives in Paradife."

LETTER XLIX.

IT was about ten o'clock when we entered the village of St. Pierre; and, as the Convent of St. Bernard was but three leagues diftant from this place, we determined

mined upon making our visit immediately, and returning to St. Pierre in the evening. We requested our hostess to prepare us a supper. The good woman talked of honey and goats-milk;—we questioned her upon the articles of bread and meat; she assured us that there was neither butcher nor baker in the town, but that she would send up to the mountains to kill a sheep for our accommodation. It was indeed our fate, wherever we stopped, to spread slaughter and devastation. We had scarcely entered our quarters at St. Blanchier, when the most dismal screams assailed us from the hen-roost. Scarcely had we quitted St. Pierre, on our route to St. Bernard, before we saw a remorseless clown, deputed to that service by our hostess, scaling the mountain, and seizing the affrighted and defenceless sheep. We blushed for the disorders we had introduced into these Arcadian regions, where all was innocence as in the age of Gold, and the peaceful reign of Saturn. Here the flocks seemed ed proprietors of the mountains, and the wants of men were satisfied without the effusion of blood; here the woods appeared sacred to solitude and silence.—

>—Where the rude axe with heaved stroke
>Was never heard the nymphs to daunt,
>Or fright them from their hallowed haunt.

In leaving St. Pierre the track divides—that to the left, opening into the Valsorey; that to the right, conducting to St. Bernard. From these opposite directions issue two streams, which are severally denominated from the Valsorey and the St. Bernard; and which uniting a little below, form that torrent which pours along the valley of Entremont. St. Pierre is the last village of the Valais in this route; and from this to the Convent of St. Bernard, they estimate three leagues or hours. Soon after leaving the village, we entered upon a coarse and rugged plain, strewed with fragments of stone, which had been washed down from the

the heights; and from this we continued to ascend over rocks of shapeless asperity. In passing these I was indebted to my mule, whose dexterity in running up the steep declivities excited my astonishment, and I ought to add, my gratitude. The most provoking property of these animals is, that they will always coast upon the precipice. I more than once laboured to force my mule to abandon this dangerous system, but he taught me acquiescence, by either making a full stop, or, if I persisted, in betaking himself to a fit of kicking. I am persuaded that no one ever reached the heights of St. Bernard in this mode of travel, without having learnt more of passive obedience and moral resignation, than he would ever have acquired from Sir Robert Filmer, or the Whole Duty of Man.

We had now climbed about two leagues and a half over a very rugged and flinty track, discovered rather by the industry of our guides and the recollection of our mules,

than

than by any veſtiges of former footſteps. We at length croſſed the torrent which takes its riſe a little above us, and now entered upon the moſt dreary and melancholy ſcenes. The mountains on every ſide were rugged and naked, except where the ſnow continued undiſſolved the whole of the year, nearly a quarter of a league. Before we reached the Convent, we paſſed through a track of ſnow, many parts of which were more than a foot deep. This ſnow liquidates very ſlowly: it is a part of the mountain expoſed to the north, and which enjoys but for a few moments the rays of the ſun. A few years paſt it continued undiſſolved the whole of the ſummer; and the pious fathers began to feel alarm, left it ſhould accumulate and form a Glacier.

We arrived by three o'clock at the door of the Convent. Our guide demanded admittance, when one of the order came to the door, and invited us to enter and partake of the refreſhment of their " pauvre hoſpice."

hofpice." He was indeed particularly forry it fhould have been a day of penance, and feared left the kitchen could not afford us a fuitable repaft. He accompanied us over the Convent, fhowed us the feveral apartments, library, chapel, &c. We were feated in a gloomy faloon, after due obfervation of the rarities of the place; and a very frugal meal was ferved up,—the brother of the order himfelf waiting upon us. We urged him to partake with us—he excufed himfelf, by faying—that he had dined at their ufual hour of half paft ten. We entreated him not to ftand; he refifted our entreaties, by affuring us—that it became him, and fupplicating us to receive the hofpitalities of the Convent " au nom de " Dieu"

LETTER L.

OUR venerable hoft had, in the interval of preparation for dinner, conducted us round the environs of the Convent, and wretched indeed was the scenery which furrounded thefe pious fathers. The whole mountain is of fo obdurate and untractable a nature, that no art or labour can render it a fubject of cultivation. There were two or three fmall interftices between the rocks, in which thefe induftrious men had difpofed fome mould imported from the foil of St. Pierre; by means of which—with the greateft difficulty—they raife a few vegetables. The whole crop would have fcarcely filled an ordinary plate: but elevated into thefe regions of cold and folitude, they have recourfe to any little expedient which may occupy their hopes, and diffipate the *ennui* of perpetual imprifonment. Theirs is indeed

a fate,

a fate, though self-imposed, beyond the rigors of the severest punishment.

> ———From the cheerful ways of men
> Cut off, and for the book of knowlege fair
> Presented with an universal blank
> Of Nature's works, to them expunged and rased.

The good father who performed the honours of the place, told us, that he had been twelve years in this Convent; and, though he was not in reality more than thirty years of age, his countenance was so haggard, so sallow, and so sickly, that he appeared quite a veteran. We asked him after the rest of his comrades; he said, they were gone " se promener."—It is diverting to hear of a promenande, in regions where every step leads to fresh dangers, and every change of scene is only an aggravation of horrors. He spoke of a journey to St. Pierre, as a boy would of his holidays; and made as much of an excursion to Martigny, as an Englishman would of a trip to Newmarket.—" On y va," said he, " des fois pour *s'egayer*."

He

He shewed us a small lake near the Convent, in which they had attempted to keep some fish; but the coldness of the water almost instantly killed them. This lake is, he said, seldom free from ice, and was frozen over last year so late as the month of August. Indeed the water he gave us to mix with our wine was prodigiously cold. He assured us it was two degrees below the standard of freezing. We were shewn a spot upon which once stood a temple of no mean fame, and the ground is still scattered with fragments of stone.

It has been a subject of much dispute among the learned what route Hannibal pursued in crossing the Alps. An attempt has been made from the evidence collected on these ruins, to fix this route in the passage over St. Bernard. This opinion is not new, as M. Saussure has remarked. It was prevalent in the time of Livy, and he opposes it as destitute of foundation. Pliny was afterwards of opinion, that he passed

by

by the Mons Jovis, or Penninus. The latter of thefe appellations is referred to the Celtic word *Pen*, which fignifies high. M. Sauffure fpeaks of numerous ex-votos, which he has himfelf feen; the greater part of which are of bronze, and bear infcribed, fome, JOVI PENNINO; others, JOVI POENINO. From the latter of thefe it has been concluded, that Hannibal erected a temple here to the God of his country, in teftimony of gratitude for the difcovery of the paffage. The ftatue of the Jupiter in queftion, is proved to have been deftroyed by Conftantine, from a pillar which now ftands at the foot of the mountain at St. Pierre: it is infcribed to Conftantine the younger.

St. Bernard was a Savoyard, and archdeacon of Aofte in the year 962. Since his time the *hofpice* has been twice deftroyed by fire. This inftitution was formerly very opulent; it poffeffed lands in Sicily, England, the Low Countries, &c. of which it is

now

now pretty well shorn. For its support at present, it is in great measure indebted to the alms collected in different parts of the country. There is upon the mountain near the Convent, a stone, which marks the boundary of the Vallais on the one side, and the king of Sardinia's estates on the other. The contiguity of this Convent to the latter has produced some altercations; and, at the beginning of this century, the king of Sardinia disputed with the Swifs the right of nominating a Provost, or Head. This, after much opposition, was decided in favour of the Swifs; who deemed it of importance, that a foreign king should not nominate to a benefice within their dominions,—particularly to one so important, as that of St. Bernard has always been esteemed.

I know not the precise number of this society: they are all regular Augustines: the Provost is elected by the Chapter, and confirmed by the Pope. He resides at Martigny. Next to him, is a Prieur Clauftral, who acts as President, and resides at the Convent. Besides these, there is a Sacristan, who has the care of the chapel; a Cellerier, who superintends the provisions; a Clavandier, who distributes to travellers; and an Infirmier, who takes charge of the sick. Usually not more than eight or ten reside; and powerful must be that motive which determines men, who can exist elsewhere, to such a mode of life.

LETTER LI.

THE principal duties of these Bernardines fall in the season when snows and storms are most frequent. At that time they are constantly in the habits of watching occasions for the exercise of their hospitable functions: a servant, whom they call the Maronnier, goes before the travellers' who pass this way during the perilous season, with a large dog, peculiar to the mountain. This dog is of an enormous size, and of singular

singular sagacity. We saw two of them at the Convent. Thefe dogs have the wonderful talent of difcovering the way through fogs and fnows, as alfo of fcenting out the bodies of thofe who have perifhed by the feverity of the cold. During the whole of the winter, the brothers at the Convent are employed in fearching for miferable objects who have loft their way, or have been buried in the fnows, by the terrible *avalanches* which happen in the fevere feafon. Each is furnifhed with a ftick pointed with iron. With thefe they found, wherever the dogs direct; and by fhaking, chafing, and other remedies, they frequently reftore thofe who are fortunate enough to be found before animation is totally extinct.

The height of this mountain is eftimated at about 7542 Englifh feet perpendicular above the level of the Mediterranean. The nature of their fituation expofes them to a thoufand maladies. Indeed they looked like the family of death. It was fo cold in the Convent, that they requefted permiffion to kindle a fire for us; and yet it was the third of August. I confefs to you, I could not view their fituation, nor hear the detail of their fufferings, without afking myfelf the queftion, whether the fervices rendered to fociety by thefe men were at all proportioned to the pain with which they are effected. I am of opinion that few would, in modern days, undertake a pilgrimage over St. Bernard, if they were not fure of *three* * days entertainment on the way: and I cannot think highly of an inftitution calculated only to keep alive an almoft obfolete fuperftition. M. Sauffure has taken fome pains to defend this inftitution in its prefent ftate; and certainly if, as this author affirms, the paffage of St. Bernard is of great importance to the Vallais on one fide, and the Lombards on the other; if the communication between thefe two divided countries be of fuch reciprocal advantage; the labours of thefe religious, and their

* So much is allowed by charter to every pilgrim.

feclufion

LETTER LI.

feclufion from fociety, merit the approbation of the world.

There was fomething fo unufually dreary and ungenial in the afpect of this place, that we were impatient, after due gratification of our curiofity, to leave it. We had ordered our mules; and while thefe were preparing, the fkies blackened prodigioufly, and a heavy ftorm of hail and thunder came on. The monks were urgent with us to pafs the night in the Convent; but we were unanimous in wifhing to take our leave of thefe grim and ftormy regions. We defcended through a deluge of rain, from which we fhortly iffued, and left behind us the ftorms and the hail, to drench the Convent of St. Bernard. Doubtlefs thefe fathers muft be actuated by fome powerful principle, in fixing their abode in thefe regions of mifery: by their voluntary fufferings here, they no doubt hope to mitigate the pains of purgatory hereafter. I know not what purgatory is, but I fhould think it almost worth hazarding, rather than endure the penance of a residence during life upon the mountains of St. Bernard. Milton has attempted to give us some idea of another place; and I could not dismiss the images from my recollection, when I turned my eyes upon this miserable scene,

> " A dismal situation, waste and wild;
> " Regions of sorrow, doleful shades; where peace
> " And rest can never dwell;—hope never comes,
> " That comes to all."

Descending partly upon our feet and partly upon our mules, we arrived in the evening at St. Pierre. The activity of our hostess and her co-adjutors—for it appeared by the bustle that she called in the assistance of the neighbourhood—had prepared our supper. On the following day we had, on our way to St. Blanchier, an opportunity of seeing the full display of mulish resistance. A watch had been left by one of the party at St. Pierre. We were now a full league from the place, and the guide was directed to return

turn in search of it. The guide prepared to return, but his mule said, " NO."—At every effort the *former* made, the *latter* added his " VETO." He used every measure of violence, but he might as well have attempted to flog the Trojan horse into a gallop. Much manœuvring was displayed on both sides; at length victory declared in favor of the beast, and the great Pierre Balmat—who had so often conquered mountains—was himself compelled to yield to the invincible stubbornness of his mule.

LETTER LII.

THE appearance of St. Blanchier is picturesque indeed, but partakes too much of the horrid. It stands upon the borders of the Drance, at the confluence of three vallies, and in the very heart of mountains, which project in awful forms over its cottages, and seem to menace its destruction. It was a festival with the inhabitants; the church bell was ringing a hollow sound, and the peasants were crowding the porch, in order to consecrate the festivities of the day by an act of devotion. As we passed through this village, we were alarmed by an explosion, the effect of which among the mountains was tremendous. We took it for thunder, and its echoes were prolonged by the reverberation of the rocks with which we were enclosed. A volume of smoke issuing from a distant eminence convinced us, that it was but the report of gunpowder.

Martigny, where we reposed ourselves and mules, is considered as of some importance in the Vallais; they called it a city, and spoke of it in high terms. It has, however, from the figure it makes, no great pretensions to distinction. It is the head-quarters indeed of business and gaiety in this country. Our landlord introduced us into a very spacious room, in one corner of which sat a man, whose figure and manner
rather

LETTER LII.

rather excited our curiosity. We had taken from the table a large pair of flappers, and were severally offering our conjectures upon their use, when, observing our embarrassment, the stranger came up, claimed the flappers, and told us, they were " pour at-
" traper lés papillons."—The inn-keeper informed us when he had retired, that it was a German baron, whose *penchant* for butterfly-hunting was extraordinary; that he exposed himself to a thousand dangers and fatigues in this whimsical pursuit; " et, Mes-
" sieurs, (continued he,) ce baron là mettroit
" huit jours pour attraper un seul papillon."

Our host was a lank meagre man: his figure was remarkably tall, ghastly, and puritanical: his head was crowned with a white cap, which did not diminish the solemnity of his appearance. He harangued us the whole of dinner upon the different pursuits of mankind. He treated the butterfly-hunter with the most sarcastic contempt.—" A fellow, said he, who runs
" over

"over bogs, lakes, and brambles after a "shadow; a phantom; a being that is not "touched without falling to pieces; a "thing that has neither body nor soul." Our landlord argued, and we fed; and his harangue finished only with our dinner. We then resumed our journey to Bex.

I have not seen during my excursion many goitrous or idiotic persons. At Salenche I saw some few of the latter; and in different other places I have observed the former. You know the opinions of medical men are much divided upon the probable causes of these wens, and of the concomitant disorder of idiotism. These phænomena have by many been referred to snowy or calcareous waters, which are here drank by the inhabitants—by others to the marshy air, &c. but M. Saussure affirms, that in the higher parts of the mountains, where the snows and ice for the most part prevail; and in the vallies open to the plains, where the marshes are principally found; neither wens nor idiocy are common. These are almost solely to be met with in the vallies elevated a little above the plain. In order to account for this phænomenon, M. Sauſſure ſuppoſes, that the warmth which the encloſed air receives in this ſituation, relaxes the fibres of infants; and produces theſe inflations of the neck, and that *inertia*, which is the ſtrong characteriſtic of the Cretin. This he eſtabliſhes, by remarking, that on the ſide of the valley, where the heat from direct and reflected rays is greateſt, theſe diſorders moſt abound; inſomuch that it is now cuſtomary for thoſe whoſe circumſtances are not too contracted, to ſend their wives to lie-in, and their infants to be nurſed upon the mountains; and this experiment has, in no inſtance, failed of preſerving the health and faculties of the children.

LETTER LIII.

WE were now entered into the valley of the Rhône, and shortly arrived upon that plain, consecrated to fame by the cascade of the Pissevache. The body of water rushes between the divided projections of a rock, whose summits are rounded off, and overspread with a picturesque umbrage. Its waters dash with the force acquired by a fall of near three hundred feet against the rocky fragments below, and remount in a cloud of foam. In comparison of these stupendous phænomena of nature, how little are the atchievements of art!

St. Maurice, through which we now passed, is the last town of the Vallais; and is famous for having been the Agaunum of the ancients, where the massacre of the Theban Legion happened. The Roman bridge

LETTER LIII.

bridge of one arch, built across the Rhône, is still in existence. Their excellencies of Berne, whose territory here commences, have a small garrison in the place; and some frivolous questions, of our names, country, designs, &c., put by a few invalids, notified our entrance upon this sovereign soil. We arrived in the evening at Bex, and finally dismissed our guides. Before I take my leave of them, let me commend their activity, fidelity, and gratitude. Men more ready to serve, and more disposed to be satisfied, I have never yet met with: their understandings are in general good, their information sound, and their manners pleasing and ingenuous. This is an eulogium due to the guides of Chamouni.

Bex is famous for the salines, or salt works, which are carried on in its neighbourhood. We visited these the following day, having obtained permission from the superintendant. Our char-a-bancs carried us to the foot of the mountain which contains

tains thefe falt fprings, and a guide conducted us to the mouth of thofe caverns by which we were to enter the heart of the mountain. I muft obferve, that it is now one hundred and twenty years fince thefe fprings were difcovered; and the Seigneurs of Berne, who are the proprietors, have fpared no expence to derive from them every poffible advantage. The great Haller had for fome years the fuperintendance of thefe works, which are now under the direction of Mr. Wild. It was fuggefted to the republic, that there muft be fome bed of falt funk deeply under the mountain; becaufe, in proportion as they dug into the earth, the water ran more copious, and was more ftrongly impregnated with falt. An experiment was therefore made at an immenfe coft; and upon digging below the bed of the Rhône, they heard the found of a fpring, to which they feemed faft approaching. This animated their labours: they penetrated to the fpring, and

to

LETTER LIII.

to their infinite mortification found it perfectly *sweet.*

A labourer met us at the entrance of the mountain, and furnishing us with frocks and lamps, conducted us along a narrow passage bored through the solid rock, and lined with sulphureous matter. After viewing in our way the reservoir, we continued along this channel, which kept ascending, till we came to the centre of the mountain. Here a large wheel of thirty-six feet diameter was playing with the ease of a clock wheel, and the sky was visible above, the mountain being here pierced from the summit to the centre. We now descended from this eminence, retracing our former steps, till we came to another bore of the mountain which opened a passage to the right. This, our guide told us, penetrated one thousand feet, and we should, he added, find the workmen extending it still farther. We entered upon it, but had not gone many paces before we felt a great difference in the atmosphere.

mosphere. As we advanced, we found the air still less fit for respiration: our lamps went out frequently, and we felt a painful pressure upon the lungs. Yet here the poor labourers were employed in chisselling the hard rock, and hewing out a passage, in an air poisoned by sulphureous exhalations, and to us—unfamiliar with its vapours—totally suffocating. We were at this moment, as the guide informed us, four thousand feet deep in the mountain. These poor people have but eight batz, or about one shilling per day. Their day consists of eight hours; at the expiration of which, the set that goes off, is succeeded by another, without interruption; so that the works are never suffered to stand still. We hastened to emerge from this dismal dungeon; and were on our way, when a hollow sound rumbled through every cavity of the mountain, and was conveyed to our ears in thundering claps. We were thrown into alarm, and imagined that the sulphureous air had kindled from the lamp,

and

and occafioned the explofion; nor did we find ourfelves much relieved by the intelligence of our guide, that it was *only* occafioned by fome labourers below, who were blowing up parts of the rock with gunpowder.

LETTER LIV.

Such was our exterior when we left the hollow windings of the Salt Mountain, that we were obliged to perform half a dozen luftrations before we were reftored to humanity. What will not curiofity atchieve? A more difagreeable expedition could not have been undertaken. A frock, thick-fet with greafe, hanging over our fhoulders—our heads bent, to watch our footfteps over the rank fmoke of a lamp—noxious exhalations hovering round the walls—and a contaminated air entering into our lungs.— Such were the circumftances attending our defcent descent into these abodes of misery and horror. Speaking in the language of a traveller, it is one of those objects which it is more pleasant to *have* seen, than to *see*.

Bex is a town of no great extent, pleasantly situated, in a soil that has enriched its inhabitants to a degree incommodious to the traveller. Their indifference to further gain is such, that they will rather suffer their cattle to continue unemployed, than let them out to strangers at a reasonable payment. The grand eatable at Bex is potatoes. These they grow of an enormous size, and a very admirable quality. They usually serve them up, dressed in various ways, in the same course. Some troops were entering this town, at the moment in which we were quitting it. The occasion was sufficiently whimsical. A dispute had arisen among the inhabitants, respecting the church pews. This quarrel had at length assumed a serious shape, and a holy war was expected. Their Excellencies of Berne had been

LETTER LIV.

been requested to march some troops into the town, in order to quell those religious feuds, and reduce this church militant to a peace establishment. I suspect that the spirit of discontent, which is gaining so rapidly among the provinces dependent on the government of Berne, has excited them to this measure of precaution; and the struggle for church pews, has only afforded the pretext for putting it in execution.

We now passed by Aigle and Villeneuve to Vevai. This was a very delicious part of our journey. It was on this day that we regained our view of the Lake of Geneva, at the extremity of which Villeneuve stands. Between Bex and this last mentioned place, we saw the entrance of the Rhône into the lake. There is nothing peculiarly striking in this, beyond the consideration, that this river continues its course through the Lake till at Geneva—a distance of more than forty miles from the point of entrance—its waters are again collected into a stream, acquire a new velocity, and move in a rapid current towards the sea.

We passed the Chateau de Chillon, as we drove to Vevai. It is a very beautiful ornament to this part of the Lake, and reminds one forcibly of antient fable. This Chateau is built upon a stupendous rock, running far into the Lake; on the other extremity of which are the heights of Milleray, immortalized by the pen of Rousseau. It was in this Chateau that the bailiffs of Vevai had their antient residence; and, previous to the introduction of artillery, this fort was considered as impregnable. The garrison has lately been augmented by the providence of the Bernois, who do not view, without strong symptoms of apprehension, the eclat which the French revolution has obtained in the different provinces dependent upon their authority. We passed the night at Vevai—a very lively little town upon the banks of the Lake, furnished with

very

LETTER LIV.

very agreeable promenades—and the next morning arrived at Laufanne.

I have now brought my journal of this expedition to a conclufion. Nine days were fpent in accomplifhing this object; and fuch has been our induftry, that we have in the courfe of this fhort period gone over a track of near two hundred miles. I retrace the journey with great fatisfaction. The fcenes with which it has been crouded, will never perhaps, in my experience, meet a parallel. Where fhall I feek again the contiguous elements of heat and cold? Where fhall I find the tranfparent pyramids of Boiffons, or the icy magazines of Montanvert? What climes will fhow me a parallel to the chryftal arches over the Arveron, or the magnificent varieties of the valley of Entremont? Where, in its darkeft moments, fhall the mind borrow more fombre colours, than from the caverns and perforated rocks of Bex, or the flinty deferts of St. Bernard? My foul is chilled when I confider the wretches who toil in the one, or reside on the other. But Heaven has moulded us to every variety of situation; and, when the wishes of man are bounded by his wants, there are few situations which can exclude pleasure; when they are not, no condition can banish pain.

LETTER LV.

Lausanne, Aug. 26, 1791.

WHAT a wonderful country is this! He who has sojourned on the banks of the Leman Lake, will tell you, that the scenery around presents an ever-fruitful, ever-varied picture to the eye. The wonders of the universe seem here to be combined in one magnificent groupe, and all the sublimities of nature collected into a focus. Each recovering day gives birth to some new beauty. The clouds are distributed into more fantastic forms. The mountains are
illumined

illumined with a richer luftre, and the trees are embrowned with deeper and more vivid tints. But it is in the rocks of Millerai that enthufiafm delights to dwell—thofe rocks where the wild and difconfolate St. Preux uttered his accents of defpair. Oft as my eye fixes upon thefe awful precipices, the lover of Heloife is prefent to my view. I fee him frantic with the agonies of difappointment, meditating, amidft thefe frowning heights, the rafh refolve, as he furveys the gulph below. His notes of anguifh feem ftill to live in faint and languid echoes—
" Les rochers font efcarpés, l'eau eft pro-
" fonde, et je fuis au defefpoir."

I fhould tell you, perhaps, that thefe mountains face directly that part of the Lake upon which our villa is planted; and it is among the chief amufements of the place, to pafs *en bateau* to the very mountains themfelves. The paffage is eafily effected in three hours; and a romantic repaft is made on the fhelving declivities of Millerai. The baths

baths of Evian form the principal rendezvous; and here, on the Sunday evenings, the song and the dance are celebrated. Numbers pafs the Lake from Laufanne and its environs, to partake of thofe feftivities in Savoy, which the rigid police of the country denies them at home.

It has been remarked by many travellers, that Switzerland would form a very noble fchool of painting; and it is a matter of aftonifhment to thofe who furvey the very rich and exuberant fcenery of this country, that it fhould not yet have excited the labours of the pencil, and that the canvas fhould not hitherto have glowed with its original beauties. The author of the " Tableau Pictorefque de la Suiffe" indulges in the warmeft raptures upon contemplating the general ftate of the country—which he calls an abftract of the known world; and then, adverting to the manners and genius of the inhabitants, he breaks out into the moft indignant ftrain of invective: " Et
" pou;

" pour qui cette superbe et magnifique ga-
" lerie? pour qui cette etonnante et riche crea-
" tion? pour un peuple insensible, apatheque,
" et froid—pour un peuple qui ne sent rien,
" qui n'imagine rien, qui ne pleure jamais,
" qui rien n'affecte; pour un peuple inca-
" pable d'emotions vives, de passions pro-
" fondes; pour un peuple qui ne connoit
" jamais le delire, l'enthousiasm de la poesie,
" de la peinture; ni les transports, les de-
" lices, les douces fureurs, les accens frené-
" tiques et brûlans des sentiments paf-
" sionnés."

Those who have studied more closely the manners of this people than I have been able to do, will better decide how far this delineation of character is accurate. A very different, and far more favourable picture of this nation, is drawn by the masterly pen of the Chevalier Mehegan, which I am disposed to believe does them no more than strict justice. " La habite un peuple sim-
" ple, bienfaisant, brave, ennemi du faste,
" ami

"ami du travail, ne cherchant point d'ef-
"claves et ne voulant point des maîtres."
Society is unqueftionably in many families
upon a very civilized footing, and all the
agremens of polifhed life are cultivated with
fuccefs. The peafants preferve for the moft
part the fturdy traits of antient character.
They live principally on vegetable diet; are
frugal, induftrious, and, generally fpeaking,
inoffenfive. Their habits of economy are
not wholly exempt from the meaner foibles
to which it is allied. Frugality too often
degenerates among them into a fordid attachment to gain, and renders it difficult to
difpute the truth of that characteriftic pro-
verb—" Point d'argent, point de Suiffe."

LETTER LVI.

Lausanne, Sept. 20, 1791.

THE harmony of this place muft now fuffer interruption. Political intrigues have been carried on, to introduce fome changes into the government, and, as it is rumoured, to effect a revolution, upon French principles. Great rejoicings were made at Rolle, a town not far diftant, upon the anniverfary of the French Revolution. At this feftival were found fome of the moft confiderable people in the Pays de Vaud; and toafts were drank, which carried no fmall terror to the ruling Powers. Since this memorable day, a very high tone of language has been held by many, whofe influence in the country is great; and in private parties and public affemblies, no fcruple has been made, of reprobating ariftocracy, and holding up to ridicule the government of of Berne, which they ftile "Le gouvernement "d'Ours."

There were not wanting among the females of the higher rank, thofe who efpoufed warmly the caufe of France, and carried into public upon their head-drefs the national colours. The air of " ça ira" was demanded upon every occafion when mufic was to be had; and this was danced to in their numerous affemblies, with a degree of enthufiafm which threatened ferious confequences. The Genevefe have for fome time paft prohibited this dance; and thofe who have feen the effects it produces when performed in the fpirit and with the vivacity of the nation from which it is derived, will not confider the profcription of fuch an air as a meafure of contemptible precaution.

At Laufanne the government flumbered, or feemed to flumber. The libraries were reforted to for political difcuffion. There the French gazettes were read and debated. To fo great a licence had the fpirit of the people

people proceeded, that the tranfactions of France were not commented upon without fome bold application to their own government; and projects of reform, nay even, of revolution, were more than whifpered. At length the alarm was given, and the energy of the ruling Powers was awakened. It is not, indeed, to be fuppofed, that they continued idle fpectators of the game that was playing. It had, however, the appearance of neglect, nay even of timidity. This might be done with the defign of fuffering the plot to attain maturity, in order to meet the full mifchief, and crufh, with more fuccefs, the partizans. News was quickly circulated, that the Bernois were now marching three thoufand men, and feveral pieces of artillery, towards Laufanne, where they fhortly arrived, and were encamped before the town. Meafures the moft vigorous were adopted, both civil and military. Laufanne had all the appearance of a befieged town: Cannon were planted at the gates, with lighted matches,

matches, in a state of preparation. A species of inquisition was instituted; and no ceremony was used in quartering a sufficient number of soldiers in the houses of those who were suspected to have been concerned in the intended revolution. Some people of consideration were arrested; and, if report may be credited, their treatment was marked with the most rigid severity. The Chateau de Chillon is the Bastile of the country: to this prison have been consigned, those who were considered as principals in the plot; and informations are still paid for at the price of fifty crowns.

What this plot was, which has brought a camp to our gates, and an inquisition into our houses, I am not able to inform you. The government of Berne does not make manifest the details of its proceedings, and some people have affected to regard the whole as a bubble. This, however, must be said, that very strong symptoms of discontent were discoverable for some time
previous

previous to the arrival of the troops; and the general turn of converfation demonftrated, that fome movement might fhortly be expected. It is I think fufficiently clear, that the lower ranks of people in this country never felt themfelves interefted in the projected revolution. The punifhments have entirely fallen upon families of a certain rank; and the peafants are obferved to continue their labours of hufbandry, without occafioning or receiving moleftation.

Indeed, the grievances alleged have never appeared to me capable of interefting the community at large: they are principally felt by perfons of condition, and relate, for the moft part, to civil and military rank. As a province dependent upon Berne, it enjoys not the full privileges of the fuperior country; and officers are impofed upon them, both in the civil and military departments, to the exclufion of thofe among the natives who afpire to fuch rank. This is what I have heard ftated by one who had the reputation

putation of being a principal in the conspiracy, as the most formidable species of oppression. However invidious and unjust this may be—however it may wound the pride, and provoke the resentment, of the higher classes—it cannot be supposed that a rough and hardy peasantry, who are not oppressed by taxes, nor abridged in the enjoyment of the fruits of their labour, should take any interest in reforms, which sought the redress of such grievances. The influence of their lords, and the eclat of the French revolution, might seduce the abject and capricious; but the wiser, and by far the greater part, would continue, as they appear to have done, firmly attached to the government, under which they enjoy tranquillity and protection.

LETTER LVII.

Lausanne, Oct. 2, 1791.

THIS country is now in its full beauty: all the sloping parts towards the Lake are covered with vines, the grapes of which are advancing fast to maturity. The vines are remarkably low, and planted very thick. They are supported by sticks; and such indeed is their exuberance, that they stand greatly in need of support.

As I have understood, the cultivation of the vineyards is done upon this principle. The farmer undertakes the whole of the labour and expence; in recompence of which he receives half the nett profit made upon the produce. This secures the estates from pillage. The farmers are very active in protecting the vineyards, which lie sufficiently exposed to depredation. It is difficult to make an excurſion, in any direction, without paſſing through many acres covered with vines; and the heat of the weather, added to the very ſeducing aſpect of the fruit, renders it not a little difficult to abſtain from acts of plunder. As the vintage is now approaching, more than ordinary diligence is uſed to guard this ſacred property; and men, ſuitably armed, are on the watch day and night.

The heat here is very oppreſſive, except when the *Biſe*, which is a north-eaſt wind, blows. This is extremely ſharp; and paſſing over the ſnowy mountains, comes charged with a very penetrating cold. Though we have now been a conſiderable time in this part of Switzerland, and are indeed looking forward to our departure, I have not had opportunity to make any excurſion beyond the Glaciers and the Lake of Neuchatel. But indeed the whole of Switzerland has been ſo accurately delineated in the journals of Mr. Coxe, and ſo warmly painted by the

Marquis

LETTER LVII.

Marquis de Langle, that I could not flatter myself with being able to tread to advantage the same ground, without borrowing largely from the industry of the one, and the animation of the other.

Such is the severity now adopted by the government of Berne, that the French language is in many regiments forbidden to be spoken. Some gentlemen, lately returned from an excursion into the heart of the country, related to me, that upon entering an inn where the officers of a Swiss regiment were quartered, they requested as usual to be shewn the room where the company supped. They were scarcely entered, when the Commandant demanded of the landlady in a very angry tone, " Qui sont ces Mes-
" sieurs là ?" " Ce sont des Anglois," replied the matron. He looked stern, and with some degree of harshness rejoined, " il est
" defendu à mes officiers de parler Fran-
" çois;" and they supped together without exchanging a word. Proscriptions are now going

going on with great difpatch; but all is conducted with fo much fecrecy, that it is difficult to arrive at a knowledge of particulars. Thus much however is certain, that fociety has very confiderably fuffered by thefe political machinations; and many individuals of the firft character have been put under arreft. This change of meafures in the ruling powers has abridged very greatly the freedom, and even the convenience of ftrangers. The libraries are put under a new law: all the gazettes from France, deemed dangerous or offenfive, are profcribed; and a notice has been affixed to the walls, prohibiting the difcuffion of political queftions—threatening the librarian with a fevere penalty, if he neglected to fee the order enforced. The uniformity of my prefent mode of life, and the ftrict military law under which we now are, will not allow me to tranfmit to you more interefting details—and the dulnefs of the place muft be my apology for the dulnefs of the letter.

LETTER LVIII.

Laufanne, Oct. 16, 1791.

I TOLD you in my laſt, that the pleaſures of reſidence in the Pays de Vaud had been very much abridged by the colliſion of political intereſts. It was my fortune to have fallen under the particular patronage of the obnoxious party, and the deſtruction of their conſequence has thrown me very much upon myſelf for amuſement. Societies are indeed not totally annihilated; but all the frank and open intercourſe of life is at an end: the ſhadow yet ſtalks abroad, but all the delicious ſubſtance is extinct. If any deſigns of a revolutionary nature were ever ſeriouſly projected, it is difficult to ſay whether the weakneſs of the projectors or the wiſdom of the governors appears to have been the greateſt. Diſguiſe is conſidered ſo

eſſen-

essential to plot, that nothing but respect for the pointed cannon of their Excellencies of Berne can prevail upon me to believe, that half a dozen families of indiscreet enthusiasm had really conceived the design of detaching the province they inhabit from its alliance to the mother country. The ruling powers have at all events stolen a march upon them; and whether the necessity may have been real or imaginary, it is certain that the government has sustained no loss of influence by this interference.

The livery of nature is now changing rapidly in this delicious country, and the completion of the vintage has stript the long hills of their best ornaments. With the swallow I am now lingering in impatient anxiety for the signal of departure to a warmer and more cheery clime. The cabals of state, by arresting the stream of amusement, have driven me to the elements of a new language; and I shall hope to mix with a new people, not indifferently prepared

LETTER LVIII.

prepared to enjoy their fociety. My mind is big with that expectation which books and reports have taught me to form of the country to which we tend. Endeared by the fame of its heroes and its poets, and exalted by the character of its local beauties, it now fills up the void which banifhed pleafures have left; and my mind embraces, in thefe its moments of folitude and feclufion, a thoufand fairy vifions.

Some deduction muft doubtlefs be made from anticipation, and proportionable allowance muft be admitted for circumftances of change and deterioration. Such would, however, deftroy the pleafure of anticipating at all, which is then only exquifite, when it fees no limit; and as I have yet to encounter a few more blafts of the cutting Bife, before I approach the *reality*, I am yet anxious to preferve the *vifion* entire.

Your amufement cannot have received any fpecial addition by my late communications. The uniform progrefs of my days opens no discovery in circumstance or reflection; and you have little to expect on the score of novelty, till the Alps are between us.

LETTER LIX.

Turin, Nov. 7.

I WAIT your congratulations on having passed the Alps. I feel as though we had performed no mean atchievement. Unluckily so many have been beforehand with me, and so many are likely to follow, that my travelling pride must suffer, I fear, on the reflection, a great abatement.

We lingered too long upon the northern frontier to find a ready passage over this mountainous barrier. It was not till the evening of the 28th ult. that we determined upon this enterprize. The *Bise*, which is a very savage kind of wind, had blown

blown for some days, and carried off the last remains of autumn. Our friends had severally struck their tents, and had quitted our neighbourhood in succession. Solitude, a barren soil, and the blasts of winter, now prompted our final resolve, and at the close of the day we bid adieu to the environs of Lausanne, and, passing the night at Morges, arrived the next morning at our old quarters in Geneva. As friendship is said to divide the pains and double the pleasures of society, we agreed to unite with two agreeable companions, of whom we had some previous knowledge, and who were, as we found, loitering between resolution and apprehension in the hotel at Geneva. The remainder of my day in that city was passed in seeking out those from whom I had on former occasions received marks of hospitable attention. Madamoiselle A. had arrested me at Rolle in the interim of preparation for breakfast. I profited of an hour's conversation with her on the state of French politics.

politics. Her talents for drawing had enabled her to indulge her veneration for some of the leading characters at Paris, whose portraits, in some cases from recollection, in others from engraving, she had designed with much spirit. These she descanted upon as she severally exhibited them with enchanting volubility. " Voila " des gens," said she, " comme il y en a " peu!" On La Fayette she was most liberal in her encomiums. " C'est un homme " fait exprès pour la revolution." My time was limited. Our political dialogue was interrupted by mutual adieus and reciprocal professions, " d'une amitié la plus sin-" cere."

Geneva was rendered unusually gay by a vast influx of company from the neighbourhood to attend the comedy. This is, to be agreeable to report, the last season of theatrical indulgence; and, by a decree of the Council, no dramatical exhibitions are hereafter to be tolerated within the jurisdiction

of

of the republic. Theatres are, according to Rouſſeau, only juſtifiable in great cities; and I am of opinion with the puritanical legiſlators of Geneva, that the permiſſion of a theatrical corps, in a town regulated even by the ſtricteſt police, may yet ſerve as a paſſport for the introduction of thoſe vices which the indolence and the diſſipation of this profeſſion are too well calculated to encourage.

But I have detained you too long at Geneva, impatient as you muſt no doubt be to puſh acroſs the Alps. Bear then with this delay in the outſet, and I promiſe you that my narrative ſhall now move with as little interruption as the inequalities of the way will allow.

LETTER LX.

REPORTS had reached us the night previous to our departure from Geneva, that heavy falls of snow had been observed on the route, and that dispatch was necessary, lest the pass should be rendered impracticable. We made therefore every preparation to enter upon Savoy at an early hour, but were after all compelled to put up for the night at a village called Frangy. This is about sixteen miles from Geneva. Here we had early experience of that inexpressible misery characteristic of the inns of Savoy. The rooms into which we were conducted were strewed with clods of grass and dirt, and the supper was made up of vile morsels steeped in garlic. Our next day's journey brought us to Chamberri. The air was clear, and the mountains began to

be

LETTER LX.

be diftinctly vifible. Aix les Bains, which lies between Frangy and Chamberri, arrefted our attention for half an hour. This town is remarkable for the excellence of its hot fprings. They are fulphureous, and reputed to poffefs very falubrious properties. The baths are very commodioufly conftructed. Excepting fome emigrants who have fought afylum here, very few ftrangers were to be feen.

Chamberri, where we next lodged, is, as you know, the capital of the duchy of Savoy. Its fituation is not among the leaft of its beauties, commanding noble and varied views of hills, plains, and vallies. I faw the town in a difadvantageous hour. It was a faint-day, and the rain fell hard. Thefe were two circumftances equally unfavourable to the refpect of a trading town, which is only rendered cheerful by the fpirit and activity of commercial occupation. The fhops were clofely barricadoed, and no doors were feen open but thofe of the churches.

churches. Here I followed the multitude, and encountered a host of beggars, more ragged, importunate, and clamorous than any of the fraternity of mendicants I ever met with. I ought to remark, that, agreeably to custom, this should have been the first stage from Geneva; and the accommodations here are at least such as ought to silence complaint. Our third day brought us to Aigue-belle, in the course of which we passed through Montmelian, sufficiently known in the contiguous countries for the excellence of its wines. It is at Chamberri that the valley opens which conducts to the foot of Mount Cenis. Down this valley the river Aar pursues its course, and moves with considerable rapidity. In some points it is worked into foam, and breaks its way with all the violence of the most impetuous torrent. In the journey of this day the Alps began to open upon us, till on our arrival at Aigue-belle they showed themselves in all their majestic and tremendous forms.

LETTER LX.

Our fourth day brought us to St. Jean de Maurienne, where we found no contemptible quarters.

From St. Jean to St. André, for we were now roving amidſt the reſidences of the ſaints, we toiled the fifth day. The valley, as we advanced, gradually narrowed, and the mountains as regularly augmented in number, height, and horrors. The torrent of the Aar we paſſed a variety of times, in the courſe of this day, upon wooden bridges, of what appeared to us the lighteſt conſtruction. We hinted ſome apprehenſions reſpecting our ſafety, but were aſſured that their ſtrength was ill-judged of by their appearance. The road was as little calculated to inſpire confidence. It coaſted almoſt uniformly along the moſt hideous precipices, exciting at times lively emotions of terror, and exhibiting, through a frightful alternation of aſcents and declivities, all the varieties of difficulty and danger.

LETTER LXI.

IT was not till the evening of the fixth day that our proceffion arrived at Lannefbourg at the foot of Mount Cenis. Nothing but miferable fights of human infirmity had occurred in this latter part of the valley. From St. Jean de Maurienne to Mount Cenis I faw little befides fallow countenances and emaciated forms. St. André appeared, indeed, the head-quarters of goitrous idiotifm and wretchednefs. Mountains on either fide feemed to comprefs, within a moft gloomy and infalubrious fort of dungeon, thefe woe-begone inhabitants, who called to my mind

the wafteful hoft
Of pain and ficknefs, fqualid and deform'd.

You will readily conceive that great falls of fnow could not much improve a track which paffed over the declivities of mountains. Sixteen miles performed between the hours of ten and four, will enable you to judge of our pace and patience. The diverfity of fhapes and magnitudes, which the vaft cluf- ter of Alps, among which we were now moving, prefented, under a deep coating of fnow, made a very curious appearance.

In a village through which we paffed, fome violent fhouts excited our curiofity. We found they were occafioned by an event of great importance to the inhabitants,— the fhooting of a bear, which had made fre- quent defcents upon this wretched hamlet, and borne off confiderable booty; till the lofs of an infant, whom he was fuppofed to have ftolen, enraged the peafants, who purfued this inhuman depredator into the favage wilds in which he refided, and, at the moment of our arrival, Bruin was drag- ging in triumph through the village.

The approach to Lannefbourg offered a curious fpectacle. The valley through which

which we had been journeying for some days, and which had gradually narrowed, now appeared to terminate; and the mountain over which we were to pass seemed to oppose, by the trackless snow which inveloped it, an insuperable barrier. We entered Lannesbourg before the day closed, and were instantly surrounded by a number of men, who demanded permission to pull our carriages to pieces by royal authority. I respect governments wherever I go, and would not wantonly pour contempt upon any of his Sardinian Majesty's subjects; but I think in my conscience, that an assemblage of more ill-looking wretches never acted under government authority. A commissioner soon showed himself at the head of these raggamuffins, and throwing out a tariffe, in length " a full cloth-yard or more," gave us our choice of travelling accommodations, with the prices settled by order of the police. Our negociation with him was expedited by the pressing desire of finding

the

the comforts of a blazing fire, and a trout fiſhed out of the Lake of Mount Cenis. A very converſible madamoiſelle, the daughter of the landlord, attended on us at ſupper, and did credit to the vivacity and naïveté of the Savoyardes.

The hotel, which is newly ſet up, ſtands a very fair chance of ſucceeding; for, in addition to the bad reputation under which the other labours, of being the worſt and moſt impoſing inn in Chriſtendom, I have no where ſeen a little ſyren better calcu- lated for detaining travellers, who are not violently preſſed to croſs the mountain.

LETTER LXII.

IT was not by the aid of mules and porters, ſedans and ſledges, that the hero of Car- thage made his *entrée* into Italy: and yet I much queſtion whether the Carthaginian ſoldiers complained more emphatically of cold,

cold, fatigue, and inconvenience, than we did. I am impatient to carry you over this mountain, or I could expatiate very largely upon the murmurs I uttered and heard in the afcent from Lannefbourg. The air was indeed impregnated with particles of intenfe cold, and made its way through all the armour with which we were provided. One hour brought us upon the plain, when, to recover from the effects of thefe feverities, we were conducted to a fhed, in which a fire recovered us to fomething like good humour. From this fhed we were feverally drawn in a fledge to the fouthern extremity of the plain, by mules who trotted with confiderable fwiftnefs through the fnows. The poft is fituated a mid-diftance on this route, and was carefully announced to us by the guides and muleteers. At the Grande Croix, in the extremity of the plain, were fome objects upon which I could not but beftow a fhare of attention. To the right was the lake fo celebrated for

the

the excellence of its trout; to the left, the hôpital.

This hôpital was founded, like that of St. Bernard, for the relief and refreshment of those pilgrims whom devotion might induce to seek the shrines of Loretto, or solicit the benediction of Christ's vicar. At some distance stood the "Chapelle de transfis"—a coemetery constructed for the burial of those who may chance to perish on these pious expeditions. Numerous huts are also raised upon different parts of this mountain, the residence of shepherds during the summer, as very excellent pasture is found in the bosom of those rocks which inclose the upper level, and whose points rise to a very considerable height. In fact, when upon this plain, which covers the summit of the mountain, we seemed to be in a valley, enormous ridges of rock rising on either side, some of which appear to bear the snows of ages. It was from this point, the beginning of the "descente des Echelles,"

that

that we entered the sledge, in order to slide down in the whimsical fashion in usage here, when the sides of the mountain are incrusted with snow. A hundred travellers have told you what this mode is, and by what expedients and under what fears it is effected. I shall not, however, be deterred from telling you what I found it. You are then to imagine me seated in a sledge. To this sledge are fastened two sticks pointed with iron, in the form of a shaft. The guide seated in the front, by the assistance of these shafts, and his feet, which are also eminently serviceable, hastens or retards the motion of the machine, conducts it along precipices with wonderful dexterity, and makes, as occasion requires, yet oftener to show his skill, the most sharp and difficult turns. In some parts we descended with vast rapidity; and the zig-zag course which these ingenious conductors sometimes pursued, in order to pass each other on the way, was really diverting.

This

LETTER LXII.

This was a very pleasant as well as novel descent. The objects by which we glided composed an assemblage of wild and grotesque scenery—a torrent amongst these issuing from the brow of that plain which we had quitted, precipitated its stream in the form of a beautiful cascade. Ten minutes brought us to the miserable village of Ferriere, the regular descent to which is called an hour. The sledges were discharged here as no longer useful, and the remainder of the distance to Novaleze performed on foot. The whole of this descent is estimated two hours or leagues, for time and space stand for each other in these countries; and thus reckoning the commencement of the rise from Chamberri, the height which is ascended by a track of twenty-five leagues, is descended in two. In this calculation, the perpendicular height of the mountain may be reckoned at more than seven thousand English feet. Our journey, though fatiguing, abounded in objects of curiosity and interest.

The memory of the great hero who, two thousand years ago, fought his way through this valley, was frequently a prop to my declining patience. What were our toils, in comparison of those sustained by men who had to scale the towering rock under the pressure of arms, exposed to the surly tempest, with no resources but the habit of combating danger, and the hopes of future conquest!

While I was entering my sledge at the point of descent, I eyed the opening through which Hannibal, probably, pointed out to his exhausted followers the spoils that awaited them in the delightful plains of Lombardy: for all circumstances conspire to fix the passage of the Carthaginians into Italy across the Mont Cenis. The line of separation between Savoy and Piedmont is the little Doria, a stream which rises in the Lake of Mont Cenis, and afterwards uniting with the great Doria, the waters of both are borne to the Po, at a little distance from Turin. At Novaleze, our carriage dissected

at

at Lannefbourg was very dexteroufly and completely re-conftructed,—a fubject of juft congratulation, when it is confidered how much more difficult it is to reftore than to deftroy. The courfe of the little Doria conducted us to Suze, a town agreeably fituated, and in high reputation among the inhabitants on the northern fide of the Alps; who furnifhed us with no article of luxury or convenience, but what they pretended to import from the fruitful treafures of Suze. This town has the reputation of being founded by Pompey. A triumphal arch is among the monuments of antiquity which it ftill preferves, and which is by Gruter carried up to the time of Tiberius. Our equipage paffed rapidly through this place, in order to reach the inhofpitable village of St. Ambroife; but in this the convenience of the horfes was much more confulted than that of their mafters, the ftages of our journey being regulated by the diftribution of the pofts.

LETTER LXIII.

THE road in paſſing from Rivoli, the laſt village on the route to Turin, gradually opens into a conſiderable width, and announces with much magnificence the approach to a great capital. Turin cannot be too handſomely ſpoken of as a town. Regularity and beauty are terms appropriate to its character. I was extremely diverted by the appearance of the inhabitants. Dreſs, air, countenance, and language were full of novelty. Etiquette here holds ſovereign ſway. I ſaw numbers, whoſe thread-bare ſuit could ſcarcely maintain its place, ſqueezing with the utmoſt formality a *chapeau bras*—a burniſhed ſword vibrating by their ſide.

Turin wears all the marks of a vigilant police. Every quarter of the town is tranquil

LETTER LXIII.

quil in the night. I went the morning after my arrival to view the palace. His Sardinian majefty was there, and we could not be admitted till he fhould fet off for his *maifon de Chaffe*. The firing of guns, and the beating of drums, fhortly announced his majefty's intention of quitting the palace. All who were on the fpot drew themfelves up in order and formed an alley, through which his majefty and his fuite paffed. This obtained me a fight of the monarch; but the fqueeze was fo great, that I had little leifure to take cognizance of the royal features.

I am not in general very curious in examining the interior of palaces, except fo far as they are reputed to enclofe the works and monuments of art. I was however unexpectedly gratified in this inftance, by the uncommon fplendor and rich decorations of the apartments. The number of them was prodigious, and they formed a labyrinth almoft as intricate as that of Crete. I shall

shall only mention a few of those rarities which struck me most forcibly:—Victor Amadeus, an equestrian statue. This monarch himself, in bronze, is mounted upon a horse of marble, trampling upon the bodies of slaves in chains, with all the wild barbarity of a conqueror and a tyrant. One stands astonished at the corruption of that mind, which can find a feast in such base and unfeeling adulation. " Parcere subjectis," was the favourite maxim of Henry IV. of France; and the arts are miserably degraded, when they are employed to celebrate the abettor, rather than the vanquisher of tyranny, and to immortalize him who imposes, rather than him who breaks the chains of servitude.—The four seasons, by Albani, were curious objects of speculation. There appeared to enter much ingenious composition into these works of the pencil, and you will readily perceive, that a fine imagination can alone embody those phantoms of the mind. I know not whether Albani has executed these

these pieces as well as he ought; but I cannot conceive how he could have executed them better. The portrait of Charles I. of England, and his children, is a fine *morceau*, from the animated pencil of Vandyke. But my attention was very highly engaged by a small groupe which passes for the *chef d'œuvre* of Gerard Dow. The subject is a dropsical woman seated in a chair. The physician is examining the water. The maid servant is at the same time administering a spoonful of physic to the patient; and casting her eye upon the afflicted daughter at her mother's knee. Every circumstance, the most minute, is expressed with an accuracy, and a finish, which surpasses conception. This piece is said to have cost the late king twenty thousand livres.

LETTER LXIV.

TRAVELLING, like age, is garrulous; and merely to fee, without relating, is but to have half feen. I have made my debut as an Italian connoiffeur, and am now about to appear in my new character of an antiquary. My knowledge is about equal in the one and the other fcience; but a man cannot travel fouth of the Alps, without either being, or becoming fo much of both, as to take off that ftupid ftare with which a perfect-novice regards the works of art.

From the palace of his Sardinian majefty we went to the univerfity, fituated in that very handfome ftreet, the Strada di Po. The univerfity is announced by a portico, bearing the infcription, " Regium Athe-" næum," and confifts of an extenfive range of buildings, comprehending various objects;

jects; among which the "Museo del Re," or "the King's Musæum," was pointed out to us as an object of importance to travellers. This Musæum forms indeed a very extensive and valuable collection of antiques in every kind, statues, busts, and ancient fragments. Among a great variety of elegant works in bronze, were a delicious little figure of Venus in the whimsical attitude of cutting her toe-nails: this is executed with the most perfect accuracy and beauty. The famous Tripod, which contracts or increases its dimensions at pleasure. A foot of a horse of the natural size, of the most exquisite execution: this, together with the leg of a man, supposed to be its rider, were purchased by accident of a founder who had employed the other parts to make bells, and was about to convert these precious relics to the same use. There are also some thunders of Jupiter, which yet retain strong vestiges of the brilliant gold with which they once glittered: to these must be added, vases vafes of filver, and fepulchral lamps, in all the forms which ingenuity could fupply.

The collection of Egyptian antiquities is alfo extremely curious and valuable: numerous penates, talifmans, &c. are here depofited. The objects which were held up as of the greateft eftimation, were, " a head of " Ifis, and the Ifiac table." The firft is of bronze admirably executed, and covered with hieroglyphics. The fecond, or Ifiac table, is confidered as one of the moft precious monuments of ancient times, which Italy preferves. It is of red copper, nearly four feet long, and fomething more than two in width. Ifis, who is reprefented fitting, forms the principal figure in this table, which thence derives its name. She is fupplied with two bulls horns as fymbols of fecundity. It appears to have been, in its original ftate, adorned with filver plates, as fome of thefe ornaments ftill remain; and it is like the head of Ifis before named, and, indeed, any relic of Egyptian origin, covered

LETTER LXIV.

vered with hieroglyphics. This mysterious table has furnished a wide field of discussion and enquiry for the learned, to whom hieroglyphics yet continue an inexplicable language. The most rational opinion yet offered, respecting the design of this table, is, that the Egyptians, who came to settle in Italy, formed it, in order that the epocha of their worship, their ceremonies, habits of their priests, &c. might not pass into oblivion. This solves, however, no part of those mysterious symbols which croud the table; for, after all the efforts of antiquarian research, or happy conjecture, the Egyptian continues, in respect to his hieroglyphics, yet master of the field.

The collection of medals appeared to be numerous and well arranged; the greater part of these, and of the valuable antiques in general, with which this musæum abounds, were taken from the ruins of "Industria," a well-known colony of the Romans, whose scite and vestiges were not discovered till the year 1745. The attendant at this musæum was an Abbé, intelligent and polite, who declined any gratuity offered, as contrary to usage. The stranger is, however, permitted to indulge his liberality to the servants at the door, the objects of whose bows and forward civilities cannot easily be mistaken.

I thought to have drawn the curtain upon Turin in this letter, but the musæum has carried me beyond the bounds I had prescribed, and I have too much respect for the Italian opera to mention it in a postscript.

LETTER LXV.

THE Italian opera is the touchstone of fashion; and no man, who has any regard for his reputation, would venture to dislike what good breeding obliges him to approve. The serious Italian opera is, in

the

the judgment of profeffional men, better prefented on the Englifh than upon the Italian ftage. This arifes from the liberal encouragement given to all the fingers of reputation, and from the very expenfive decorations which thefe exhibitions receive in a country whofe refources and prodigality feem to keep equal pace with each other.

The Buffo, or Comic Opera, is that which a ftranger will vifit to moft advantage in Italy, this being the fpecies of compofition in which modern fingularities are held up to ridicule; while the ferious opera reforts to fome tale of ancient hiftory, choofing, for the moft part, that into which the greateft number of fplendid characters can enter. I went, the evening after my arrival at Turin, to the Theatre di Carignano, and was agreeably entertained with a comic reprefentation of La Serva Inamorata. My knowledge of Italian is as yet but very flender; neverthelefs, without underftanding any confiderable portion of the dialogue, I found

I found an excellent scholium in the gesture, play of the muscles, and musical expression, with which the whole was accompanied. To judge from the only two specimens I have as yet had, the Italians have a very extraordinary talent at musical inflection upon subjects of humour; and can render, with the greatest effect, by artificial modulation, the easy familiarities of colloquial wit. On a foreign stage the same freedom is not felt, because it is with reason supposed, that what will be ill understood where humour is concerned, cannot be highly relished; and every attempt to methodize or accommodate, must in such cases destroy those features of nature which he who studies mankind would wish principally to find.

Italian dancing has been frequently commented upon with great severity: and indeed, the measure of censure has never yet reached the demerit of the performance. Such outrageous strides, jumps, and somersets,

merſets, I never before had witneſſed, as were exhibited in the ballets annexed to the operas. The dance formed a direct contraſt to the ſong, and produced in me as lively emotions of difguſt, as it did in the audience of applauſe. A dance of ſavages round a cannibal banquet could not have been more wild and extravagant. I could not but feel aſtoniſhed, that a people, who excel ſo decidedly in the arts of muſical expreſſion, ſhould judge ſo corruptly on a ſubject which appears to turn upon principles ſo nearly analogous.

LETTER LXVI.

I HAVE ſpoken with ſufficient emphaſis of the general beauty of Turin, and I ought to add, that the details will not ſuffer by examination. They reckon 110 churches in this capital, of which many are of great architectural beauty.

The *place* or square which precedes the palace presents a magnificent appearance. Eight streets there concentre; and continued arcades, or piazzas, favour the expofition of every kind of merchandize. The place San Carlo divides, at nearly its centre, the Strada Nuova, and adds confiderably to the fplendour of the city. The promenades are delicious. They confift in an efplanade between the town and the citadel, and alfo in a beautiful diftribution of the ramparts. The ftreets are for the moft part wide, clean, and regular; and many of the houfes are conftructed upon a grand fcale.

The Po, near the city, appears not yet to have recovered from the commotion into which the mufe of Ovid has thrown it. Addifon tells us, on the authority of fome botanifts, that larch-trees, and not poplars, are thofe which fhed a gum, and are found on the banks of the Po. And Apollonius could not have been very accurate when he tells us, that the thunderbolt of Jupiter fo affected

affected the waters, as to render it fatal to a bird to fly acrofs the ftream. But this was a favourite image with the poets; and, the lake of Avernus was not efteemed by Virgil fufficiently corrupt without this quality. There is a pleafure of no common magnitude in contemplating thofe realities which have been wrought by claffic fancy into fuch fplendid vifions. It would afford a ftill higher pleafure, if it were poffible to diveft them completely of the veil which covers them; for after all that Hefiod, Apollodorus, and ftill more rationally Ariftotle, and others, who have improved upon this fyftem, have taught us, the fable of Phaeton, and the combuftion he occafioned, is one among thofe amufing myfteries whofe machinery is enchanting, whofe moral is obvious, but whofe precife meaning has perifhed with the records of the times.

The fpirit of trade feems to be very active at Turin, if any judgment may be formed from the lively buftle of the ftreets. Articles

ticles of English manufacture are vended in every part of the town, and a very considerable traffic is reported here to be carried on with Great Britain. How greatly is the state of empires changed since Virgil pronounced the Britons " penitus toto di- " visos orbe?" I am aware that their insular situation formed a part of that sentiment; but the very striking contrast which modern Britain presents to the more general construction of the expression, I am called upon continually to remark. Briareus-like, she now extends her hundred arms over the different districts of the continent, and maintains, by the vigour of her commerce, and the extent of her political influence, a connection with every nation of the globe.

LETTER LXVII.

Feliffano, Nov. 11, 1791.

AT the end of two days journey, we have got into a miserable village, and though shivering with an aguish cold, contracted amidst the snow of Mount Cenis, I shall endeavour, by attention to my journal, to forget my maladies. Imperious circumstances, rather than choice, shortened my stay at Turin; and as I had foreseen that our departure might be precipitate, I had availed myself of every opportunity to gratify my curiosity upon objects of interest and information. Being either too little or too great to quit without notice the capital of Piedmont, in attempting to cross the bridge over the Po, we were suddenly commanded to halt, and take off a pair of horses, it being contrary to the established rules of the place to suffer one man to drive out four

four horses. This was rather a trial of pride than of patience, for the remainder of the town was of no great length; and our horses being again put to, we proceeded in quiet pace along the banks of the Po.

It was morning, and all that remained of dying vegetation was illumined by a clear and temperate sunshine. Although the season of the year has greatly abridged the beauties of the scenery, objects were not wanting to inspire the landscape with interest. A charming distribution of country villas covered a wide and variegated tract. The Alps, at distance, presented their snowy summits in a vast and stupendous chain, while beside us rolled in peaceful motion the turbid waters of that stream, consecrated to classic fame. Imagination was not idle in these moments so favourable to fancy. All the fictions which had crowded my childish memory embodied themselves before me; and I seemed to be moving over enchanted ground, till I arrived at Villa Nuova.

LETTER LXVII.

Nuova. I muſt tell you, that I never yet entered any town at ſo late an hour. For upon aſking the *padrone* of the inn the time of the day, he aſſured me it was leaſt 3 and 20 o'clock.

On remarking to our hoſt that this was a ſmall village, he replied, with ſome degree of diſpleaſure, *padrone!* This word *padrone* is a term of moſt comprehenſive ſignification; inſomuch that I, who am but an *inceptor* in the language, feel ſome difficulty in determining the intention of the party by whom it happens to be uſed. In the ſalutation of friends, I have obſerved *padrone* enquired on the one part, and the ſingle term *padrone* returned on the other; and, in this caſe, it implies the " How do " you do?" and the " Pretty well, thank " you," of the Engliſhman. But the ſenſe in which my hoſt employed it was, as I have ſince underſtood, a very common and a very civil one; namely, " I beg your par- " don." In order to impreſs me more

ſtrongly

strongly with the importance of the place, he added, that it contained a convent. I was not quite fatisfied with this proof; but fearing that my Italian might not bear me out in the difpute, and dreading the confequences of an attack upon the church, I fuffered myfelf to be beaten out of the field. It was in our plan of this day's journey to reach Aleffandria, but the inevitable flownefs of our pace, from the extreme badnefs of the road, and the counfel of an old man, who was queftioned upon the remaining diftance, determined us to ftop at Feliffano for the night. Two beds of ftraw, with fcanty coverlids, juft leave fpace for a ricketty table, upon which my pen is now moving; and the chilling winds, which enter by the papered cafement, are playing moft wantonly about my fhoulders.

If ever you fhould be tempted to crofs the Mont Cenis, at a period when the fnows are almoft knee-deep, and one or both of your boots may happen to admit
water,

water, let me caution you not to exchange your carriage for your feet. A raging fever of laſt night, and a thouſand aches and ſhiverings all this day, enable me to aſſure you that the pains attending on ſuch indiſcretion, are as ſevere as thoſe which puniſh ſome of the moſt important follies of human eccentricity.

LETTER LXVIII.

Caſtel San Giovanni, Nov. 13, 1791.

OUR hoſt at Feliſſano made up in attention, for the deficiences of his miſerable accommodations. Aleſſandria, through which we paſſed in our road to Tortona, detained us no longer than was neceſſary to procure a dinner, for which we paid at a rate which left no room for regret on the part of the landlord. The country from Aleſſandria is for the moſt part flat, and in

a ſtate

a ſtate of high cultivation to Tortona, where we arrived in the evening.

I am not in the habits of retailing the articles of proviſions which I find on the way, but our yeſterday's fare may ſerve as a ſpecimen of what I am given to underſtand is conſidered as an excellent Italian ſupper. A diſh of macaroni was our firſt ſervice. This was followed by a ſaucer containing ſome ſcraped parmeſan. A plate was then introduced with ſome morſels of pigs liver, and a ſecond adorned with omelettes and garlick. Three ſmall birds, and a handſome deſert, cloſed this *petit ſouper*, which, however deficient in weight and eſſentials, may, in the language of the Latins, be at leaſt allowed to have been " *numeris* abſo-" luta fuis."

Horace has told us of ſome meals in his time, in which variety appears to have been not leſs conſulted. Naſidienus's ſupper made certainly a better figure; and was on that account more deſerving of recital: but I

think

think that, taken upon a fmall fcale, the gufto of antient times is not badly preferved in the modern arts of Italian catering. As I have brought Horace upon the ftage, in vindication of my bill of fare, I fhall make him do me another fervice before I difmifs him. His vifits to Mæcenas were frequent, and their repafts convivial. Some animating topic had engaged him at one of thefe " noctes coenæque Deum ;" and inattentive to the objects of fenfe, which were doubtlefs fet before him in profufion, he imprudently fwallowed fome garlick. How he felt upon that occafion, his mufe has amphatically told us. My feelings are fo perfectly in unifon with his, upon all that relates to this naufeous vegetable, that though I am not prepared to confider it as a fufficient punifhment for the crime of parricide, yet I can never fee it cordially digefted without exclaiming,

   O dura mefforum Ilia!

LETTER LXIX.

Piacenza, Nov. 14, 1781.

A VERY diverting Signora, who attended upon us at Tortona, gave us the firſt ſpecimen of the Italian face, ſuch, at leaſt, as I have been taught to expect it. It is not beauty, or rather it is not lovelineſs; but it poſſeſſes great ſymmetry, and there is much in it to excite admiration. I remarked to the Signora that the town muſt be dull, as I underſtood from her that it could boaſt no theatre. She replied, that at preſent there was indeed but one battalion of ſoldiers at Tortona, but that their uſual compliment was three. One was gone off towards France, and another into Savoy. I found by this, that a red coat was not without its charms beyond the Alps; and that the Signoras of Italy were of an opinion,

nion, not peculiar to this country, that "where troops were quartered, there could "be no want of amufement."

Our journey from Tortona to Caftel San Giovanni, where we ftopped laft night, brought the Apennines before us: but the country is in general fo flat, as to furnifh little variety. I would not fay, of any part of Italy, that it is uninterefting. It was the theatre of all that is great in hiftory for many ages; and not a fpot of it exifts that has not been the feat of fome celebrated event. The claffic enthufiafm of Mr. Addifon was able to difcover fome veftiges of its antient grandeur, even in the rudeft parts of this country. "There is," fays he, "fcarce any part of the nation that is not "famous in hiftory, nor fo much as a "mountain or river that has not been the "fcene of fome extraordinary action." I could however learn nothing of Caftel San Giovanni from any of its inhabitants. The place feemed funk in wretchednefs and po- verty;

verty; yet an old wall, mouldering into ruins, appeared to commemorate some lost importance. The strolling ecclesiastics, of whom I enquired respecting those ruins, could give me no information, though they appeared to have sufficient leisure for antiquarian studies. No less than eight churches and three convents were enumerated in consequence of my enquiries; and notwithstanding the deplorable wretchedness which covered the inhabitants, it was easy to see that the honour in their estimation outweighed the burden.

Indeed, I could not but be strongly impressed with this infatuation, upon passing a few minutes in their cathedral. It was curious to observe the contrast that appeared between the worshippers and their shrines. While the one were covered with rags, the other were invested with costly ornaments. Columns of marble supported the altars, while the thread-bare cloke scarcely covered those who knelt and crawled around it. On the

the one, precious odours were afcending in votive clouds; from the other, proceeded only the vile fcent of garlick. Yet the countenance of the worfhipper fpoke a fentiment above content. He eyed, with fomething more than complacency, the range of coftly ftatues which enkindled his devotion, and feemed to forget the depth of his mifery in the fervor of his prayers. How ftrong is the grafp of fuperftition, when it has once faftened upon its victim! The comforts of life really feemed to thefe deluded people, a very mean price for the religious trumpery they received in exchange, and the privilege of worfhipping at a golden altar: content to exift upon macaroni, and to ftretch their bodies upon beds of ftraw, provided their faints and demi-gods may feed upon frankincenfe, and inhabit fhrines of alabafter!

LETTER LXX.

Parma, Nov. 15, 1791.

I KNOW not how a town can be viewed to lefs advantage than during a fall of undecided rain. By undecided rain, I mean that diftillation which fcatters a dufky mift over all the works of art. Such was the ftate of the atmofphere upon my arrival and during my ftay at Piacenza; and perhaps it is to this that I owe the impreffion of dullnefs which I have brought away with me from that town. It is not, however, without its ornaments.

The Piazza Publico (which is a fquare) partakes of the grand; it is difficult, however, to be fatisfied with more than one of its fides. Two noble equeftrian ftatues commemorate in bronze, at two angles of this fquare, the virtues of Aleffandro I. and

his

his fon. I ought to have admired, as books inftruct me, the painted cupola of the cathedral; but, alas! the height of the cupola, and the gloom of the cathedral, had ravifhed thofe beauties from my fight. I was obliged to content myfelf with gazing upon an object which had the advantage of a better light—I mean the dial; as this was the firft I had obferved defcribed after the Italian method of keeping time, and prefenting on one circumference the twenty-four hours of the day. I was very much pleafed with a fmall painting of the Virgin and Child in a glafs frame, and hung over one of the altars in the church of St. Francifco il Grande; it had fo much in it of fweetnefs and nature, that I cannot but hazard a word in its praife, though I have not yet found it in that lift which travellers are inftructed to admire. A very elegant altar in the fame church attracted my particular curiofity; it was defigned with art, and finifhed with beauty. The richeft marble,

marble, and the pureſt alabaſter, were here expended with equal ſymmetry and profuſion. I was anxious to know what Saint or Martyr claimed this altar. If it were my lot to be canonized, I know not a ſhrine I ſhould more earneſtly covet. A little invocation, and ſome few inſcriptions, ſoon led me to its lawful claimant, who was no leſs a perſonage than St. Anthony, the great apoſtle to the fiſhes. All the good things in the province of Milan ſeem conſecrated to this powerful Saint, whoſe head-quarters are at Padua. He was ſpoken of in very high terms upon the tablets which beſtrewed this altar, and repreſented as very dear to Jeſus Chriſt, and a great favourite of the Holy Virgin.

The church of San Agoſtino is a riſing ornament to the town of Piacenza, and promiſes to end in a building of great taſte and beauty. The ſide aiſles are fitted up in a very elegant ſtile, and the new front which it is now receiving, preſents the outline

line of a noble façade. The Augustines, to whom this church belongs, are in possession of vast property. It is at their expence that this church is now receiving its finish. " The façade," said an old mendicant, " has already cost 14,000 sechins."—" What then," said I, " these gentlemen " are rich?"—" Rich!" said he, " richis-" simi-sono i nostri principi."

As the distance from Piacenza to Parma was not considerable, we passed from thence in the afternoon, and entered Parma in the dusk of the evening. The country in the whole of this route was delectable; not a rood of ground was to be seen, but what possessed the highest degree of cultivation.

LETTER LXXI.

Parma, Nov. 16, 1791.

MY speculations of to-day upon the curiosities of this place have been so extensive, that though I burn with impatience

tience to communicate, I scarcely know whether the late hour at which I attempt this sketch will allow me to complete my report. It was a grand day at the cathedral, so that I had the pleasure of hearing high mass performed. The church of San Giovanni Evangelista, which I next entered, was very highly ornamented, and the pencil of Correggio has pourtrayed upon its cupola some animated figures; that of St. John is eminently beautiful.

The academy afforded me a large field of amusement. A variety of miscellaneous paintings and designs is here preserved, and some curious fragments of antiquity; amongst which was a very noble head of Jupiter. But the principal ornament of this academy, and one of the greatest ornaments of Europe I might add, is the *chef d'œuvre* of Correggio preserved here with great care, and still in high preservation. The groupe is formed by the Virgin, who has the Infant in her lap. Mary Magdalen

len is to the left of her, having her head reclined. St. Jerome, an angel, and the Infant Baptift, enter into the compofition, and a more exquifite production never iffued from the fchool of painting. I did not think it poffible for imagination to pourtray a countenance of fuch delicacy, grace, and fweetnefs. She feemed to be occupied in affection, veneration, and rapture. Thefe paffions were blended like the mellow colours of the immortal painter into the happieft unity. The bold figure of St. Jerome, the attitude, the folidity and fainted gravity of his countenance, compofed a ftriking counter-part to thefe fofter paffions. The infant was vivacious and benign. The Magdalen penfive and dejected; melancholy veiled the full luftre of her countenance, and preferved the proprieties of her character. The angel was what an angel fhould—I had almoft faid, all that an angel can be. Such is this wonderful painting. If I might make fo free with the terms of art, I would say, that it has all that softness, finish, keeping, and vigour can contribute to animate the works of the pencil. Days and years might be spent in admiring it; and genius might exhaust the power of language in its praise. A copy is now taking of this inimitable groupe, which promises to catch some portion of its spirit. But, alas! such are the imperious limits of this art, that no transcript can be made of its excellencies; and the pencil of the artist can alone perpetuate his own fame.

The theatre which joins the academy is sufficiently known as a building of wood, particularly constructed for the conveyance of sound without echo or confusion; and reports of travellers are perfectly correct as to this fact: for upon experiment made in a whisper at one end, the words were distinctly heard at the other. The form of the theatre is light and elegant. It is now, however, falling into decay, and the sole
use

LETTER LXXI.

use to which it is at present applied, is the occasional exhibition of Naumachiæ, for which the arena is very conveniently adapted. I could descant upon a second production of Correggio's, to which I was introduced after quitting the academy, but I am fearful that my epithets would scarcely hold out through another description; and, indeed, to speak the truth, it succeeded the other too rapidly to find a particle of admiration disengaged.

I have been relaxing this evening at the theatre, being previously acquainted that a tragedy of Shakespeare's would be performed, and wishing to know in what manner our immortal bard would be handled by these cognoscenti. The tragedy was nothing less than Amletto (Hamlet); and, alas! my poor countryman has seldom fallen into worse hands, since Voltaire attempted to translate him. The jokes and the idle play of words which were the side-arms of this poet, were all that this caterer

for

for the Italian ſtage had reliſhed or underſtood. Theſe were laviſhed, and not without effect, upon the audience, who ſeemed to have taken the whole for a burleſque, and expreſſed their approbation of theſe flights of humour with tremendous peals of applauſe. It was only in ſome moment when Hamlet himſelf occupied the ſtage, that any thing like gravity appeared in the houſe. Then, indeed, a call of ſilence was raiſed and echoed from different parts, and attention was erect till Hamlet, who was dreſſed in black, and brandiſhed a white handerchief in his hand, had done ranting. So much for Italian tragedy.

It is painful to ſee ſuch inattention to the convenience of travelling in countries of ſuch wealth and fertility. A ſmall deduction from the palace would clear the peaſant's path. Almoſt all the rivers in theſe opulent duchies, are deſtitute of bridges, and ſome are not paſſed in ferry-boats without danger.

LETTER LXXII.

Bologna, Nov. 18, 1791.

UPON commencing our route to Modena, we entered upon the old Æmilian way. I amused myself, during this part of our journey, with reading a letter of Pliny to Trajan, in which he mentions the Cura Viæ Æmiliæ as an object of great advantage, and thanks the Emperor for having given the appointment to a friend of his. It was some addition to this train of pleasurable images to be informed, that on passing through Reggio, I was viewing a place which, besides its antient fame, was revered as the birth-place of Ariosto. Modena is a delicious town, and has every advantage of buildings and situation. Tassoni, in his poem of the *Secchia Rapita*, has given a very

very animated and juſt deſcription of this his native place:

" Modana Siede in una gran pianura," &c.

The cathedral is rather ſingular than handſome, and ſufficiently ſombre for all the purpoſes of occult devotion. One of thoſe who ſtand in the place of Levites, and ſerve about the altar, offered to conduct me to ſome objects of curioſity. They conſiſted of a number of antient mauſoleums, whoſe inſcriptions were not difficult to decipher. My guide was however ſo intolerably ſtupid, that I got no information from him as to their hiſtory. They were all found in the town, he aſſured me; and when I aſked him how long it was ſince their diſcovery, he talked to me of more centuries than I ſhould chuſe to repeat. All that I could draw from him was, that they were " tro-
" vati nel piazzo," (found in the ſquare,)
" tranſportati qui," (conveyed here,) " &
" tutti di marmore," (all of marble.) This laſt

LETTER LXXII.

laſt he repeated with great energy. He next introduced me, having previouſly lighted two candles, into a chapel, which he called the Chapel of San Geminiano.

This ſaint, of whoſe hiſtory I cannot inform you, is in great eſtimation among the Modaneſe, as Petronius is at Bologna. Taſſoni, in his poem before quoted, calls the former *Gemignani*, as he does the latter *Petronj*, from theſe reſpective ſaints:

"Che tolſero a' i Petronj, i Gemignani.
CANTO I.

This chapel was ſufficiently curious. There were two very well executed portraits in it. I wiſhed to know the artiſt, but the only anſwer I could get was " San Geminiano," and " tutto di marmore!" My guide now led me to the back part of that monument, on which the portraits were hung, and pointing to a ſmall door, reſembling the entrance into a vault, he rehearſed a hiſtory reſpecting it, which I was far from thoroughly comprehending. He ſpoke of creeping and
crawling

crawling upon his knees, and accompanied his words with geftures, which made me conclude that this was the opening into fome fubterraneous paffage. He afked me, if I would enter it? I made no objection; on which he unlocked the door, and pointed to the infide. I was furprifed on looking, to find that it was but a fmall area under the monument or vault, the roof of which was fupported by fix or feven marble pillars, at fuch intervals as to leave room for a perfon to crawl on his knees. Upon feeing me hold back, he explained the whole of the myftery, by telling me " Chi vuol' " obtenere una grazia di Dio bifogna fer- " pere qui." (He who would obtain a bleff- ing from God, muft creep through here.) And ftooping down, I obferved that this operation had actually worn a channel upon the marble. I afked him how long it had been the fafhion to creep among thefe pillars? He told me, five hundred years. Whether his chronology was accurate or

not,

LETTER LXXII.

not, I had no opportunity to afcertain. The man feemed not a little aftonifhed at my retiring without making this religious tour. Unfortunately he detained me fo long in his recital of miracles performed at this tomb, and in the exhibition of a moft marvellous and wonder-working crucifix, that I loft the opportunity of feeing the *Secchia*, which is preferved among the archives of this cathedral.

It paffes for a fpecies of miracle, that the mere theft of a bucket fhould become the foundation of a war; and it does at firft fight prefent a fubject of furprife, that the blood of nations fhould be fpilt for " un " infelice e vil fecchia di legno." It is however to be feared, that in reviewing the wars of Europe, too many cafes will be found, in which fo valid a pretext cannot be affigned for the effufion of human blood.

LETTER LXXIII.

Florence, Nov. 21.

BOLOGNA is a town, the remembrance of whose beauties will not readily be effaced from my mind; and yet I have seen so small a portion of them, and been compelled to take so rapid and cursory a glance, that I almost blush to attempt any thing like an enumeration of its curiosities.

The churches are usually in all places the first object of attention: and I had heard so much of the celebrity of St. Luke at Bologna, that I immediately requested to be conducted thither. The path to this church is a continual ascent; but pilgrims of all ages, and labouring under whatever infirmities, seemed to tread it without reluctance or fatigue. The church bears the name of the Madonna di San Luca, from the

the famous portrait of the Virgin, painted by the hand of the Evangelift, and which it is the boaft and glory of the Bolognefe to poffefs. A portico of three miles conducts the pilgrim to this object of adoration. This portico has confiderable beauty, and ftill more convenience, as it affords at once the means of fhelter and of reft. It was raifed by voluntary contribution; fix hundred and forty-eight arcades compofe the whole range; all of which were built at different periods by the zealous devotion of private perfons, or different corporations, and they were conftructed in reference to each other, fo as now to compofe an uniform piazza to the entrance of the church, adorned with frefcoes, fome of which have no fmall merit.

The church is an elegant building, and bears on its walls fome tablets, commemorative of miracles performed by this marvellous picture. This ineftimable treafure is provokingly covered with a cafe, ornamented

with jewels, and different offerings of devotion; so that I could only judge of St. Luke's pencil by its miraculous effects. A string of beads, which I purchased to escape the suspicion of heresy, entitled me to a little tract, written by the Abbé Calindri, from which I learned the very high value set upon this precious deposit, the solemnity with which it is venerated at Bologna, and the innumerable benefits which have been derived by this city from its residence among them. The Abbé, speaking of the annual ceremony of carrying this image in procession, says, " Molte altre volte é stato, " &c. *i. e.* This ceremony has also been " performed in cases of public emergency, " as was the case in 1779, on account of " repeated earthquakes. The consequence " was, that though these shocks were so " violent, and so frequent as to agitate the " country for three years, the city of Bo- " logna sustained no sensible mischiefs from " this scourge, which, during its continu-
" ance,

LETTER LXXIII.

"ance, committed such ravages in the cir-
"cumjacent cities."

The Abbé, full of the authenticity and influence of this magical picture, has annexed to his abridged account of this history, the means by which it passed into the hands of those who founded the present church. As such a curiosity may not often come before you, I will endeavour, for your amusement, to put this portion of monkish Latin into a decent English dress*. "In

* Anno Domini millesimo centisimo sexagesimo, Die octava intrante Madis. Actum in Monte de Guardia sub heremato Domne Azoline & Beatrixie, presentibus Domno Rambertino de Guezis, Domnus Marcheximus Ottonellus, Judex; Domnus Angelettus de Ursis, et alii plures testes, Domnus G. Episcopus Bonon dedit et assignavit supradictis Azoline et Beatrixie unam capsulam de ligno, cum tabula, ubi picta est imago Beate Marie manu beati Luche Evangeliste, quam portavit de Constantinopoli, in civitate Bononie Theoclys Kennya hermitanationis Grecus ibi presens ad conservandam, tenendam, et custodiendam in heremitatico de monte de Guarda pro se et earum successoribus, in dicto heremitico ad honorem Dei et dicte imaginis. Prenominati Dominus Episcopus et Theoclys heremita hoc instrumentum assignationis ut super legitur scribere rogaverunt. Ego Vitalis Biblicie Dei gratia dicti Domni Episcopi notarius interfui; et hanc cartam instrumenti consignationis rogatus scripsi et sigillavi cum sigillo dicti Domni Episcopi indictione octava.

"the

" the year of our Lord 1160, and the 8th
" day of May, in the Monte di Guardia, at
" the hermitage of the ladies Azolina and
" Beatrice, and in the presence of Signior
" Rambertino de Guezi, Signior Marche-
" sino Ottonello, Judge, Signior Angioletto
" del Orise, and many other witnesses,
" Gerard, Bishop of Bologna, gave and
" assigned to the aforesaid Azolina and
" Beatrice, and their successors, a box, con-
" taining a tablet, upon which is an image
" of the blessed Virgin, painted by the hand
" of St. Luke the Evangelist, and brought
" by Theocles, a Greek hermit, then and
" there present, from Constantinople, to
" have, to hold, and to keep in the hermit-
" age of Monte Della Guardia, to the ho-
" nour of God, and of the said image.
" The afore-named bishop of Theocles,
" the hermit, have called upon me to make
" out the foregoing instrument. I there-
" fore, Vitale di Beliesa, by the grace of
" God notary of the said bishop, 'have
" written in their presence, and at their in-
" stance,

"stance, this instrument of conveyance, and have sealed the same with the seal of the said bishop, in the 8th indiction."

I must allow you to take a moment's refreshment after so tedious a journey through the scrolls of superstition. And as the whole resembles so strongly the structure of a fable, I think you will not object to its usual appendage—a moral! I am free to confess, that I could neither view, nor can reflect upon the whole, without concluding, that when religion is addressed to the senses rather than the understanding, there is nothing too ridiculous to become the object of adoration; and, for my own part, I can discern in the rationality of this species of devotion no difference between the tomb of Mahomet and the cross of Calvary—the image of Diana that fell down from heaven, and the portrait of the Virgin painted by Saint Luke.

LETTER LXXIV.

AMONG the advantages I derived from my visit to St. Luke, were the extensive, varied, and delicious views which I obtained of Bologna and the environs, from different points of the arcades. Numerous villages are scattered over the circumjacent country, which is adorned with the richest cultivation. The next object of attention which I found in my excursion, was the grand and beautiful church of St. Paul. It is not easy to imagine a more impressive piece of sculpture than that which stands before the grand altar, and represents the decollation of St. Paul. The hand of the executioner is raised to strike, and the neck of the calm and intrepid apostle is bared to receive, the blow. This group is disposed with such just attention to light and eleva-

LETTER LXXIV.

tion, that no part of the effect produced by the energy of the artift is loft.

The academy (L'Inftituto) being only viewed to advantage during a clear light, was the next fcene to which my intelligent and managing lacquey conducted me. This is a collection which, as it might not be curforily viewed, fo it ought not to be lightly criticifed. Among the more valuable treafures of this mufeum were a large variety of defigns and fketches, by different mafters of the Bologna fchool. I know fcarcely any pleafure equal to that of tracing the growth of a noble thought from the rude outline to the laft perfection. In viewing the random fketches of the pencil, one is enabled to feparate genius from art, and to difcriminate between imagination and mechanifm. I wifhed to have dwelt longer upon the contemplation of thefe draughts, but I was obliged to obey the fummons which called me to the Hall of Antiques, where my eye was loft in beholding ftatues, and limbs of ftatues,

tues, pigmean heads, coloſſal feet, Roman wells, idols, tablets, and tomb-ſtones. I had ſcarcely time to wonder, before I was hurried into a library, ſaid to contain twelve thouſand volumes, beſides MSS. With the ſame rapidity, I laſtly viſited various cabinets of minerals, petrefactions, and philoſophical inſtruments, halls of wax-work, chambers of fortification, and naval tactics.

Of palaces I ſaw but one, viz. the Sampieri, where the Labours of Hercules, by the Caraccis, the Crucifix in ivory, by John of Bologna, and other productions, attracted their portion of admiration; but my attention was chiefly fixed upon three paintings. The firſt of theſe was the very affecting ſcene of Abraham diſmiſſing Hagar, by Guercino. All the emotions which their reſpective ſituations could inſpire, have been attended to by the painter. Sternneſs on the one hand, and diſtreſs on the other, were never expreſſed in a manner which could ſpeak more powerfully to the feelings.

LETTER LXXIV.

ings. There are dufky tints in the colourings of this mafter which affort well with the graver fubjects. The fecond was a portrait of Chrift, and the Pharifee who brought the tribute-money. The countenances could not be infpired with jufter expreffion; plaufibility and artifice reigned in the one, caution and penetration prevailed in the other. The painter appeared to have nicely ftudied the fhades of fentiment and character, and to have well diftinguifhed between fubtilty and fagacity, between the fpecioufnefs of art and the fobriety of truth. The laft is a painting, whofe fame is not confined to the fpot which contains it. I mean the celebrated production of Guido, in which St. Paul is reprefented rebuking St. Peter. Any other performance would have acted in vain upon my nerves, whofe vibrations began to fail, exhaufted by repeated impreffions of the fublime; but this was irrefiftible. The firft glance quickened my fenfes, and all my powers of admiration fuffered a refurrection.

I declare

LETTER LXXIV.

I declare to you, that in contemplating this interesting work, I seemed to enjoy an interview with the very personages whose portraits were expressed on the canvass. And what an interview! With what characters! and on what occasion! Two apostles whose equals for piety and christian heroism are yet to be sought—men who, from the similarity of their views, their motives, and their labours, must have entertained for each other the highest reciprocal affection and esteem— are here found in a situation the most critical and interesting. " I rebuked him to his " face, said St. Paul, for he was to be " blamed." I thought I saw in the countenance of the first, an inflexible attachment to virtue and to truth, which silenced the pleadings of private feeling; and obliged him to reprove the errors of a man, unequalled perhaps in the christian church, excepting by himself. In the latter I marked manly sorrow and sober penitence. While the former stood with his hand raised, his finger pointed, and his attitude bold, the

latter

LETTER LXXIV.

latter sat with his head reclined, resting upon his hand, and his eyes turned with confusion from the countenance of the rebuking apostle. So much life, vigour, and interest, such an union of sentiment and pathos, I have never yet seen in the productions of the pencil: and I am much deceived if the impression which this excited, will ever be surpassed by any of the master-pieces of art which may yet lie before me. However that be, I cannot but felicitate myself upon having acquired that fund of noble images which the recollection of this painting supplies: and if I could with the pilgrims persuade myself that the sight of a picture would quiet my conscience, and settle my faith, I should make no scruple of turning my back upon the Madonna di San Luca, and seeking my absolution at the Palazzo Sampieri.

LETTER LXXV.

BOLOGNA is reputed to contain as many paintings as Rome itself, and some are of opinion, even more. The churches of Giovanni in Monte, that of the Dominicans, St. Agnes, Corpus Domini, and Petronius, were the chief of those which, in addition to the Cathedral and that of St. Luke, I had leisure or even disposition to visit.

The first of these could not be neglected. Respect for the Cecilia of Raphael carried me there, and I was repaid by the sight of a countenance full of serenity and beauty. The church of the Dominicans contains the Massacre of the Innocents, by Guido. This is held to be one of his best productions, but it is a subject which excites horror. The church is one of the handsomest buildings in its kind that I have ever seen. A very elegant

gant tomb of pure marble here pretends to preserve the relics of that Saint to whom the church is confecrated. The guide unlocked a small door, in order that I might apply my hand to the place where the body lay, and obtain, as I fuppofed, full demonftration of the fact. In compliance with his wifhes, I made the experiment, but not feeling all that anxiety to be convinced, which he fhowed to convince me, I did not obtain fufficient evidence to remove my infidelity. I ought to obferve that the Dominicans have lately poffeffed themfelves of a very beautiful painting, reprefenting the death of the Virgin. It is a production full of fweetnefs and delicate expreffion, and may be regarded as a valuable acquifition to the treafures of this monaftery. The martyrdom of St. Agnes has given fufficient celebrity to the church of that name: and the powers of Dominichino are in this bold defign very ably and fuccefsfully exerted. St. Petronius had nothing to fhew me but the

the meridian line drawn by Caffini, and the figure of that fon of Mars whofe hand was arrefted in an attempt to wound the Virgin. The hiftory is given at length by Moore.

The opera was very brilliantly fupported by fome fingers, who will, I prefume, in due time, follow the fortunes of their brother Sepranos, in England. Crefcentini is the favourite, and the Dilettanti have great expectations from his promifing talents. Bologna is indeed the fchool of Italian mufic: and as the air is foft and temperate, the voice muft have an advantage the lofs of which is much felt in England.

I regret that the fhortnefs of my ftay fhould have deprived me of the power of communicating more extenfive information upon the interefting curiofities of this delightful town. Its general afpect is ftrongly prepoffeffing, and its details are fubjects of ftudy. We left it yefterday morning, and began to afcend the Appennines. Thefe mountains are diverfified by a rich and la-

boured

boured cultivation; and the two days paſſed between Bologna and Florence were enlivened by ſcenes of magnificence and beauty. The lambent and ſulphureous flames of Pietra Mala, riſing near the village of that name, and cònſtantly burning, lighted us as we approached Cavigliaro, the boundary of our firſt day's journey: and early in the morning of the ſecond, we deſcended amid the rays of the riſing ſun upon the turrets, palaces, bridges, gardens, and all the majeſtic ſcenery of this celebrated capital.

LETTER LXXVI.

Florence, Nov. 25, 1791.

THERE is nothing that requires more art than a juſt ſelection of local curioſities. It is difficult to diſcern the faireſt where all are fair, and to fix upon the moſt uſeful

VOL. I.   B B   where

where none are without their use. Florence abounds so greatly in objects of interest to travellers, is so rich in natural scenery, monuments of architecture, and cabinets of art, that the mind is rather distracted than directed, by those catalogues which undertake to do the duty of guides. Whether I have yet visited one tenth part of its nominal, or digested one hundredth part of its real beauties, I am not anxious to know; my time has been wholly employed in seeing, and much of what I saw has filled me with wonder. The gallery,—the great monument of Tuscan liberality, and the first resort of strangers,—has furnished me with a large fund of study and amusement. The princely bounty of the Grand Duke, who has enlarged the salary of the guides, to throw open the gates of this invaluable musæum, is a subject which calls for the traveller's eulogium. All who have crossed the Appennines, have indulged in the praise of this gallery; and, though the rarities of its cabinets have been

so

so often and so variously served up, I cannot deny myself the pleasure of reporting to you in what manner I was affected by them. The Tribune, which is usually the *last* displayed, was that into which I accidentally entered *first*. I knew not the name of the cabinet, and had followed some strangers. " This (said our conductor) is the Tribune, " and here," pointing to a statue that stood before us—" is the Venus de Medicis." Thus taken by surprize, I remained for some time in silent contemplation of this " statue " which enchants the world," and which is considered as the perfection of sculptural art. Carrying my speculations back to the first rudiments of this wonderful production, I pictured to myself, with the Abbé Du Palli, the birth of this design in the mind of the sculptor, and the enthusiasm which fired him when he first viewed the mass. Kindling as I gazed, I traced the progress of the chisel through all the stages of its formation. I admired the genius which actuated, the art

which

which guided, and the delicacy which managed the sculptor's hand. Such circumstances must combine to give perfection, and perfection is the only attribute which can characterize this statue. The Arrotino or Whetter, who stands to the left of the Venus, is a subject both of admiration and perplexity. Position of body, cast of countenance, and circumstance of occupation, denote some mystery which they do not develop. He is resting on one knee, and whetting a knife or cutting instrument. His head is elevated inclining to the left, as though he were listening to something said. It is curious to observe what ingenious conjectures have been indulged upon the history of this Arrotino: he is listening to Cataline's conspiracy, he overhears the plot of Brutus's sons to restore the Tarquins: it is Cincinnatus; it is Manlius Capitolinus; and lastly, as though there were not already sufficient hypotheses to obscure the fact, the Abbé Palli has found out that it is the Scythian who assisted

LETTER LXXVII.

at the duet between Apollo and Marſyas, and who afterwards flayed the latter. Now, that he is liſtening, cannot be diſputed: and that he may be liſtening to the Catalinarian or the Tarquinian faction, are conjectures equally probable. And whether or not he repreſents the Scythian who was to flay Marſyas, it muſt be owned his heart ſeems ripe for a murderous deed. The hiſtory of this character is, in ſhort, among thoſe records which have ſlipped through the fingers of time, and whoſe place can only be ſupplied by fancy and conjecture.

LETTER LXXVII.

Florence.

As I have ventured ſo far into the field of deſcription, it would be treaſon to the remaining ſtatues not to allow them ſome ſhare of encomium. The Wreſtlers, ſo oft and so deservedly admired, is a most beautiful and energetic production of the chisel; the mind of the artist must have been filled with the justest conceptions of human proportions and anatomical accuracy. My ignorance of antient sculpture had led me to form false and vulgar expectations of this groupe. The figures are of a moderate size and a perfect form; and exhibit an happy union of beauty and strength, of grace and vigour, of muscular force and personal comeliness. The inter-twining of the limbs is most artfully rendered, and evinces at once the power of the superior, and the disadvantage of the fallen combatant: while the countenances respectively express, by emotions of confidence and agony, the triumph of the victor and the despair of the vanquished. The dancing faun is certainly the most facetious and mirthful character ever brought out of marble. This grotesque figure is presented with one leg elevated, in the attitude of dancing. His head is inclined with much

much natural expreffion, and in his countenance is painted a lively image of luxurious joy. Every lineament difcovers the abfence of folicitude and the annihilation of care. It is indeed a charming ftatue, full of antient thought, and in perfect unifon with the feftive imagery of the Grecian mufe. I might now conduct you, as I was conducted myfelf, through a feries of cabinets feverally furnifhed with diftinctly arranged curiofities. Among others were thofe that contained collections of precious ftones and minerals wrought into a thoufand varieties of form. Here were columns, vafes, and urns of agate, rock-cryftal, lapis lazuli; and, in fhort, a large profufion of antient and modern valuables, diftributed and afforted with great tafte. The cabinet of portraits was not among the leaft interefting of thefe fecondary departments. Thefe portraits are of different painters, painted by themfelves. Madame Le Brun and Angelica Kauffman are not among the leaft attracting. The very

very noble urn di Medicis, on which is reprefented, in relievo, the facrifice of Iphigenia, forms a grand central ornament to one of thefe faloons. The Cabinet of the Hermaphrodite, and the Hall of Niobe, containing this defcendant of Jupiter and her fourteen children, are treafures of ineftimable value. Amongft a variety of urns, fepulchral fragments, and different *morceaus* of antiquity, are the known and celebrated bufts of Alexander the Great, and Brutus, the laft of which may well deferve a place amongft the productions of the Grecian fchool. Thefe bufts have alfo fet the learned afloat upon the occean of conjecture. The firft of thefe is the buft of a coloffal figure, and bears in the countenance a ftrong expreffion of agony. What circumftance this alludes to in the hiftory of Alexander is the queftion at iffue. " He fighs for new worlds," fays Mr. Addifon. " He is difturbed, *beyond a doubt*, fay " others, with remorfe for the murder of " Clitus." There is certainly an expreffion of pain in the countenance more deeply coloured than the fretful emotion of pining difcontent could infpire; and fuch as might be expected from the man, who had rafhnefs enough to kill, and fenfibility fufficient to repent. The buft of Brutus has alfo furnifhed work for the critics. The buft is excellent, but *unfinifhed.* All the myftery is, why fhould Michael Angelo have left it in this ftate? Cardinal Bembo has affigned a reafon which will fcarcely pleafe beyond the pale of a court.

Dum Bruti effigiem fculptor de marmore ducit,
In mentem fceleris venit, et abftinuit.

But Michael Angelo has left many unfinifhed works. All his figures upon the tombs in the chapel of St. Lorenzo, are uncouthly and imperfectly fculptured. Perhaps this great man, enamoured with the rougher ftrokes of his chifel, and pleafed with the expreffion of his outline, would rather leave the buft unfinifhed, than efface the bolder parts by an addition of the laft polifh.

LETTER LXXVIII.

Florence,

THIS city appears conſtructed, in all its parts, to fill the eye of the traveller with pleaſure. The ſtreets, which are paved with even flag-ſtones, chiſeled as occaſion requires, for ſafety—are generally clean; and where they open upon the Arno, are illumined by wide and varied views, extending on either ſide of this noble ſtream. The entrance from Bologna is not improperly called a deſcent upon the town: for at the diſtance of ſome leagues the whole appears extended below the brow of the Appennines; and the traveller ſeems to be plunging from the lofty precipice into the boſom of thoſe viſtas and parterres, which interſect and adorn the vale below. A triumphal

umphal arch receives him at the foot of this defcent, and announces his entrance into the Tufcan capital. The palace Pitti, refidence of the Grand Duke, is fombrous in its afpect, but has an air of Gothic majefty. The interior is noble, and adorned with all that art, riches, and good tafte can contribute to dignify the palatial refidence. Here Pietro de Cortona has lavifhed the fineft touches of his pencil upon the ceilings; and among the pendents is preferved the Madonna of Raphael, to which the connoiffeurs affign the higheft rank. It is but juftice to the patron of this palace to fay, that it is exhibited with the fame liberality as the gallery: and that ftrangers are conducted through all its chambers with an attention and refpect, which in other places is confidered as involving the expectancy of an exorbitant fee. The palace Ricardi is a ftructure of noble architecture, raifed, for the moft part, upon the defigns of Michael Angelo. It is impoffible not to be delighted with the very elegant and mafterly pieces

of

of Luca Giordano which cover the fpacious roof of the grand faloon. Of the four Evangelifts painted by Guercino, each had its proper merits; but the portrait of St. John was a faithful tranfcript of the Evangelift's pen. It was a countenance animated with as much fire and intelligence as can confift with fweetnefs and fenfibility. Of other palaces I can only fpeak from a view of their exterior, and the reports of others. Their inhabitants are reputed to hold an high rank in polite accomplifhments; and, thofe who have leifure to cultivate their fociety by a longer refidence, bear teftimony to their domeftic hofpitality. Amufements of every defcription are in this city at their zenith. Their opera has indeed its feafons, and the tide of gaiety its flux and reflux; but from what I have feen—and ftill more from what I have heard—no city has a fairer ground of pretenfion to detain thofe travellers, whom *ennui* and *hypochondria* have driven to feek the cure of their melancholy from the hands of pleafure.

LETTER LXXIX.

Florence.

THE cathedral of Florence is a very large and ponderous edifice, conftructed of black and white marble, and therefore prefenting a very fhadowy afpect. The ftatues of the twelve Apoftles, and the noble baffo relievos which furround the altar, hardly compenfate the gloom which over-hangs the general mafs. The brafs gates which adorn the baptiftery, an octagonal building detached from, but belonging to this cathedral, were by Michael Angelo deemed worthy of opening and fhutting the entrance to Heaven. Next in order is the church of San Lorenzo. Here, in the chapel of the princes, are the two celebrated tombs of Michael Angelo. They are, like his buft

of

of Brutus, imperfectly sculptured; and prefented to me little beyond the rude outline. Two figures of bold defign adorn each of thefe monuments—the firft of which reprefent Day and Night—the fecond Crepufculum and Aurora. The chapel di Medicis in this church is defervedly efteemed amongft the ornaments of Florence. It contains fix tombs conftructed upon the defigns of Michael Angelo. The form of the chapel is octagonal; and the monuments are, in point of defign and execution, ftriking and magnificent. Oriental granite of the moft beautiful vein, lapis lazuli, coral, and, in fhort, every fpecies of ftone and mineral is here difpofed and arranged by the hand of a mafter. And were the chapel completed in a ftyle fuited to the original plan, the world would not be able to fhew fo perfect a model of tafte and magnificence. The church of Santa Annuntiata is adorned with fome handfome altars of marble, and paintings of no mean execution. The *bas reliefs* in bronze

bronze by Jean de Bologne, compofe rather an interefting than fplendid ornament to the Chapelle de La Vierge, in which an image of high character is depofited. The flagellation of Chrift is, among thefe brazen tablets—an extraordinary effort of genius, replete with vigour and fenfibility. Among the contiguous cloifters are fome admirable frefcoes. The wafteful hand of time, and expofure to the damps and dews have brought into decay a beautiful Madonna of Andrea del Sarto, whofe buft and epitaph are affixed againft the walls of this cloifter. The church of the Dominicans is of inferior reputation to the convent. This contains a grand elaboratory for balfams, fimples, &c. and is efteemed to produce fome of the beft effences and perfumes which ever fhed their fragrance around the perfons of beau or belle.

The church of San Spirito, prefents a bold defign of folid but fimple architecture. It is as yet fo little advanced, that the paintings it contains are perfectly eclipfed. It promifes, mises, however, to exhibit in its finished state that species of grave and decent edifice, which corresponds with the rational idea of a Christian Temple. My register of the churches shall close with that of the Santa Croce. It had for me only two objects— the first of which was the monument of Michael Angelo—a monument worthy of the subject. Three of his scholars united to form this memorial of their illustrious preceptor—equally skilled in the rival arts of painting, sculpture, and architecture. The tomb of the great Galileo was the second. A simple bust and tablet of marble record his memory. Peace to his ashes! May no sacrilegious hand destroy the pile on which his name is inscribed! may his memory for ever flourish! and may it appear from the concurrent plaudits of all succeeding ages, how perishable are the decrees of superstition and error, how immortal the discoveries of reason and truth!

LETTER LXXX

Foligno, Dec. 1.

IT was not without great reluctance that I left Florence, after so short a stay. An offer of introduction to some of the principal inhabitants, rendered this abrupt departure still less palatable; but change and reverse are the lot of man, and the chances of travel, like those of life, are not all in favour of the adventurer. It was by a tardy movement of more than two days, that we reached the antient and venerable town of Peruggia.

The journey to Rome, by this route, is less frequently taken, than that of Sienna, as it is a track extremely circuitous; but those who study the wear and tear of horses and carriages, prefer this route, as more than compensating for its length, by the fuperiority of its roads. Among the curiofities of this place, are to be feen many of the productions of Pietro Perugino, the mafter of Raphael, whofe beft and greateft works are here preferved. At the church of San Francefco, is one reprefenting the Refurrection, on which I fixed with a great degree of admiration. The outline was faithfully fketched ; and there appeared a great degree of accuracy and chaftenefs in the drawing, and difpofition of the colours. In what I had ever before feen of this mafter, there was fo great a drynefs and formality, that it was difficult to trace, without a deeper knowledge of the art than I can pretend to, any thing like the touches of an able and animated pencil. But from this and other fpecimens at Peruggia, it appears, that Raphael may have ftood confiderably indebted to the leffons of his preceptor. Superadding to his own genius the principles of Pietro, he has fhewn the fublime effects which refult from the union—too feldom exifting—

of

LETTER LXXX.

of strong talents and attentive study. This church was rich in excellent paintings. From viewing some designs, more remarkable for their quaintness and antiquity, than their merit, I passed to the contemplation of an assumption of the Virgin, which passes with me for the best Raphael I have yet seen. The Virgin is represented in Heaven, and Jesus Christ placing the crown upon her head. The Apostles below are collected about her tomb, and gazing upwards with countenances full of attention and rapture. There was in this painting a sort of expression, which made its way more successfully to my admiration, than the Cecilia at Bologna, or the Madonna at the Palace Pitti. I had formed very erroneous conceptions of the pleasure I was to derive from the productions of Raphael—expecting to know them at first sight, and to worship them almost by instinct. Painting has however its mysteries, I find—and it requires some study and knowledge of its principles, to be able to admire what is moſt excellent. Like the ſiſter arts of poetry and muſic, it ſeems to hide its excellencies from thoſe who are ignorant of its laws. A good painting ſeems therefore to ſtand very much in the predicament of a good poem, and a well wrought concerto. Some ſimple delineation ſhall faſcinate in the *firſt*, beyond a regular and ſtudied production; while in the *laſt*, an artleſs tale and a popular air ſhall pleaſe more, than the ſtately muſe of Milton, and the learned melodies of Pergoleſi.

At a palace belonging to the noble family of Della Penna, I was gratified with the ſight of ſome of the beſt and moſt finiſhed pieces, from the hand of Salvator Roſa. Numerous productions of this extraordinary maſter were ſhewn me, in which all the wild and groteſque fancies which genius could create, were brought upon the canvas. To theſe were added four landſcapes in his beſt ſtile, two of which preſent nature in leſs uncouth forms, and are

LETTER LXXX.

in all refpects deferving of the higheft eulogium.

I was completely occupied, during the time we paffed in this town, with the various and valuable fpecimens of art which I had opportunity to vifit. The town is fufficiently gloomy in its afpect—the marks of antiquity, defertion, and decay, are ftrongly vifible in all its extent: and it is among the very few cities in Italy which are ftruck out of the lift of the travellers route. It is however certain, that though little vifited, it wants not its importance in the fcale of art. Its churches and its palaces have indeed little to boaft of fplendor or ornament: the intelligent traveller will, neverthelefs, be repaid, for entering apartments feldom inhabited, and churches little frequented, by defigns and ftudies appropriate to this place, and of a clafs which is in vain fought for in cities of greater refort.

LETTER LXXXI.

Terni.

FROM Foligno to this place, the road was flanked on either side, by sloping lands of rich and laboured cultivation. Foligno is a town of some traffic, and much fraud. The British minister resident at Florence, (Lord Harvey,) was by some accident passing on this route. Whatever be the subject of his journey, it is certain that he went *incog.* to the confines of Rome, and is returning to Florence by this little-frequented route. The politicians of this place are greatly perplexed to account for his Lordship's appearance amongst them; under such circumstances, they regard it as full of mystery. He paid us a visit with much politeness, and I had an opportunity of laying before him a specimen of that sort of information which the

LETTER LXXXI.

the politicians of Foligno poſſeſſed. For in a newſpaper of the place, which I was not a little ſurprized to meet with, it was hinted with ſome confidence, that an union was in agitation of the crowns of England and France, by the marriage of the Prince of Wales with Madame Royale. This may ſerve to ſhew you, how much theſe people are admitted into the ſecrets of ſtate.

I roſe early on the following morning, in order to obtain, before my departure from Foligno, a ſight of the Madonna of Raphael, preſerved in the convent Des Comteſſes. My guide and myſelf had concerted the hour and the means, but alas! when I approached the door of the chapel and demanded admittance, a number of Franciſcans, who were aſſembled at their devotions, growled refuſal.

From Foligno to Spoletto the track conducted us through a country whoſe beauties have not diſappeared in the month of December. The air was ſoft, the ſky deliciouſly ſerene above us, and every where around

around were scenes of that ornamental description, which confound, in the traveller's eye, all diſtinction of ſeaſons. In proportion as we advanced, the ſtate of the country ſtill improved; mountains of the moſt picturesque forms preſented themſelves. Emboſomed upon the heights of theſe, were caſtles, monaſteries, and towns, interſperſed with olive gardens, the bloom of whoſe fruit reflected in various hues the rays of the ſun. We alighted on our route, to view the little temple by the road ſide, conſecrated, as the lovers of antiquity affirm, to the god Clitumnus; and as men of leſs enthuſiaſm, and therefore probably of more judgment, ſay, to ſome modern Divinity. Spoletto was the boundary of this day's journey, and the hour of our arrival was ſufficiently early to viſit the Gothic Aqueduct, which here connects the mountain of St. Francis with Spoletto. It is a ſtupendous building of ten arches, the loweſt of which is eſtimated to ſtand more than ſix hundred feet above its founda-

LETTER LXXXI.

foundation. Its hiftory is carried back to the times of Theodoric, and it forms in its prefent ftate, an object of great magnificence. The mountain againft which it refts, has many wild and picturefque beauties. A loofe and irregular fhrubbery overfpreads it from the fummit to the narrow channel below; and intermixed with the maffes of ftone which hang upon its flopes, the tangling fhoots exhibit thofe light and negligent ornaments, which art can never fuccefsfully imitate. I was given to underftand that a portrait of the Virgin by St. Luke, was among the ineftimable rarities of Spoletto—but I heretically contented myfelf with the report of its miraculous properties; and, glancing fimply at the pompous infcriptions which announce the pride of this place, as the "caput umbriæ," and the town fo celebrated by the flight of Hannibal—compofed myfelf to an anticipation of thofe beauties which I was to fee in the Cafcade of Terni.

LETTER LXXXII.

Citta Caſtellana.

THE Caſcade of Terni is formed by the fall of the Velino into the Nera, (antiently the Nar—" Narque albeſcentibus aquis—in Tiberim properans." *Sil. Ital.*) The Velino is a pretty conſiderable river of a navigable depth, and takes its riſe in Monte Abruzzo; ſeparating, in its paſſage to the point of deſcent, the town of Rhieti, from its ſuburbs. There are many circumſtances attending this Caſcade, which render it not only an object of aſtoniſhment to the traveller, but of intereſt to the naturaliſt. The river Velino once formed a marſh in the valley of Rhieti, highly prejudicial to the country, and whoſe waters had the ſingular property of petrifaction. This circumſtance is atteſted by Pliny: " In lacu Velino lignum dejectum lapideo cortice induitur." The channel

nel through which the Velino now paſſes, in its way to the point of defcent, was dug by order of Clement VIII. The calcareous particles with which the water is impregnated, have here concreted in their paſſage, and overlaid the whole fuperficies of this bed with a fubſtance refembling the folidity of marble. Hence this level has acquired the name of Piano del Marmore, or the Marble Level; and the Cafcade itfelf, La Caduta del Marmore, or the Marble Cafcade. The track from which it is approached from the town of Terni, is fingularly picturefque. Cut for the greater part out of the folid rock, it purfues a winding courfe, and furnifhes, by a gradual yet conſtant afcent, numerous and varied views of the furrounding fcenery. The rapidity of the river in that channel, which is hewn out of the rock to give paſſage to its waters, is fcarcely to be imagined. It is here that the fpectator is ufually conducted firſt, in order that he may fee the quantum of force with which this

body

body of water haftens to its fall. It is impoffible, to regard without dizzinefs, the extreme velocity of this part of the current. Stones of confiderable weight are buoyed up by the rapidity of the motion. The next point of view, is that which from a fmall terrace conveys to the eye this powerful ftream, precipitated from the extremity of its marble level with all that violence which it has already acquired by the compreffion of its waters. The ftream thus precipitated is received in a rocky bafon, fcooped out by the force of the waters, and from whofe bafe it is difcharged to a fecond receiver, amidft a vaft profufion of foam and uproar. Defcending thus with a rapidity regularly diminifhed by the re-action of two fucceffive rocks, the river enters the Nera, and proceeds to join the imperial Tiber. A fcene of greater and more terrific magnificence cannot be pictured by the imagination. The force and velocity of the current, in the point preparatory to its defcent, is moft tremendous.

ous. It is difficult to decide—so different are the calculations upon this subject—its accurate measurement. The Pere Carrara has fixed its total height from the Piano del Marmore to the level of the Nera, at 1871 Roman palms. The tumult of its waters, reverberated in a thousand directions;—the frothy clouds which issued from the valley;—the arching rocks which overhung the gulph;—and the luxuriant shrubs which scattered their delicate shades;—formed together a picture of romantic sublimity, too impressive to be easily supplanted by any scenes of secondary beauty.

LETTER LXXXIII.

Rome, Dec. 7.

IT was between Spoletto and Terni, that we passed the highest point of Appennine upon this route, and we have been since regularly descending. I could not pass through Terni,

Terni, without feeling an emotion of classical pleasure. It was the birth-place of Tacitus, and the mind is forcibly impressed with scenes thus connected with those it has learned to admire. Johnson has expressed, in his masterly imitation of the Roman poets, the same sentiment:

> Struck with the spot which gave Eliza birth,
> We kneel, and kiss the consecrated earth.
>
> IMIT. Sat. 3. Juv.

Our route from Terni lay along the beautiful valley which connects this town with Narni. The waters of the Nera, gracefully discomposed, and rendered musically sonorous by the influx of the Velino, roll along this charming vale, in their way to the point of junction with the Tiber. The ruins of the great bridge, which once connected the two opposite mountains, and over which passed the high road to Peruggia, stands at no great distance from the town of Narni. The only entire arch which now remains, discovers it to have been, whatever were its form,

LETTER LXXXIII.

form, of bold and sublime construction. Blocks of stone composed without cement, and compacted into an apparently solid mass, convey an high idea of the perfection to which the arts were carried in the age of Augustus. What was once Otriculum, is now a little dirty post town, and preserves more of its name than its substance,—still retaining the appellation of Ocricoli. Numerous vestiges of ruined monuments are visible in its environs, and different sides of the roads yet shew the remains of antient fabrics, and heaps of crumbling materials. The very serpentine course which the Tiber pursues, engaged particularly my attention in passing from Narni. The level surface of the country allowed the eye to observe the flexions of this stream over a considerable space. The beauties of cultivation gradually disappeared as we approached Citta Castellana. It was from this miserable town, once the capital seat of the Falisci, and taken by Camillus, A. U. 359, that we yesterday finished our journey

journey to this metropolis. Scenes of natural beauty had been for some time receding; and now, in proportion as we advanced, the aspect of the country increased in that deformity which neglected agriculture and reduced population have introduced into the most fertile and productive soil under the Heavens. A few scattered huts, and these for the most part sinking into ruins, serve rather to heighten the picture of desolation; and to awaken a more lively degree of sensibility in the bosom of the contemplative traveller. At length the dome of St. Peter's rising amidst this weary waste, indicated our approach to ROME, which received us by an entrance majestic, and expressive of the genius of this antient capital.

END OF THE FIRST VOLUME.

www.ingramcontent.com/pod-product-compliance
Lightning Source LLC
Chambersburg PA
CBHW051851300426
44117CB00006B/348